THREE TIGERS, ONE MOUNTAIN

Just As Well I'm Leaving
Doing without Delia
Sushi and Beyond
Eat, Pray, Eat
The Almost Nearly Perfect People
The Meaning of Rice

THREE TIGERS, ONE MOUNTAIN

A Journey through the Bitter History and
Current Conflicts of China, Korea and Japan

Michael Booth

JONATHAN CAPE
LONDON

3 5 7 9 10 8 6 4

Jonathan Cape, an imprint of Vintage,
20 Vauxhall Bridge Road,
London SW1V 2SA

Jonathan Cape is part of the Penguin Random House group of companies
whose addresses can be found at global.penguinrandomhouse.com.

penguin.co.uk/vintage

A CIP catalogue record for this book is available from the British Library

ISBN 9781910702956

Typeset in 11.5/14.75 pt Dante MT Std
by Integra Software Services Pvt. Ltd, Pondicherry

Printed and bound in Great Britain by Clays Ltd, Elcograf S.p.A.

Penguin Random House is committed to a sustainable future for our
business, our readers and our planet. This book is made from
Forest Stewardship Council® certified paper.

Two tigers can not share the same mountain.

Ancient Chinese proverb

Contents

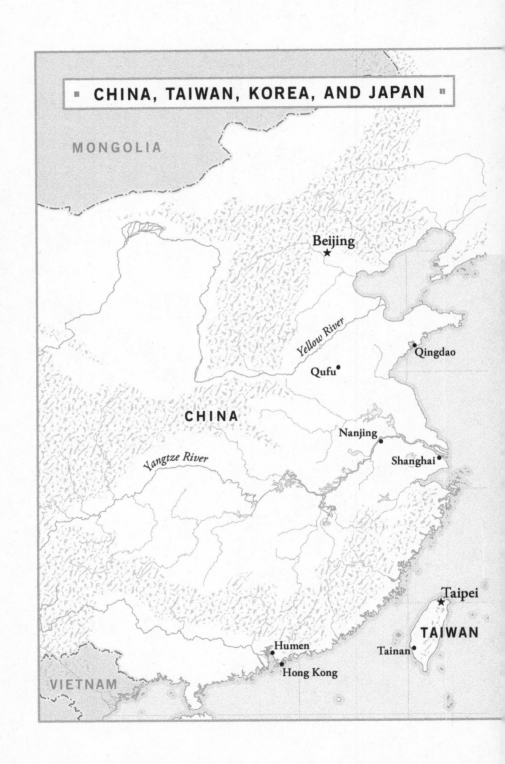

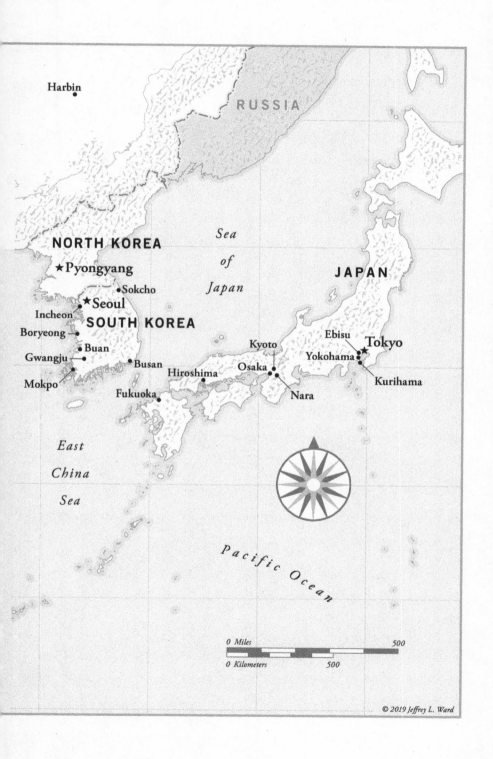

Harbin

RUSSIA

NORTH KOREA

★Pyongyang

•Sokcho

★Seoul

Incheon

SOUTH KOREA

Boryeong

•Buan

Gwangju

•Busan

Mokpo

Fukuoka

Sea
of
Japan

JAPAN

Ebisu

Kyoto

Tokyo

Osaka

Yokohama

Hiroshima

Nara

Kurihama

East
China
Sea

Pacific Ocean

0 Miles   500

0 Kilometers   500

© 2019 Jeffrey L. Ward

PROLOGUE

The two tiny dots of blue icing, each barely a millimetre in diameter – they were the problem. They were a component of a rather appetising-looking mango mousse entitled Spring of the People, which, it had been announced, was to be served at a dinner in honour of the leaders of South and North Korea. The dots were virtually invisible, but the Japanese spotted them and they were not happy.

'It is extremely regrettable and not acceptable,' said a Japanese foreign ministry spokesperson when news of the dots leaked ahead of the historic meeting in April 2018. 'We have asked that the dessert not be served.'

The Japanese made a formal complaint and lobbied hard for the mousse to be struck from the menu, but to no avail. Indeed, on the day of the dinner, Moon Jae-in, the president of the Republic of Korea, and Kim Jong-un, leader of the Democratic People's Republic of Korea, applauded with especial enthusiasm as their pudding was served.

The reason for the Japanese indignation was that the dots were part of a chocolate map of the Korean peninsula and represented a group of disputed islands, really not much more than a few lumps of rock, located 177 miles off the east coast of South Korea. In Korea the rocks are known as the Dokdo Islands, in Japan as Takeshima, and in the English-speaking world as the Liancourt Rocks. Ownership of the islands is hotly disputed between Japan and South Korea. Korea's claim goes back to the twelfth-century *Samguk sagi*, the chronicles of their Three Kingdoms era. The Japanese say that the islands have been used by their fishermen for hundreds of years and point out that South Korea's claim was turned down by the Americans at the 1951 San Francisco Peace Conference.

Though the leaders of the two Koreas were technically at war at the time of their official dinner, and though one of them was a despot threatening the security of east Asia and responsible for the deaths of thousands of his own people, on one topic they could agree wholeheartedly.

The Japanese could go whistle.

To the Koreans, North and South, those two dots of icing sugar represented defiance of their former oppressor; to the Japanese they were a needless provocation; to the Chinese, doubtless monitoring events closely, they were a heartening sign of the ongoing hostility between their two neighbours, as a strong Japan–Korea alliance would be highly threatening to Beijing.[1]

I watched all this unfold on the TV news in my hotel room in Taiwan at the very end of my journey around this troubled neighbourhood. With all I had seen and learned of the region's history by that stage, I had a fair idea of what the dessert meant. In those two little icing dots I saw tens of millions of innocent people dead; I saw the destruction of cities and the fall of empires; I saw oppression, occupation, exploitation and, above all, a festering animosity which at any moment could explode into a devastating regional war with consequences for the world.

So why can't the nations of east Asia get on? How deep, really, is the enmity between Japan, Korea and China, and what keeps it alive today? Whose interests are served by sabotaging the peace between these three Asian tigers? These are some of the questions which had prompted my journey through a part of the world that has fascinated me throughout my adult life.

---

[1] The South Koreans are highly adept at this kind of sly dinner diplomacy and had deliberately leaked the name of the dessert, with professionally taken photographs and everything, knowing full well that it would annoy the Japanese. A few months earlier, while on a state visit to Seoul, Donald Trump had tucked in to a starter at a state dinner featuring shrimp which had been farmed on Dokdo. Trump was utterly oblivious to the symbolism of the shrimp but the Japanese weren't. They got cross about that too.

The Chinese, Koreans and Japanese, along with a fourth tiger, Taiwan, would appear from a distance to have everything to gain from harmonious relations: economic prosperity, cultural and technological exchange, progress and peace in all its forms, and yet they seem constantly to be on the brink of serious conflict. Many believe that if there is to be a World War III, it will most likely begin here, perhaps following some convulsion within North Korea or a confrontation or accident in the Taiwan Strait, which has long held the dubious status of the world's number one military flashpoint. It could just as easily kick off with someone doing something silly on Dokdo.

Barely a season passes without a diplomatic spat between these nations, a public protest on the streets of Seoul, Beijing, Taipei or Tokyo, trade sanctions being imposed, military jostling. The rhetoric is ramped up by political leaders and diplomats seemingly at will, their constituents react accordingly, and the rest of the world sighs at the predictable futility of it all. And the tension is building. China is rapidly building the world's largest military, and its navy dominates the region's oceans; Japan's rulers are attempting to overturn its pacifist constitution to permit an aggressive military capability; and a unilateral declaration of independence from Taiwan would almost certainly prompt China to invade, with the potential to draw in America, which has tens of thousands of military personnel stationed in the region. And then of course there is Little Rocket Man in Pyongyang, with his fat fingers still supposedly poised over a nuclear button. And the bad blood in east Asia is not limited to its governments and military leaders. Hatred – proper, visceral, blind hatred – simmers among the people of these countries, every once in a while erupting into violence.

In 2012, in the Chinese city of Xi'an in Shaanxi Province a man called Li Jianli, aged fifty-one, was dragged from his car and beaten almost to death by a mob following the Japanese government's nationalisation of some other disputed rocks in the sea, in this case the Senkaku Islands – known to the Chinese, who claim them, as the Diaoyu Islands – which lie between Taiwan and Okinawa.

Li wasn't even Japanese; he just happened to be driving a Japanese car. The Japanese ambassador to China was fortunate to escape when his car was attacked in the streets of Beijing the same week.

Some of the popular protests are weekly affairs. During my journey I spent some time at a demonstration by a couple of hundred protesters outside the Japanese embassy in Seoul against the sexual enslavement of women by the Japanese military during World War II, an event which has taken place every Wednesday since 1992. A large part of the crowd comprised schoolchildren. One expects florid anti-Japanese rhetoric from the North Korean regime, but how is anger concerning events which took place over seventy years ago still so fresh among young South Koreans? Who is stoking that and why? And the hatred of Japanese by Koreans is reciprocated, at least by a minority in Japan. Earlier on in my trip, in Yokohama, a convoy of black minivans had passed me, a tirade of anti-Korean invective spewing from their loudspeakers. This wasn't the first time I had seen such things in Japan. For many years various right-wing factions have been taking to the streets of cities to threaten and insult ethnic communities, particularly in Osaka, home to the country's largest Korean population. But what could the Japanese possibly have against the Koreans? Were these merely tit-for-tat demonstrations, or was the hatred as deep on both sides of the Sea of Japan?

The disputes do not always involve Japan; they are multi-directional. The installation in 2017 of an American missile defence system on a golf course south of Seoul antagonised Beijing, resulting in an immediate and precipitous drop in tourists travelling from China to Seoul, enough to shake the South Korean economy. Although the missiles were ostensibly intended to counter the threat from North Korea, the Chinese felt menaced by the presence of yet more American military technology so close to their borders and made their neighbours pay with unofficial trade sanctions.

These hostilities of course have their roots in the region's history, which since the late 1800s has been a litany of man-made hellishness featuring war, massacre, mass rape, chemical weapons, firebombing, totalitarianism, famine, destitution, political oppression, torture and atomic destruction, all of which remain vivid in the collective consciousness.

Commemoration and remembrance of the kind which takes place at Hiroshima is one thing, but historical memory takes many, often more controversial and divisive forms in this part of the world. Before I set off on my journey I knew for instance that in the heart of Tokyo was a shrine, Yasukuni, where Japanese citizens, including occasionally prime ministers, pay their respects to war criminals along with thousands of others who died fighting for Japan. This seemed to me odd and distasteful but did not really explain the broader picture of the destructive relationships within the region. I also knew that, more than seventy years after the end of World War II, China and South Korea were still seeking an apology from Japan for its crimes. But numerous Japanese prime ministers, as well as their emperor, had offered many variations of 'sorry' to their former enemies, expressing 'remorse' or 'deep regret' on numerous occasions. Was there a bat squeak of insincerity, only audible to Koreans and Chinese, which meant that Japanese contrition was never deemed sufficient?

From the outside, this can be perplexing. When most of us in the rest of the world think of the Far East we automatically draw up a list of all that's wonderful and fascinating in its cultures: the artistic treasures of ancient civilisations, the wonderful food, a carnival of contemporary temptations from kimchi to Hello Kitty, 'Gangnam Style' to smartphones. We think of the people who live there as industrious, ingenious, dutiful, respectful of traditional family values and justly proud of a cultural heritage far older than our own. With the obvious exception of the 'mad neighbour' North Korea, nowadays these countries tend not to be prone to religious or ideological extremism. There is so much to admire: China will soon be crowned the world's largest economy; South Korea has gone from economic basket case to the world's leading producer of our favourite high-tech consumer products, and in 2017, with the election of Moon Jae-in, showed itself to be a paragon of grass-roots democracy; while Japan remains the most civilised and courteous society on earth, its products – physical and intangible – in demand around the globe. And not to forget Taiwan, the little island that has flourished against all the odds.

South Korea, Taiwan and Japan ought to be the firmest of allies. All three are democracies with developed economies and significant mutual trade; all are allies of, and militarily dependent upon, the US, and share grave concerns about China. Yet the South Koreans can at times seem hostile to the Japanese to the point of derangement. If it weren't for the Americans, many believe they would ally with Beijing against Tokyo. On the other hand, although there are obvious ideological and political differences between communist China and its neighbours, they are deeply intertwined culturally, genetically and historically in ways which have been mutually beneficial for millennia. China has given its neighbours Confucian philosophy, rice cultivation, Buddhism, porcelain manufacture and tea, as well as the secrets of metallurgy, written language and the art of calligraphy.

In more recent times, Korea and Japan have returned the favour. From Korea has come K-pop, histrionic TV dramas and cartoonishly violent films, all of which have become massively popular throughout China, Japan and beyond – the so-called *Hallyu* phenomenon. In the last seventy years Japan has provided the economic model (as well as financial support and know-how) for South Korea, Taiwan and more recently China, to develop their manufacturing and exports. Wherever you travel in east Asia, you find Japanese restaurants, as well as retail brands like Uniqlo, Hello Kitty and Muji. Since I started visiting Japan twenty years ago, I have seen the streets of Tokyo fill with Chinese and Korean tourists there to eat and shop. On a recent visit to Japan I sat next to a young Chinese couple in a restaurant in Osaka. They had come to Japan, they said, because they wanted to get their wedding rings made here. Everything was better quality in Japan. There are now an estimated million Chinese living in Japan, making them the country's largest ethnic minority – the Koreans are second.

In terms of who should shoulder the blame for this noxious family feud, most point with a good deal of justification to the Japanese and their early-twentieth-century expansionist crimes, yet no other people seem to me today to be as peaceful, kind, respectful and trustworthy. I recognise the solipsistic folly of extrapolating one's own, by definition limited, experience of a nation of 127 million in this way, but the Japanese really are so *nice*. Honestly. They are *ridiculously* nice. How could anyone not like them? It genuinely troubles me that they are so loathed by their neighbours.

Before I set off, I believed I had a reasonable grasp of the charge sheet against Japan. I didn't, as it happens; it was worse than I thought. But if Europe and Israel could come to terms with Germany's war crimes, and the Philippines, Indonesia and other countries also occupied by Japan no longer seemed to harbour huge animosity towards the Japanese, if India and Britain could rub along, if the Indonesians could consider the Dutch friends, why did Korea and China persist with their grudges? The disputed islands were a tricky issue obviously, and South Korea also has an ongoing issue with the Chinese over some other half-submerged rocks, not to mention a dispute over Yeonpyeong Island in the Yellow Sea with North Korea, but if Spain could tolerate British rule in Gibraltar and the two Cypriot communities could co-exist surely some independent, international commission could adjudicate in such matters?

Whose interests were served by perpetuating the hatred? Was it born of a genuine popular feeling, or was this geopolitical Mexican stand-off being manipulated by the elites in Seoul, Pyongyang, Tokyo and Beijing? The mass tourism, mutual trade and exchange of cultural soft power would seem to suggest the latter, but a 2016 Pew Research Center survey suggests the former. According to the poll, 81 per cent of Chinese people had an unfavourable impression of Japan and 86 per cent of Japanese felt the same way about the Chinese, while 77 per cent of South Koreans had an unfavourable view of the Japanese.

I should mention one extra little toxic ingredient to add to the mix: notions of racial superiority. The Japanese believe they are special because their emperor is directly descended from the sun goddess, with their early-twentieth-century elite, led by Emperor Hirohito, parlaying this national foundation myth into a divine right to colonise their 'lesser' neighbours by force. The Koreans, meanwhile, are convinced *they* are special because of what they believe to be their unique racial or blood purity, evidenced by the fact that over half of them share one of five surnames – Kim, Park, Lee, Seok and Choi. The Chinese believe that they are the centre of the universe and are taught from an early age that their culture is five thousand years old. And the leaders of Taiwan once believed they were the rightful rulers of China, though these days not so much.

I happened to watched the Korean summit dessert fracas unfold on television in my hotel room in Taiwan, where I was nearing the end of my journey around this beautiful, intoxicating, toxic part of the world. This was ironic because it turns out that the Taiwanese actually quite *admire* the Japanese. They build statues to *honour* their former colonial rulers, not to shame them like the South Koreans do. How could this be? But, rather dispiritingly, in Taipei I also discovered yet another antagonistic relationship in the region, one I had been entirely unaware of prior to setting off. I don't want to spoil it for you, but it turns out that the Taiwanese absolutely *loathe* the Koreans. As if they didn't have enough to worry about with China meddling in their elections, attempting to sabotage their economy and threatening to invade at any moment, the Taiwanese still find the energy to harbour a major beef against their neighbours to the north even though they have never crossed swords.

As I set out from Tokyo back at the beginning of my trip around this neighbourhood from hell, I have many puzzles and concerns but put my faith in curiosity, an open mind and asking better-informed folk stupid questions. Above all, I am just excited to dive into this incredible region and visit these cultures, albeit slightly nervous about the ferries, and the mud festival which awaits me in South Korea.

The plan is to drive through Japan to Fukuoka, then take a ferry to South Korea, which I will explore in a zigzaggy fashion up to the border with the North, before travelling again by sea to China. In China I will journey by train from Beijing to Harbin in the north, then back down to Hong Kong through the cities of the eastern seaboard which were the main focus of Japan's invasion of 1937–45. From there I will cross to Taiwan, before ending up back in the Japanese capital. I am looking forward to it all enormously, but there will be some dark waters to navigate. I realise that at times I am going to have to stare into the heart of that rising sun which has so captivated me in the past, and that I may end my trip with a very different view of the Japanese.

I begin my journey not in a place but a year, 1853. And at the start of my trip I am quite certain about one thing: if you go back far enough, everything is the fault of the Americans.

JAPAN

1

Kurihama

The assembled samurai and shogunate officials of the court of the Emperor Komei were captivated, watching intently as the American engineers Mr Gay and Mr Danby spent the morning laying a circular railway track on the Yokohama harbour front and attending to the Norris Works miniature locomotive with the focus of bonsai pruners. When, finally, the engine's boiler had been lit and the required pressure achieved, its resulting motion and accompanying clouds of steam were indeed a novel and thrilling sight. The Japanese onlookers were 'unable to repress a shout of delight at each blast of the whistle'.

The train was a scale model, its carriages too small even to accommodate a child, but this was not going to cheat the samurai of their ride. Dressed in all their feudal finery they 'betook themselves to the roof', sitting atop the carriages, robes billowing, swords held carefully at their sides, to experience this Western technological marvel as it lapped the 350-foot, 18-gauge track at speeds of up to 20 miles per hour.

This was the famous exchange of gifts between Commodore Matthew Calbraith Perry, envoy of President Fillmore of the United States, and the representatives of the Tokugawa shogunate, rulers of Japan, with the Emperor Komei present as the country's symbolic head. As well as Perry's own report, from which I quote, there is a splendidly evocative painting of the events of March 1854 by a Japanese witness, a panel of twelve scenes depicting this seismic clash of civilisations, the very moment Japan commenced its turbulent journey to modernity.

On its first visit the previous summer Perry's fleet of 'Black Ships' had dropped anchor at Kurihama, a little south of Yokohama just around the headland flanking the entrance to Tokyo Bay. Perry and his men were on an extraordinary mission to prise open a country which had been shut off to the world since the 1630s, an era known as the *sakoku* – 'closed country' – period. I had read of this event many times, which always evoked for me levering open a stuck kitchen drawer or an obstinate oyster, but why and by what means did a sailor from a far-off land unilaterally dictate an epochal shift in foreign policy to a sovereign nation without a single weapon being discharged in anger?

For the why, we need to go back to 1848. Mexico had lost its two-year war with the United States and would forfeit California, the final piece of the USA's west-coast puzzle, the Americans having relieved the British of Oregon a couple of years earlier. The US now eyed the Pacific greedily. Beneath its waves there were whales galore, whose oil illuminated and lubricated the rapidly industrialising world and accounted for roughly 20 per cent of the entire American economy at the time. But the more whales they harpooned – up to three thousand a year in the mid-1800s – the further the Americans had to sail out into the Pacific. If they sailed far enough, the riches of China awaited: tea, silk and porcelain. With colonies ranging from India to Singapore and Hong Kong, their great rivals the British had grown rich on the China trade, and America badly needed a foothold in this part of the world.

Looking in the other direction, to the east, the journey overland across America was now the shortest route between China and Europe, making it 'a highway for the world', as one contemporary report put it. But there was a problem. On the same latitude as the whaling port of San Francisco, in the way of China and its riches, lay a two-thousand-mile-long hitherto impenetrable barrier: the Japanese archipelago. Japan had been effectively closed to the world since Portuguese missionaries had excited the locals with their radical ideas and threatened the power of the Tokugawa shogunate, the country's feudal military government. Christianity had been banned, along with all potentially meddlesome foreigners aside from a handful of docile Dutch traders on a couple of hectares of artificial land in Nagasaki harbour – and the Chinese of course. Not to trade with China would have been unthinkable. Any Japanese who left the islands without official permission faced death upon their return. Any foreigner attempting to land on Japanese territory was sent packing, if they were lucky.

In 1846 US Commodore James Biddle had ventured close to the entrance of Tokyo Bay, seeking permission for American whaling ships to be allowed to refuel and repair in Japanese harbours. He had suffered the indignity of being towed back out to sea by the Japanese. Russian attempts to make contact had been similarly rebuffed. The other key Western powers – France and Germany – were also keenly aware that whoever had access to the harbours of Japan controlled the Pacific.

But the seas around Japan's rocky coast were uncharted and notoriously dangerous, with treacherous currents and whirlpools. In 1848 the American whaler *Lagoda* had been wrecked off the coast of Hokkaido, Japan's northernmost main island, and its crew imprisoned. Several had died during their incarceration, and the rest had been forced to trample upon a crucifix to prove their rejection of Christianity. A US naval ship had eventually arrived and persuaded the Japanese to release the survivors, but there had been outrage in the American press at their treatment.

America's response to the *Lagoda* incident and the snubbing of Commodore Biddle not only transformed relations between Japan and the West for ever, but would eventually destabilise the long-established order in east Asia, with cataclysmic consequences which still reverberate today. Seeking to sort out the Japan problem once and for all, in July 1853 Commodore Perry's four heavily armed ships sailed into Kurihama Bay on the Pacific coast of Japan. Japan was believed to be rich in minerals, particularly gold and copper, but also, vitally for the new steam-powered ships, it had coal.

*

I am here now, on the waterfront at Kurihama where the Black Ships first dropped anchor, staring out at the sea, trying to think big thoughts about nations and cultures, colonial legacies and the sands of time, but the modern world is conspiring against me. There is the young family trying their best to make the most of their out-of-season trip to the beach, digging doggedly in the chilly wet sand a few feet away; there is the FUCK THE POLICE graffiti (quite unusual in Japan) on a fisherman's hut over to my right; and a cement works and electricity pylons blot the horizon. None of these is helping to conjure the epochal moment when Perry sailed into this modest bay south of Tokyo and changed the world.

I turn away and walk across the road to a small park. In the middle is a large grey rock like one of Obelix's menhirs, on a plinth, with on one side vertical white Japanese text and on the other an English translation in a, I suppose, rather apt, Wild-West-style font.

THIS MONUMENT
COMMEMORATES
THE FIRST ARRIVAL
OF
COMMODORE PERRY,
AMBASSADOR FROM THE
UNITED STATES OF AMERICA
WHO LANDED AT THIS PLACE
JULY 14, 1853

A nearby plaque expands:

On July 8, 1853, Commodore Matthew Calbraith Perry, USN, Commander-in-Chief, the United States Naval Forces East India, China and Japan Seas, who anchored offing of Uraga, landed here at Kurihama Beach and delivered the letter of President Filmore [sic] to the then Japanese government. Next year, the US Japan Treaty of Peace and Amity had been concluded at Kanagawa. Such series of events became motive power to bring back Japan, who unilaterally shut its diplomatic door to other countries by the then Japanese government, to the world.[2]

I have come to Kurihama because I am looking for a place to start my journey, somewhere with historical resonance, and to me, at least at this stage of my impending trip through the region, the moment when the Americans muscled their way into Japan seems the most resonant of them all.

When Perry sailed into Kurihama he inadvertently set off a chain of events which would result in the complete inversion of the Confucian geopolitical hierarchy which had held in the region for most of the previous two millennia. China had long been the Middle Kingdom, font of all knowledge, technology and civilisation; Korea was its primary tributary, the elder sibling, while Japan was a vaguely barbaric little brother. But the Black Ships' arrival lit the fuse for a quasi-revolution in Japan, followed by rapid modernisation and militarisation, leading ultimately to a catastrophic attempt to build an empire on the Western model.

For Japan this event was the equivalent of one of those alien invasion movies in which colossal spacecraft blot out the sun. Perry's squadron dropped anchor with 'guns placed in position and shotted, the ammunition arranged, the small arms made ready, sentinels and men at their posts, and, in short, all the preparations made, usual before meeting an enemy'. The Japanese were shaken to their foundations by the towering ships, which were up to forty times the size of Japanese vessels and belched diabolical smoke. With their matchlocks and spears, they could only stand impotently by as Perry delivered what he described as a 'manly, yet respectful'

---

[2] Perry's ships arrived off Uraga on 8 July but he actually came ashore on the 14th.

letter from the thirteenth president of the United States to the emperor of Japan.[3]

The Japanese had been warned by the Dutch that the Americans were on their way and, via a mixture of French, Dutch and Chinese, quickly informed Perry that he must leave or at least go to Nagasaki at the far south-western end of the country, where they had officials for negotiating with foreigners a safe distance from the capital, Edo (Tokyo). Perry refused. He was prepared to wait. The Japanese sent artists to draw the Americans' ships and equipment as talks continued about how and where the president's letter would be handed over and a response given from the emperor.

Almost a week later, following many bottles of brandy shared with Japanese functionaries on board the *Susquehanna* (Perry noted that the Japanese's 'studied politeness' was employed as much between themselves as with their visitors, that they somehow knew of the Panama Canal being built on the other side of the world and took detailed notes when shown the workings of the ship's steam engines), they had finally thrashed out the details of an agreement right down to whether the commodore would present the letter with his own hand to the Japanese commissioner, and, amid great ceremony, Perry, two hundred sailors and a marching band landed on the beach here in Kurihama and delivered the president's letter to a Japanese official judged to be of equal standing to a commodore of the United States Navy.

To the letter Perry added a threatening little postscript for the emperor: 'Many of the largest ships-of-war destined to visit Japan have not yet arrived in these seas, though they are hourly expected; and the undersigned, as an evidence of his friendly intentions, has brought but four of the smaller ones, designing, should it become

---

[3] I had always assumed Perry and his mini-armada sailed from the west coast of America, but in fact they went the long way from the naval yards of Annapolis in Maryland on the east coast, across the Atlantic to the Canaries, then around the Cape of Good Hope, stopping at Mauritius before continuing to Ceylon (Sri Lanka), Singapore, Hong Kong, Macau, Shanghai and what is today Okinawa.

necessary, to return to Yedo [Edo] in the ensuing spring with a much larger force.'

Having wintered in Okinawa, Perry returned to Kurihama in February 1854 to receive his answer. He came with eight ships this time, and was rewarded with a letter from the emperor promising 'we shall entirely comply with the proposals of your government.'

The Japanese were all too aware of the fate which had befallen the Chinese at the hands of the English, who had secured Hong Kong in 1842. They capitulated, giving US ships permission to visit Shimoda, south of Tokyo, and Hakodate in Hokkaido, and for a US consul to take up residence in each port. Shipwrecked sailors would be treated hospitably, and American ships allowed to buy supplies. On 31 March 1854 Perry signed the Treaty of Kanagawa to this effect, celebrated on shore with a show by sumo wrestlers ('twenty-five masses of fat', according to Perry), a gift of hundreds of sacks of rice from the Japanese, a minstrel performance by American sailors and the aforementioned miniature steam locomotive.

As Perry later wrote, 'The vigorous grasp of the hand of America which was proffered in a friendly spirit, but thrust forward with an energy that proved the power to strike, as well as the disposition to embrace, had stirred Japanese isolation into a sensibility of its relationship to the rest of the world.'

But Japan had also been humiliated. Its sense of itself had been thoroughly undermined, and its short-term future plunged into uncertainty. The Tokugawa government had caved in at the merest hint of military threat but Perry's initial treaty was just the start. In 1858 another treaty permitted the Americans to set up consulates in several Japanese ports with their own jurisdictions under US law, to set trade terms favourable to themselves and to worship as Christians on Japanese soil, the first time this had been allowed in three centuries. Within a couple of years, the English, French, Dutch and Russian governments had also signed similar 'unequal treaties' imposing their terms on Japan, with Yokohama emerging as the largest centre for foreign trade.

The foreigners' extraterritorial status, meaning that they were not subject to Japanese law or its courts, would lead to various abuses and conflicts. As the British diplomat C. Pemberton Hodgson wrote of Japan in the 1860s: 'Insults, threats, words of doubtful celebrity, met the quiet and wonder-struck Japanese as often as they endeavoured to pacify their indignant guests.' Japan was traumatised and divided by the arrival of the barbarian foreigners. One faction advocated the violent removal of this alien presence, and there were several attacks on foreigners in the early 1860s. In 1862, in Yokohama, samurai of the Satsuma clan, a notoriously belligerent bunch from Kyushu, killed a British merchant, C. L. Richardson, when he refused to dismount from his horse out of respect to them. In retaliation, the British bombarded Kagoshima, at the heart of the Satsuma territory in far south-western Japan, forcing the clan to pay compensation.

In 1866 the Satsuma formed an alliance with the Choshu (from today's Yamaguchi, not un-coincidentally the home prefecture of current prime minister, Shinzo Abe), and rose against the Tokugawa shogunate in the name of the emperor. The ensuing revolution sought to restore the emperor from his centuries-old position as a powerless ceremonial figure to a central role in the modernising elite, with Shinto, Japan's ancient indigenous religion, as the nation's guiding belief system. The Meiji Restoration, as the revolution was later known after the posthumous name given to the emperor, Mutsuhito, who reigned at the time, came about with relatively little blood spilled, thanks to a turn of events which saw both the ruling shogun, Iemochi, and the then emperor, Komei, die within that same year. Iemochi's successor, the Tokugawa Yoshinobu, the last shogun, ruled for just one year. The alliance rid Japan of the samurai class, and restored the emperor to the head of what would become a highly militarised, industrialised, modern Japan. Initially, the victors planned to return Japan to its state of seclusion, epitomised by the slogan 'Revere the emperor, expel the barbarians,' but they soon realised that the best strategy would be to absorb the new technologies of the West. As the Charter Oath read at the enthronement of Emperor Meiji, put it, 'Knowledge shall be sought all over the world, and thereby the foundations of imperial rule shall be strengthened.'

The foreigners were allowed to remain, and forty-eight Japanese officials and fifty-eight students embarked on a two-year mission to Europe and the USA to learn the secrets of the Western imperialists. Dozens of Western engineers were invited to Japan to help with the process of *bunmei kaika* – 'civilisation and enlightenment' – embodying another motto of the era, '*Wakon Yosai*' – 'Japanese spirit/Western technology.' Japan rejected Asia and turned towards the West. It has never really looked back.

The emperor moved his seat from Kyoto to Edo, which was renamed Tokyo. Japan was divided into prefectures to be run by government-appointed governors. With the founding of a national conscript army, the samurai had to get jobs – or not, as was the case for many who died in poverty. And, for all the revolutionaries' bluster about ridding Japan of evil foreigners, within a decade of Perry's arrival the Japanese had begun to dress like Westerners in starchy collars, top hats and tails, eat curry and schnitzel, trade at Western-style banks and were learning how to make whisky and play golf. Above all, the Japanese came to believe that to be a modern nation, to be respected on the global stage, meant becoming an expansionist colonial power.

By 1876, Japan was able to do to its neighbour Korea precisely what America had done to it two decades earlier – open up the country and impose unequal treaty terms. More astonishing still, by April 1895 the Japanese had defeated the Chinese Qing army in the First Sino-Japanese War, fought to decide who would 'protect' Korea. By the ensuing Treaty of Shimonoseki, China was forced to hand over control of Taiwan to Japan. And in 1905 Japan became the first outside nation to defeat a Western power, Russia, following a conflict over present-day North Korea.

Encouraged by this military success, in 1910 Japan annexed all of Korea, partly as a buffer against Russia, partly to secure supplies of food and raw materials for the rapidly expanding Japanese population, and partly to give the samurai something to do. Over the ensuing thirty-odd years, the Japanese army would move into north-eastern China, and continue south to Hong Kong, Singapore and beyond. They would not return home until 1945.

At the Tokyo war crimes trials in 1946, General Kanji Ishiwara, who had been in charge of the invasion of China in 1931, referred specifically to Commodore Perry when questioned on Japan's military expansionism. 'Haven't you heard of Perry!' he told his American interrogators. '[Japan] took your country as its teacher and set about learning how to be aggressive.'

My disappointment at the lack of historic atmosphere here at Kurihama doesn't really matter of course, not least because my original hypothesis – that America was at the root of all east Asia's problems – would later turn out to be fatally flawed. I give up on my attempts to conjure sweeping evocations of history and head for the small local history museum in the corner of Perry Park, interrupting two boys' baseball practice as I cross the gravel.

Inside the museum are fascinating nineteenth-century Japanese depictions of Perry's ships, their exaggerated scale giving a sense of the artists' dumbstruck awe, along with Hogarthian caricatures of the commodore with his massive gold epaulettes like wings, and his crew with huge noses.

I look at a model of the ships in the bay and imagine the fear they must have inspired; the two massive, triple-masted steamers in particular must have seemed quite unearthly. Earlier that afternoon on my drive down the coast from Tokyo to Kurihama, I had stopped off in Yokosuka, Japan's biggest naval base, headquarters both of the largest overseas American naval installation in the world, the 7th Fleet, and the Japanese Maritime Self-Defence Force, their navy by another name. Though obviously no threat to me, I still experienced a stomach-churning frisson standing beside the massive grey bulk of the destroyers. There is nothing like viewing a ship of war up close to give you the willies.

I leave the museum and head back to my car. Kurihama is a rather straggly, workaday kind of town, with a small fishing harbour, a light-industry area and a quiet pedestrian high street. I notice that some of the paving stones are embossed with a profile of one of Perry's ships, with the distinctive steam paddle on the side. These days Kurihama's history is cherished by the town, it seems; they even have a Perry Festival every July.

My plan now is to drive west through Japan and beyond, but first I am going to retrace my steps a little, back up the coast to Yokohama, to explore a rather more contemporary social and political issue which has its roots back in the country's ambitious Meiji-era colonial expansion.

2

Yokohama

I am standing waiting to cross the road close to Yokohama stadium as the convoy of one white and five black minivans passes by. Flags flutter from the vans and red police lights flash from their roofs, but this is not an official parade. I catch a glimpse of a driver's white cotton gloves, incongruously genteel in contrast to the tirade blaring from the vans' loudspeakers, which is so loud it's drowning out the cheers of the crowds watching the baseball inside the stadium on this sunny Saturday afternoon. None of the other pedestrians around me seems to pay the noise any heed at all.

I don't know what exactly is coming from the speakers – it's usually something along the lines of 'Koreans are vermin' or 'Koreans must die', that kind of thing – but I do know that the vans belong to one of Japan's many ultra-nationalist groups. One give-away is that two of them fly rising sun flags, the one with red rays radiating from a central sun on a white background. Once the symbol of Japanese military imperialism, these days the *Kyokujitsu-ki* is often displayed by those with, let's say, a misguided sense of patriotism, and it is especially offensive to the Koreans and the Chinese. The Japanese Maritime Self-Defence Force ships also fly it, which as you can imagine causes problems when they take part in events with the Korean navy.

The name of this particular group is displayed on the side of their vehicles. It translates as 'make wind', a reference not to flatulence but to the kamikaze, the mythological divine wind which supposedly twice saved Japan from invasion from the Mongols in the thirteenth century and also of course refers to their World War II suicide pilots. The vans bear messages asserting that the Japanese constitution is that of an occupied country which they would like to 'blow away', and another referring to the Dokdo/Takeshima Islands dispute.

The first couple of times I encountered these convoys in Japan many years ago I assumed they were mainstream political parties campaigning. Finally I asked some passers-by, and they rolled their eyes and dismissed them as 'crazies'. This would turn out to be the unanimous verdict of every single Japanese person I discussed them with thereafter, but they are noisy, high-profile, persistent crazies – thugs and racists who cause a great deal of upset to immigrant communities. (I was later told by someone who once travelled inside one of the vans that the messages they play are pre-recorded and the passengers pass the time watching cooking shows on TV.)

My encounter with the ultra-nationalists is particularly unfortunate as I have come to Yokohama, Japan's second largest city, south-west of Tokyo, in search of what I hoped would be a positive story about the country's largest ethnic minority, the Chinese. There are 730,000 Chinese with legal residence status living in Japan today, although the actual Chinese population is perhaps more than one million. Yokohama's Chinatown is the biggest in Asia with about 250 shops and restaurants. It is the number-one tourist attraction in the city and is especially packed today as there is an annual festival taking place.

I enter through a massive ornate *paifang* – a Chinese-style gateway – decorated with golden dragons and green tiles, but it is soon obvious that Yokohama's Chinatown is very much a Japanese version of China. At one point I pass a large fibreglass Hello Kitty dressed in a panda suit – a touching symbol of Sino-Japanese accord, I tell myself. Souvenir shops sell plastic battery-powered pandas (which for some reason dance the lambada), and the food is 'international Chinese' rather than anything authentically regional. Everything is nice and neat and tidy, just like the rest of Japan, although some Japanese people had wrinkled their noses when I mentioned I was coming here and warned me that it would be smellier and dirtier than 'normal' Japan.

The queues for all the restaurants in Chinatown are impossibly long today, but that doesn't matter. I have alternative Sino-Japanese lunch plans over on the other side of Yokohama.

I pause, chopsticks poised twixt bowl and mouth. This is the most delicious bowl of noodles I have ever tasted, a genuine goosebump bowl. But wait, Michael. Not so hasty. Calm yourself. Remember your ramen golden rule: 'The true test is how you feel beyond the halfway mark.' Every bowl of ramen tastes good to start with, but in my heart I already know this bowl from Rishiri Ramen Miraku, an outpost of a restaurant on a remote island off the northern coast of Hokkaido, is the single greatest noodle soup I will ever taste. Slurp, slurp, ponder, slurp. I'm already feeling wistful that it is nearly over. Slurp, tilt bowl, scoop the last spoonful. Deep sigh.

I am in Yokohama's Raumen Museum ('raumen' is a common alternative spelling of ramen), more a food theme park than a museum, decorated in a Showa-era style to look like Tokyo in 1958. I have arranged to meet the museum's PR director, Masahiro Nakano, because I want to find out more about the Chinese origins of ramen, in particular how the Japanese regard the roots of what is arguably their most popular dish. The story has a familiar beginning; it is how so many stories about modern Japan begin.

'Up until the 1850s Japan was a closed country,' says Nakano. 'But China had been trading with Europe and America for a long time, so in China they had plenty of people who could speak English, French and so on. After Japan opened, Chinese people came to work as translators for the Europeans and Americans who started to come here – the special Japanese ports where foreigners were allowed, like Yokohama.' By 1899 the Westerners had all but left Yokohama for nearby Tokyo, but the Chinese remained, their community having grown over the years to around five thousand people. They had set up businesses, initially restricted to three fields: catering (with cooks from Canton), hairdressing and the textile industry.

'There was some distrust of the Chinese in Yokohama, but they were good business partners,' says Nakano, and the one place where the two business communities were always able to gather was around that great unifier, the dinner table. 'The Chinese found Japanese food difficult to eat, especially all the raw vegetables and raw fish, so they started their own restaurants. The Japanese were curious about Chinese food, particularly because they only really ate chicken, not beef and pork like the Chinese.'

In those early years Chinese restaurants were considered rather posh; it wasn't until the early twentieth century that they began to move downmarket. One of the early Chinese culinary imports would become the origins of ramen, which was sold here in Yokohama in the 1890s initially as *Nanking soba*.

So ramen, the most iconic of twentieth-century Japanese dishes, started off Chinese but morphed into something distinctly local with the addition of soy sauce and later *dashi*, Japanese stock made primarily from dried seaweed. Usually, the Chinese make a generic soup which is then used as the base of many dishes, but with ramen the soup is specific to the dish. 'Japanese people think of it as Japanese but realise that it has Chinese roots, and many Chinese think it is wholly Japanese,' says Nakano.

The Americans also had a hand in ramen's rise. After World War II, they flooded the Japanese market with cheap wheat, of which they had a surplus. This fuelled the ramen boom, as ramen uses wheat-flour noodles. Yokohama's Chinatown was also a playground for the American troops stationed in the area; still today it is home to quite a few jazz clubs and American-style bars. But the district really began to boom after 1972, when Nixon's 'ping-pong diplomacy' with China sent the Japanese into a panic. They realised that they too had to start building bridges with the Chinese and so Prime Minister Kakuei Tanaka hastened to Nanjing to shake hands with Mao Zedong. As also happened in the States, this kick-started a mini-boom in all things Chinese, and Yokohama Chinatown took off, gradually transforming into, as one local explained it to me, 'a lovable, cartoony version of China, like Disneyland gives you of America'.

As I left the museum and headed off for another appointment on the other side of the city, this all seemed to me to be a hopeful omen for the ability of different nationalities to cooperate and find common ground. But what happens when the rift is *within* one of those immigrant communities?

3

Kotobuki

'If you just peer round the corner inside that door you can see them, but best not to let them see you looking,' Professor Tom Gill, my guide to the seamier side of Yokohama, whispers as we loiter on the pavement. Checking that we aren't being observed, he gestures that I should look through a beaded curtain over a doorway just ahead. Outside is a glossy black 1970s Mercedes convertible, out of place in this shabby part of town. I sneak a look through the door as I pass, affecting nonchalance. Inside, a handful of men are gathered around a card table. They are yakuza, Tom says. It is an illicit gambling den.

This is obviously an awfully exciting turn of events as far as I am concerned, but Tom, a social anthropologist wearing an argyle sweater, glasses perched absent-mindedly on his forehead, has seen it all before. In his late fifties, he is a long-term resident of the city and has spent twenty-six years in Japan. He is a lecturer at Yokohama's Meiji Gakuin University and an expert on Kotobuki, the district we are exploring. Though adjacent to Chinatown, Kotobuki is very different. Tourists don't come here unless they get very, very lost.

As well as the yakuza, Kotobuki is home to a couple of thousand of the city's day labourers. There are versions of this Japanese skid row in several major cities, but Yokohama's is perhaps the best known; it is also a kind of unofficial Koreatown as most of the flophouses – *doya-gai* – here are owned and in part occupied by people of Korean descent.

In Japan resident Koreans are called *Zainichi*. This literally translates as 'foreign resident of Japan'. In theory the word can apply to any foreigner but in reality it strongly implies someone who is descended from pre-1945 Korean immigrants, a legacy of Japan's annexation of Korea between 1910 and 1945. During this time, hundreds of thousands of Koreans were encouraged to move to Japan to work in mining, munitions manufacturing and farming among other sectors, but as Japan's military ambitions gathered pace, many were also forcibly brought here, or tricked into coming, to replace the Japanese men who were sent off to fight. By the end of World War II, around 2.3 million Koreans, most of them originally from what is today South Korea, were living in Japan, but with the economy almost entirely destroyed, there were few opportunities for work and the majority went home. Most of the 600,000 or so who remained had come voluntarily during the earlier part of Japan's colonial rule and had built lives in Japan over several decades. Then Korea was plunged into the civil war of 1950–3, which was followed by widespread poverty, at times starvation and then brutal dictatorships in both North and South, all of which made the Koreans in Japan even less inclined to return to their ancestral homeland.

Today, there are roughly half a million *Zainichi* in Japan, although as we will see, defining who they are and how they identify themselves is complex, a reflection of the tumultuous times they lived through after the war. The *Zainichi* faced heavy discrimination in the post-war employment market. Public-sector jobs were closed to them because you needed to be a Japanese citizen to work for the government. The moment the Japanese regained control of their own country when the Treaty of San Francisco formally ended the Allied occupation of Japan in 1952, the *Zainichi* were placed in a stateless limbo which endured for many years, affecting their rights in terms of healthcare, travel and job opportunities, despite the fact that they had contributed both to Japan's war effort and its reconstruction.

When it did finally become possible to apply for Japanese citizenship the process was long and costly, which in itself excluded many. It was only when diplomatic relations were restored with South

Korea in 1965 that the *Zainichi* were given the chance to apply for South Korean passports, and many did. Later they were able to apply for 'extra-special permanent residence status' in Japan. Even so, many Japanese companies still did not want to employ Koreans and many had gravitated to working for the American-led occupiers. There was plenty of work for the Koreans in Yokohama's docks unloading the vast quantities of emergency food from ships which flooded into Japan in the immediate post-war years, and later during the Korean and Vietnamese Wars, which were hugely prosperous for the Japanese.

It is obvious that Kotobuki is different as soon as Professor Gill and I enter the first of its four blocks: there are piles of garbage by the side of the road, the buildings are notably grubbier with stained concrete and rusty windows. Chinatown was colourful, full of life, clearly a place for leisure. Kotobuki is monochromatic, not a little bleak. On one corner a couple of dozen rather dishevelled-looking men sit on the kerbside with beer cans at their feet. These are the day labourers.

'The Korean community in Yokohama never had the cash cow of a Chinatown,' Tom tells me as we adjourn to a dingy café-bar. Two men in overalls sitting at the bar drinking draught beers regard us suspiciously for a moment, then return their gaze to the TV on top of the fridge, which is showing a talent show. 'All they've had is this slum district, which most [Japanese] people don't even know is Korean, and if they did, they would use it as just another example of how "slummy" and "smelly" Koreans are.'

This prejudice persists even though people of *Zainichi* heritage have achieved prominence and success in most areas of Japanese society. The richest man in Japan, Masayoshi Son, founder of telecommunications giant SoftBank, is descended from Koreans who came to Japan before World War II; he has even reverted to using his Korean family name. But still the image many Japanese have of the *Zainichi* today – not just the day labourers but all Koreans – is of a lower-class people who make pungent food, have different traditions to the Japanese, and work in unskilled or even criminal occupations. Koreans supposedly all run *pachinko* parlours[4] or *yakiniku* restaurants (derived from Korean barbecue), or work in illicit gambling – stereotypes that the black van protesters exploit.

The *Zainichi* are now in their fourth or fifth generation and their numbers are slowly declining. Around ten thousand take up Japanese citizenship each year, often adopting Japanese names. In this they are helped by the curious situation in Japan whereby people might have an everyday name as well as a completely different official, formal name, which they don't use. There are many options for *Zainichi*: often they use their Korean name informally but maintain a legal alias – a Japanese name for official use. 'Most people would agree that having a Korean name is still going to be a minus point on your CV when you are looking for a job,' says Tom. In the past it has been difficult for *Zainichi* to rent property, and despite the positive image the Korean male has among many female Japanese thanks to the popularity of Korean romance series on Japanese TV, a Korean heritage is still often a handicap when it comes to dating and marriage.

It is a major taboo for one Japanese person to ask another if they are of Korean descent, so sometimes they have to resort to other means to find out. I tell Tom about a Japanese friend of mine who told me that his fiancée's parents, suspecting he might have Korean heritage, hired private detectives to check out his background. Tom thinks this kind of thing is illegal now but adds that it is still an issue in more traditional families. Nonetheless, many ethnic Korean Japanese residents have married Japanese people and have mixed-race children – by some estimates over a million.

Sociologist Yasunori Fukuoka has defined five categories of Koreans in Japan. First there are those who identify with South

---

[4] *Pachinko* is like pinball and is insanely popular in Japan – there are over 12,000 halls. It is illegal to gamble for money when playing, but the ball bearings you win can usually be exchanged for prizes in a neighbouring shop, also usually run by the *pachinko* parlour.

Korea. They are called *Mindan* and might even have dual Japanese/ South Korean nationality – officially illegal, but rarely prosecuted. Most remarkable from a foreign perspective is the second group – die-hard North Korean sympathisers who hope and believe that one day they will return to live in a reunified Korea run by the Kim dynasty in Pyongyang. They are called *Chongryon* or *Chongreon*. For obvious reasons, their number has declined in recent years, but there was a time, back in the 1960s and 70s, when this wasn't such an absurd position to take as North Korea still held some appeal economically and ideologically.

At the opposite end of the spectrum are those Koreans who hate their ethnicity and have changed their names to blend in; they might not speak Korean and have naturalised and received Japanese passports. In many cases their friends and colleagues don't even know they have a Korean background. There are also those who are proud of their Korean heritage – not least since the *Hallyu* cultural wave made it cool to be Korean – but don't consider themselves particularly Korean, don't affiliate to either North or South, certainly don't want to move to Korea and often don't even speak Korean. Finally there are those who don't care either way and just want to get on with their lives in peace without having to identify as anything.

There are an estimated 35,000 or so Korean residents of Japan who continue to refuse to get either a South Korean or a Japanese passport because their sympathies lie with the Great Leader Kim and his regime, and it is quite likely that a number of those who have reluctantly acquired either passport also still identify with the North. They long for the day when its totalitarian dictatorship finally triumphs, and the pure race of the 'true' Korea reunifies the peninsula. All the while the North Korean regime has been firing missiles in the direction of their temporary adopted home.

Even more extraordinary is the fact that these North Korean sympathisers run most of the sixty to seventy Korean schools which remain operational in Japan. There used to be many more North Korean-affiliated schools in Japan, but a large number have amalgamated or closed over the past twenty years. Some of these *Chongryon* schools are funded directly from Pyongyang, and some even receive Japanese state funding via their local prefectures. This is because up until the 1980s many Japanese politicians, particularly from the communist and socialist parties, fostered good relations with the *Chongryon* leadership. *Mindan* – South Korean-oriented – parents often send their children to these schools too because they want them to learn Korean language and culture. They can either send their children to North Korean schools, or abandon their cultural and ethnic heritage completely. When you realise that the suppression of Korean culture and language was a policy of the Japanese when they occupied Korea, you can understand why they might be reluctant to let that happen. 'Imagine, for decades you have seen the Japanese try to destroy your culture and national identity – they made the population speak Japanese, take Japanese names, put up Shinto shrines all over the place,' says Tom. Particularly in the latter stages of their occupation the Japanese did all they could to turn Koreans into Japanese citizens. They even referred to them not as Koreans but 'external Japanese'.

As for the South Koreans, they seem to be ambivalent about the plight of the *Zainichi*. In a 2018 poll only 7.8 per cent cited 'discrimination against South Koreans living in Japan' as the reason they had a 'bad impression' of the Japanese. Far more pressing were issues such as the sovereignty of the Takeshima/Dokdo Islands. Meanwhile, Japanese right-wing groups complain that their special permanent residence status gives the *Zainichi* undue privileges. It isn't fair that if a Korean resident commits a crime, it will be one of his aliases that appears in the newspaper, not his real name, they complain. It also irritates them that the *Zainichi* are allowed to pass through immigration using the same gates as Japanese people.

In truth, Japanese ultra-nationalists probably just use the special-resident status as a convenient stick with which to bash the *Zainichi*. What really gets their goat is the ongoing criticism of Japan's colonial past by South Koreans – by politicians, protesters, on TV, in movies, and in particular the still widespread anti-Japanese teaching in schools, plus of course the Takeshima/Dokdo dispute.

One of the more prominent anti-Korean right-wing groups of recent times has been the Zaitokukai. (Its full name translates as something like 'Citizen's Association Against the Privileges of Old-Comer Korean Japanese'.) It began around 2010, online, before moving to street protests in Osaka and Tokyo, usually in areas with large Korean populations. The slogans they have chanted outside Korean schools and residential areas (as reported in the *Japan Times*) include:

Kick Koreans out of Japan.

Push criminal Koreans into Tokyo Bay.

Come out Koreans who are listening there. Come on out so we can beat you to death. You don't fool Japanese, you cockroaches.

Come on out if you guys have pride as North Koreans. You come forward so you can get tormented to death for the sake of Kim Jong-il. Come on out so we can kill you.

As a result of this kind of thing, in 2014 the US State Department, in its country report on Japan, accused the country of 'entrenched societal discrimination' against its immigrant populations. Following further pressure from the United Nations Human Rights Committee, Japan did eventually pass a law against physical threats to people, but the law doesn't actually ban hate speech in person or online and carries no penalties for the guilty.

In Tokyo the Korean community has traditionally been centred on Shin Okubo, a small district in the shadow of Shinjuku. I go there the next day and spend an enjoyable afternoon wandering the streets around the station, which are packed with Korean restaurants. I have come to meet journalist Koichi Yasuda. I want to get a little perspective on the noisy black minivanners, who seem such an anomaly in decorous, reserved, contemporary Japan. Yasuda had been present at their genesis.

'There have always been racists here in Japan, but if you didn't look for them you wouldn't have noticed them,' Yasuda, in his early fifties and with that slightly knackered appearance typical of the news reporter, tells me. 'But this was a new group emerging. You were seeing a normal mother with her child, ordinary office workers, pensioners, saying that we were better off without foreigners. They have this excessive sense of loss, that many things have been taken away from them by foreigners and foreign countries.'

It was around December 2006 when the online hubbub moved out onto the streets of Japan, led by a man who called himself Makoto Sakurai – his real name is Makoto Takada – from Fukuoka. Yasuda did some digging on him. 'I spoke to people who went to high school with him, but they just said he was very quiet, very low profile. Most didn't even remember him, and there is no trace of him after he graduated apart from local part-time jobs, which means he probably didn't have many friends.' Takada moved to Tokyo, got a job as a security guard and somehow managed to gather a sizeable online following for his racist rants and blog posts. 'He started to engage with Koreans about the territorial issues and historical issues. He became a hero online, a charismatic patriot.'

In truth, Japan's annual immigration figures are minuscule. In 2017 the country accepted 20 asylum seekers out of almost 20,000 applications; typically fewer than 10,000 applications for citizenship are approved each year. The total resident foreign population is currently 1.75 per cent, compared to around 14 per cent in the UK. However, the number of skilled and semi-skilled foreign workers permitted to come to Japan has doubled over the last five years to 1.28 million in 2018, the largest proportion – 29 per cent – being from China, only 4.4 per cent from South Korea. Ironically this influx has been overseen by Shinzo Abe, the current prime minister, who is closely associated with right-wing nationalists. What's more, he is aiming to bring half a million more short-term, unskilled immigrants to Japan by 2025 to help with shortfalls in elderly care, farming and construction.

Takada's followers took to the streets in increasing numbers, beginning in Japan's largest Korean quarter, Tsuruhashi in Osaka, and later here in Shin Okubo in Tokyo. Yasuda picked up on the movement early on but couldn't place articles anywhere in the mainstream Japanese media. 'Editors told me that it was a marginal movement; they didn't need to cover it. Kind of "Ignore them – they will go away,"' he tells me. 'There was also a sense of "Don't give them any publicity."' But he felt they posed a genuine danger precisely because of their broad demographic. 'If it was a group of skinheads then you could have disregarded them.'

A visit by the South Korean prime minister to the disputed Takeshima/Dokdo Islands in 2012 was the catalyst for a major explosion in the number of anti-Korean marchers. As the demonstrations outside Korean schools grew to gatherings of up to a thousand people, it became impossible for the mainstream media and the government to ignore them. The Tokyo authorities eventually cracked down on the demonstrations, but by then locals had already mobilised in opposition. 'When Zaikokukai organised with seven hundred people, more than a thousand came to counter them and, just like the Zaikokukai, they were a whole spectrum of people – regular people, not unionists or communists, but salarymen, musicians, office workers,' Yasuda says.

Why did the right wing protest so much against South Korea? Surely, North Korea and China pose far greater military, economic and diplomatic threats to Japan?

'I asked a member of Zaikokukai this, and he said that it was because they had more information about South Korea. China and North Korea are further away physically but also in terms of information. Whatever is reported in the South Korean media is also reported here. The racists in Japan hear about the Korean education system [which can be virulently anti-Japanese]; they know a lot about how the average South Korean thinks about Japan. They are an easy target.'

It was all very depressing, but Yasuda-san did have some good news. 'The number of demonstrations is down. Their activity is slowing to nil.'

Hooray!

Not so fast.

'It's not because we have less racism or discrimination in Japan. The reason is, Japanese society as a whole has embraced their ideas. It used to be them saying, "Go Home, Koreans," now I hear that kind of thing from people around me. And look at the Japanese government. It's just a diluted version of the Zaitokukai. Mr Abe doesn't make crude remarks like they do – he is quite sophisticated – but his government believes that the pre-war militarism of Japan was correct, and there are so many in the local assemblies making the same kind of assertions.'

Another prominent right-wing group is Nippon Kaigi – 'Japan Conference' – founded in 1997. They are rather more sophisticated in their rhetoric than the black vanners: one expert described them to me as 'a blue-blood, upper-crust elite made up of effete reactionaries'. They fear China, want to revive the Meiji restorationists' emperor-centric view of Japan, amend the constitution so that Japan can militarise, and erase anything unpleasant about the colonial past from Japanese history textbooks. They endorse prime-ministerial visits to the Yasukuni shrine to pay respects to the war dead, including war criminals. Indeed, among their membership are many descendants of those who prosecuted the war in the 1930s, most prominently Abe himself (his grandfather was a high-ranking official in the wartime government), as well as a large number of members of the Diet, Japan's legislature.

Yasuda draws a direct line between modern-day right-wing racism and the country's imperial past. 'Japanese people have always considered the Korean peninsula as our enemy. Ninety years ago, after the great Kanto earthquake here in Tokyo, many Koreans were killed by locals.[5] We have always looked down on them as a violent people, barbaric people. I can remember my grandparents saying we should always be wary about Koreans. Discrimination: that is their history.'

Social media have also changed the landscape, of course, simultaneously isolating and connecting people with extremist views. 'These people have found what they think is the truth online. For them the media is the enemy. Whoever screams loudest and longest gets the people's attention.'

And yet Yasuda still has some hope. 'I hate the way it is in Japan today, but I believe in society. I believe that people have the power to change this trash society because it was ordinary people who stopped the demonstrations in Shin Okubo. Today, you can't conduct that kind of demonstration here unscathed. They are mocked. There is a counter-attack. Democracy has always been precarious, but I have a marginal hope – very marginal, but I hope.'

[5] As many as 6,000 *Zainichi* were hunted down and killed by Japanese vigilantes in the wake of this massive earthquake – one of the twentieth century's worst natural disasters – which struck Tokyo in September 1923. False rumours spread that the community posed a threat – that they were poisoning wells and planting bombs, and so on. Each year in Tokyo the killings are remembered in a ceremony in Yokoamichi Park in the east of the city, but in recent years some prominent Japanese politicians have been more equivocal about the massacre. The same kind of xenophobic scaremongering still sometimes happens in Japan after earthquakes, although now it is usually online.

4

Ebisu

You would think that the decades of attacks and vitriol from the Japanese right wing would have generated a strong sense of solidarity among the two main *Zainichi* factions, the *Mindan* and the *Chongryon*. But not a bit of it.

Back in the 1980s there had been an attempt to turn Kotobuki into a Koreatown to rival Yokohama's Chinatown, for instance, but the groups could not agree on a plan, despite the fact that it would have been a sure-fire economic winner with its location on prime real estate close to Chinatown and the baseball stadium. The idea was to knock down all the flophouses, sell off half the land for redevelopment into offices and hotels, and use the rest for Korean barbecue restaurants, bars and an off-course betting centre for horse- and power-boat racing. Yokohama's Koreatown would have been perfectly placed to cash in on the boom in Korean culture which swept through Japan in the late 1990s and early 2000s, anthropologist Tom Gill told me, 'but the two groups essentially hated each other's guts'. The discussion dragged on for years, until the economic crash rendered further discussion redundant.

The mutual hatred between *Chongryon* and *Mindan* rumbles on to this day. A couple of years ago a *Chongryon* school won a notable court case against one of the ultra-nationalist groups which had been inciting racial hatred outside its gates, terrorising children and staff. But did the local *Mindan* newspaper report on their success against the hate-mongers in the Japanese courts? They did not mention a word of it. And when the *Mindan* community was successful in a campaign to stop a fingerprinting identification system – which they felt was discriminatory – the *Chongryon* would have nothing to do with it, as they considered themselves to be merely temporary residents of Japan anyway, inconveniently stranded until the glorious day when they would return to the workers' paradise of North Korea.

Some *Chongryon* Koreans could not wait. Tired of the relentless prejudice and restrictions on them in Japan, they made the move to North Korea regardless. In 1959 Kim Il-sung made a famous speech encouraging *Zainichi* to 'return to the socialist fatherland', and from then until the early 1980s the *Chongryon* leadership in Japan (in the absence of official diplomatic ties between the two countries, their HQ in Tokyo was the de facto North Korean embassy) managed to persuade almost 100,000 *Zainichi* to move to North Korea. They did this with the full cooperation of the Japanese Red Cross, most of the émigrés sailing from the north-east port of Niigata.

Some of the *Zainichi* who left for North Korea later realised their mistake and escaped to China; others have 'disappeared' or been imprisoned on suspicion of spying for Japan or South Korea. But the fate of a few of these migrants is at least now well known thanks to Yang Yong-hi, a *Zainichi* film maker based in Tokyo.

Yang's father was born on Jeju Island, off the south-west corner of Korea, in 1927. Aged fifteen, he moved to Osaka to follow his brothers in search of work, as many Koreans had done. Communism was popular among Koreans in Japan at that time, understandably given its emphasis on the very equality they lacked, and Yang's father fell in with friends who had communist leanings. After the Korean civil war, the group naturally allied themselves with communist North Korea. This might seem an odd choice today, particularly as Yang's father and the majority of *Zainichi* Koreans were from the South, but the newly formed Republic of Korea, to give South Korea its proper name, was poorer than the North, where most of the Japanese factories and infrastructure had been built during the colonial era, and the South soon fell under the control of a right-wing military dictatorship. The dictatorship in the South did not care about the plight of the *Zainichi*: they saw them as collaborators, hardly Korean at all, having lived in Japan for decades at that point. Park Chung-hee, the military dictator of South Korea from 1963 until his assassination in 1979, even advised the *Zainichi* to become Japanese citizens. In contrast, the regime in North Korea had been founded by men who had fought against the Japanese colonialists and were now promising a fair and equal society free from outside influence. The North's leader, Kim Il-sung, made several more speeches directly to the *Zainichi*, promising them a better life, free education, free housing, jobs, free medical care, if they came 'home', and for many years North Korea's economic growth outstripped that of the South. Back then, North or South Korea was the VHS versus Betamex of east Asian geopolitics.

'Though most of them were from the South, more than 70 per cent of the *Zainichi* supported *Chongryon* at that time,' Yang told me when I met her in a cafe in Ebisu, western Tokyo, a half-hour train ride from Yokohama.

I had learned about her family's extraordinary history through her films, the first of which, a documentary, *Dear Pyongyang*, won the Special Jury Prize at the 2006 Sundance Film Festival. The film was shot over ten years and explored her late father's decision, back in the 1970s, to send her three brothers from Japan, where they had been born, to be educated in North Korea. The brothers never returned, and their standard of living and health declined steadily over the years. Yang was able to visit them a few times, and the footage she shot on those visits – the kind of access no foreigner ever gets in that tightly regulated country – was also used in her second documentary, *Sona, The Other Myself*, focusing on her niece. She filmed Sona before she started school, and afterwards, charting her transformation from innocent young girl into a child who, in order to survive, became a parrot of the Kim regime's propaganda.

The obvious question was, why on earth did Yang's parents send her brothers to North Korea in the first place? Sitting in a hipster cafe in Tokyo with cold-drip coffee and matcha madeleines, it seems an unimaginable decision.

'There was a very organised return project involving the Japanese Red Cross,' Yang tells me. 'It was encouraged by both governments and the media. You wouldn't believe it, but even most right-wing newspapers and magazines in Japan were describing North Korea as paradise. And the Japanese government really wanted to kick out as many *Zainichi* as possible.' The *Zainichi* were a diplomatic and social headache for the Japanese. 'And of course the Koreans in Japan were really a non-educated people. Even my father, who became active at a high level in the North Korean association, just graduated junior high. He always talked about Kim Il-sung as a great leader, and about Marx and Lenin and those thinkers, but he never read their books; he only read the pro-Korean propaganda from *Chongryon*.' By the 1970s, Yang's father had risen to become deputy of the Osaka branch, the largest *Chongryon* group after Tokyo.

Yang explains that to properly understand what happened to the *Zainichi* children who were given one-way tickets to North Korea, one needs to make a conscious mental shift away from a European way of thinking, to a Confucian one in which family hierarchy and the authority of the father are inviolable. The family outranks even obvious common sense. Yang's father, a bluff, charismatic bruiser, told his sons that they would get a better education in North Korea, a proper Korean education, for free, and that job opportunities would be vastly better there too, away from the prejudice the *Zainichi* endured in Japan. Yang only escaped being sent by dint of her gender – as a girl, her education was not considered important (she went on to study at universities in Tokyo and New York).

Yang believes her father meant well but was ill informed and later self-deluding. She clearly loved him even though his decision turned her mother into someone she described as 'permanently obsessed' with sending supplies from Japan. When she visited her brothers in Pyongyang, Yang would see the packages her mother had sent stored, untouched, like sacred relics. Why didn't her father go himself? For one thing, he had become a powerful man, more powerful in Japan than he would ever be in North Korea, but also he was holding out for reunification under the Kim regime, so that he could return to his birthplace, Jeju.

Confucian parental pressure is one of the reasons Yang and many other *Zainichi* have not applied for Japanese citizenship. 'If I had applied for Japanese citizenship, there would have been a big war in my family. My parents asked me not to change nationality, that's why I had to wait until I came back from studying in graduate school in New York in my late thirties. By then, I didn't care about it, and even my father said I should get Japanese nationality.' This was a major event, recorded in Yang's film: the moment her father accepted he had been wrong about the North.

'It was a very important, short comment. He didn't want to argue any more. Towards the end of his life, he could finally see the reality. I asked him on camera if he had any regrets about sending his sons to North Korea. I thought he would say nothing, but he said very honestly, "I was too young. I never imagined that things would be like that." That caused a big problem for him with the *Chongryon* because he had this very important post in Osaka.' But by that stage even her father could not deny the nature of the North Korean regime. Kim Il-sung had publicly admitted that his regime had abducted Japanese citizens, and the *Chongryon* organisation had come to seem increasingly sinister.

Though her films are hardly anti-North polemics, Yang has been forbidden to ever return to North Korea. 'I have been totally black-listed. I can't go; I can only write to my brothers and nieces. I was worried that my family in North Korea would get into more trouble after my documentary but so far they are OK.' Her films have been highly acclaimed and entered for international awards by the Japanese film authorities, but Yang has also experienced a backlash at home in Japan.

'Of course, for *Chongryon* in Japan it was still very, very provocative, particularly that my father is shown expressing his regrets. Because of that, I became enemy number one. After it came out, I was very worried about assassination, for me or my parents. My mother's home was attacked – stones were thrown, windows broken – and there were blackmail-type phone calls, obviously from *Chongryon* people saying, "Your daughter is really a problem, we hate her, she is a traitor, how can a graduate of a Korean school do this?"'

This was one of the reasons Yang turned to a fictionalised story with *Our Homeland* (and she is now writing a novel), although that was closely based on the true story of the return of her brother, Seong-ho, to Japan to be treated for a brain tumour – arranged following months of behind-the-scenes negotiating by her father. Sadly, her brother had to go back before he received his treatment. He is still alive but ailing, she tells me. *Our Homeland* was an even greater success than her documentaries. 'In the beginning I was told that no major Japanese stars would appear in it because it was so political and would mean their careers would be damaged – they would never get commercials again – but we got our first-choice actors. I had two big Japanese stars, so lots of people who knew nothing about the *Zainichi* came to see it, and it was written about even in fashion magazines. I realised that many good Japanese actors were bored by the simplistic stories in Japanese films.'

Though she is too modest to say, *Our Homeland* cleaned up at the domestic Japanese film awards, and remarkably, given the subject matter, was selected to represent Japan in the foreign language category at the Academy Awards in 2012. 'It was totally ridiculous. My film was not so bad, but honestly there were no good Japanese films that year. Anyway, anyway ...' she says, brushing aside my praise in a very Japanese manner, 'after that, the stars appeared in many, many TV commercials!'

And what of the *Chongryon* today – presumably, they are dwindling to the point of extinction? 'I still have friends who send their children to *Chongryon* schools,' Yang says. 'You see, if they denied or changed their ideology, they would really have to deny their entire lives. That generation, they devoted their lives to protect that *Chongryon* story, and suffered so much because of it. And now, finally, I understand a little bit. These were poor, not very educated people, living in a society which treated them as less than human, and they found a community where they could become a human being, and find something to believe in and belong to. Of course, when they finally realised the whole of this life was wrong, or an illusion ...' Yang shrugs as if to say their whole lives had been based on a phantom promise. After that had gone, there was nothing.

They lost so much: lives, time, hope, nationality, any sense of belonging, of home. Perhaps they were destined to lose everything the moment they set foot on those boats to travel to Japan. As the novelist Min Jin Lee writes in her gripping *Zainichi* family saga *Pachinko*, set during and after Japan's occupation of Korea, 'There was always talk of Koreans going back home. But in a way, all of them had lost the home in their minds for good.'

One suspects that the fate of Yang Yong-hi's siblings was shared by many of those 1970s *Zainichi* returnees to North Korea, but what of those who ignored Kim's siren song and instead attempted to find their roots in the South?

It was early in the morning, too early for any good to come of a knock at the door. Kang Jang-Heon, twenty-four, dragged himself out of bed. Three men stood outside the door of his student accommodation in Seoul. They wanted to know about Kang's friends. Would he mind stepping outside for a moment? He threw on some clothes and followed the men downstairs. Waiting on the street was an army Jeep with two armed soldiers. In those days South Korea was ruled by a military dictatorship headed by a Japanese-trained general, Park Chung-hee. People went missing in the Republic of Korea and were never heard of again.

The military police bundled Kang off to a military jail, where following lengthy interrogation he was charged with breaking national security laws. He had visited the enemy, North Korea, and received orders from the regime, said his accusers; he was the leader of an 'underground group' which wanted to foment revolution in South Korea. He was not permitted to see a lawyer, and no communication was allowed with the outside world. For two months Kang was questioned and tortured using water and electric shocks. Eventually he signed a confession.

This was 1975. Kang had been born in Nara, Japan in 1951 to Korean parents. His father had followed in his grandfather's footsteps, leaving Korea towards the end of the war, aged just fifteen, to become a clerical worker in Osaka. Kang's mother had made a similar journey and had met his father in Osaka.

Growing up in Japan in the 1950s, Kang had early on realised that as a *Zainichi* he would struggle. 'I couldn't see any light in Japan,' Kang tells me when I meet him later on in my trip in a rather dingy café in Tsuruhashi, the Korean quarter of Osaka, where he now lives. 'You couldn't get a government job. You couldn't get any work in the public sector. You couldn't enter big enterprise. I thought there would be little chance for me. That there were better opportunities in Korea.'

Despite not speaking any Korean, in 1971 Kang left Japan to study medicine at Seoul University, where he soon fell in with the pro-democracy crowd which the military junta claimed were in the pockets of the North. 'I was anti-Park and anti-Kim – I just wanted peace,' he tells me, referring to the then leaders of South and North Korea. In those days the Japanese had much better access to North Korea via regular ferry routes from Japanese ports. Kang believes this is why he was singled out and accused of being the movement's leader and a regular visitor to North Korea, despite never having set foot in the country.

He was indicted in January 1976, and over the course of the next fourteen months was tried three times, on each occasion appealing, and on each occasion the verdict and sentence handed down, not by a jury but by three judges, was death by hanging. 'At first I felt that it wasn't really happening. As each trial went on, I started to feel it was real and I grew afraid.'

Kang is now in his mid-sixties. He looks like the academic he eventually became, and currently teaches international relations at Doshisha University in Kyoto. Quiet, composed, without a trace of anger or bitterness, he speaks calmly and evenly to me about his ordeal.

He was imprisoned with murderers, thieves and rapists, handcuffed twenty-four hours a day, even while sleeping, and transferred to several different prisons over the years. At one point, denied his precious exercise time, when he had a chance to meet other student prisoners, he went on hunger strike. Guards tied him up and beat him for eight hours straight. Although the Japanese government did not initially intervene in his case, he suspects the authorities hesitated to kill him because of his connection to Japan. Many other students who were found guilty of collusion with North Korea were hanged, but Amnesty International eventually became involved in Kang's case. Friends from Japan testified that he couldn't have visited North Korea on the dates the South Korean authorities claimed because he was in Hokkaido with them. In 1982, after six years on death row, his sentence was commuted to life imprisonment, and then to twenty years. He ended up spending another seven years in prison before being released in December 1988 as the South Korean democracy movement built to critical mass and the Seoul Olympics shone a light into some of the darker recesses of the penal system.

'I couldn't sleep the night before I knew I was to be released,' Kang recalls. 'I just rubbed the wall of my cell, thinking to myself that my youth resided there. I remember in the morning passing through so many gates, so many gates ...' For a moment he looks past my shoulder to the wall behind me. 'I was a little confused but eventually I reset my feelings. The people outside had always lived their lives, but I had to catch up with my lifestyle slowly, at my own pace.'

Surprisingly Kang remains deeply attached to South Korea and to the idea of reunifying the peninsula. He is able, he says, to separate the military junta which imprisoned him from the rest of the country he loves. 'My complaint is between my family and the Korean government, not the people.' He even has a positive take on his thirteen-year incarceration. 'I got to know Korea in prison. The cell was a reflection of society. In university you tend to mix only with other students, but I learned a great deal in prison. I never gave up because my family and friends supported me all the time, and over the years I could sense that Korean society was changing towards democracy, little by little.'

Kang was only declared not guilty by the Korean authorities in 2015, with the chief judge officially finding that the charges against him had been fabricated. He is seeking compensation. 'It's not about the money – it's only about a million won per year of imprisonment,' Kang tells me mildly. 'The money doesn't pay for the hardship, that's not something I can be compensated for. The real thing I am not happy about is that the Korean government has not said sorry. They have not apologised.'

Kang still does not have a Japanese passport, but does now have a South Korean one. He visits South Korea often and has even visited North Korea (in 1992, out of curiosity, he says). To me it seems strange that he feels more of an attachment to the land which tortured and imprisoned him than the country of his birth. Why doesn't he get a Japanese passport, as he tells me his brothers have done?

'My youth is in Korea, I have friends there. I identify myself as Korean,' he says, sipping his coffee. He looks up. 'I am married and have children here, and the people of Japan are my friends, but Japan is not my country. Every time I go back to Korea, I feel like I am coming home. I think nationality is a human right, and you should have a right to choose.'

Not all *Zainichi* have been so determined to maintain their Korean identity. Tei Tai-Kin is a professor at Tokyo Metropolitan University. Now sixty-nine, the son of a Japanese mother and Korean father, he has dedicated much of his career to Japan–Korea relations, including fourteen years as a lecturer in Korean universities.

When he and I met in Tokyo, he told me he had little time for what he considers the 'victim mentality' of many of his fellow *Zainichi*. He long ago chose to take Japanese citizenship and a Japanese name – his original name was Chung.

'When I moved to Korea I realised that there was not actually much sympathy in South Korea itself,' he said. 'It was rather hypocritical.'

Tai-kin has a sister who has refused to take Japanese citizenship and kept her Korean name, Chung Hyang Gyun. Finding her career path blocked in the public sector in Japan, she took her case to the Tokyo court but lost the case.

'I think ethnic Koreans in Japan should acquire Japanese nationality,' said Tai-kin brusquely when I asked him about his sister. 'My little sister could have done this and continued to work in the Tokyo metropolitan government. [The *Zainichi*] demanded more and more, they were harassing and bullying Japan, they were hysterical, trying to punish the government of Japan. In the past it is true that being Korean in Japan meant suffering discrimination, but not all Japanese discriminated; there were always some Japanese who sympathised, and those discriminations were abolished at the beginning of the 1980s, yet still the discussion continues. My position is, rather than criticising Japan, I think it's time that the ethnic Koreans here should decide what to do with their nationality.'

5

Nara

Having spent over a week shuttling around Tokyo and Yokohama, it is time for me to hit the road properly. Driving out of Yokohama, I stop off at the Foreign General Cemetery, up on a bluff overlooking the city. The cemetery was founded by Commodore Perry himself as a place to bury one of the sailors who died on his return visit to Japan in 1854, and in the 1890s it was the base for the first British arrivals.

I always find foreign cemeteries in obscure corners of far-off lands poignant. Perhaps it is because the people buried in them travelled to the other side of the world, to a country which in Japan's case genuinely was *terra incognita* at the time. They were nineteenth-century astronauts, colonialists too of course – here to trade, exploit, enslave, or preach – but the residents of this cemetery never saw home again.

Those who did survive long enough recreated their peculiar Victorian upper-middle-class lives here in Yokohama with lawn tennis associations and cricket clubs, a horse-racing track, libraries, schools, hospitals and English-language newspapers. A small museum beside the cemetery tells some of their stories, including that of the American travel writer Eliza Scidmore, who died in Switzerland in 1928 but was so fond of Yokohama that she stipulated that she be buried here alongside her brother and mother. Scidmore is recalled today on the other side of the world, in Washington DC, as the woman who, inspired by her time in Japan, planted the cherry blossom trees along the banks of the Potomac.

I want to take the pretty route west from Yokohama today, which means sticking to the Tokaido Highway, the ancient road between

Tokyo and Kyoto. Before I set off, I imagine this to be a semi-rural, two-lane road, an historic postal route on which I will occasionally encounter small villages of wooden houses and shrines, with cobble-stones and samurai mansions, maybe a wizened old soothsayer or two, pipe-smoking priests, that kind of thing, but it soon becomes apparent that the Tokaido is the very opposite of this, an unrelenting litany of car dealerships, rusty vending machines, cheap housing, vast petrol stations, fast-food joints, light-industry parks, strip malls, pylons and billboards – all of which I have ample time to enjoy as the traffic rarely moves faster than 20 miles per hour.

Actually I don't mean that 'enjoy' sarcastically. The nature of the Japan fetishist is such that he or she can experience shivering frissons of excitement at the most quotidian of Japanese sights – a billboard campaign for coffee featuring Tommy Lee Jones floating in a bathing ring, for instance, or a timewarp 1960s shopfront – so it is no great hardship that my first day is a treacly crawl in heavy drizzle for the entire hundred miles to Shizuoka, my first overnight stop.

Shizuoka is rather lovely, squeezed between bamboo forests, mountains and the sea. Any land not built upon is given over to plump green tea bushes, a balm for the eyes, and the spaces between them are so overgrown with rapacious vines and greenery that I imagine if the people went on holiday for a week, the whole place would be reclaimed by the jungle by the time they returned.

A couple of random, motoring-related things strike me during my first day's drive. There are no roundabouts in this country but the Japanese do love traffic lights. There is a set every couple of hundred yards or so, which is enervating. Even when there is no traffic, the Japanese drive at a cautious pace: on one dual carriageway the limit is 30 miles per hour. Japanese cars and even trucks are meticulously maintained with not a speck of dirt, but they only seem to come in three colours: white, black or silver, mostly white. The car I have borrowed though is a very loud, orangey-copper colour. Amid the otherwise monochrome traffic I feel like one of those Congolese dandies at an accounting convention. More pertin-ently as far as my mission is concerned, I see not a single Korean car. Not one Kia, no Hyundai, not so much as a ssingle Ssangyong, despite the fact that South Korea is the world's fifth largest car manufacturer.

I pass some of the journey with my ongoing game of Japanese car name bingo, spotting old favourites like the Nissan Cedric, the Toyota Ractis and, for a maximum ten points, the Mazda Bongo Friendee. I wonder why nobody at Japanese companies ever bothered to run their slogans by someone who speaks English as a first language. Even back in the 1980s, when there was a rash of such names and anything foreign was deemed exotic and cool, it couldn't have been that difficult to find out that, say, Calpis and Pocari Sweat were not ideal names for soft drinks.

To me though this linguistic hubris evokes a Japan of unfettered confidence, one that felt it could mould the English language to suit its purposes. Can you imagine how great it was to have been Japanese in the 1980s? Your country had recovered from the atrocities of war, rebuilt itself from virtual bankruptcy in the 1940s, when the average annual income per capita was on a par with a Sri Lankan's, into one of the richest and most technologically advanced nations on earth with bullet trains, portable TVs and enough money to persuade Harrison Ford to advertise pretty much anything. Westerners no longer recoiled from your eating habits; indeed Manhattan was in thrall to platinum-card sushi joints, which was fortunate because Japan Inc. owned a good chunk of it.

The excesses of Tokyo in the 1980s are legendary: the members-only Ginza restaurants where high rollers ate sushi from the naked bodies of geishas; the vintage Ferraris bought on a whim and left to rot in Nakameguro basement garages; the gold leaf sprinkled liberally over *wagyu* tartare; and the old master paintings bought by the yard to hang on the walls of corporate bathrooms.

Such profligacy seems an age away now. For more than two decades the story has been of Japanese 'stagnation' and an economy doomed by irreversible demographic decline. I suspect Japanese business people have been quite happy to maintain that perception in negotiations with foreigners, but any visitor to Japan can see that things are not as bad as is made out. It still at least looks like an incredibly wealthy, highly developed country, with among the best living conditions in the world. So what is the reality of Japan's economic misadventure? What went wrong, and what's going right?

Legend has it that at the height of the boom, in 1989, the land occupied by the grounds of the Imperial Palace at the bullseye of Tokyo – an area roughly the size of Disneyland – was valued at more than all of California's real estate combined. To give you an idea of how out-of-kilter property prices had become in relation to the size of the economy, that made the palace worth approximately $5.1 trillion. Japan's total GDP in 1989 was $5.3 trillion. And then the bubble burst.

'The bubble burst.' I read that so many times but never fully grasped what it meant, why it happened, or the enormity of Japan's financial collapse. The stark figures are these: within two years the square-metre price for property in the Japanese capital had dropped by 80 per cent, in some cases more. The Nikkei, Japan's stock market, plummeted 60 per cent because companies and institutions were allowed to borrow money in quantities so great they ended up threatening the economy of what was then the second richest nation on earth. The Bank of Japan got carried away with the growth achieved off the back of industrial exports in the 1970s and loaned so much cash that it fuelled one of the greatest property booms in human history. To combat the resulting inflation, the bank increased interest rates, and all those companies with loans suddenly found they could not repay them. The government was forced to step in to prop up those deemed too big to fail. At the same time, manufacturers that had prospered in the 1970s by adding value to imported raw materials by manufacturing high-quality, high-tech products, faced growing competition from fast-developing rivals in South Korea and Taiwan, and later China too. To revive the economy, Japan resorted to increased spending financed by borrowing, which is how it has ended up today with a debt ratio of 236 per cent of GDP, when even Greece is only at 180 per cent.

In his book *Dogs and Demons: the Fall of Modern Japan* American author Alex Kerr lays the blame at the feet of Japan's ruling elite, particularly the bureaucracy and its refusal to modernise: 'Japan's way of doing things – running a stock market, designing highways, making movies – essentially froze in about 1965,' he writes. The country does appear to have been stuck in its ways, and in many respects – particularly the participation of women in the labour market, on company boards and in government – it still is.

The economy stopped growing, but it didn't actually shrink that much, and even in the dark days unemployment never exceeded 6 per cent – at least not according to official statistics. Today the *Washington Post* claims that Japan's 'economy has done so well the last few years that it has almost entirely made up all the ground it [lost] during its protracted slump in the 1990s'. But things were never as bad as they seemed. The country's declining workforce made the overall GDP figure look worse than it actually was; GDP per working age adult – the amount individuals actually contribute economically – has remained buoyant, outperforming both the UK and the US. In other words, there may be fewer Japanese people, but they are as productive as ever. The number of women working has increased by 7 per cent over the last six years too.

Government debt is still eye-popping, and low inflation doesn't help in repaying that debt, plus the declining population is going to have an impact on tax revenues in the future, but in 2018 Japan had a trade surplus of £155 billion. The debt is mostly held within Japan too, so there is little risk of a lender coming knocking. Japanese companies are also said to be sitting on at least two trillion dollars worth of cash, perhaps half the nation's entire wealth. Much of the rest is sitting under mattresses: the Japanese are notable hoarders of cash.

Reports of Japan's demise may have been exaggerated then, but the country now has one of the highest relative poverty rates of any developed nation. A sixth of Japanese people now live in relative poverty, and almost two thirds report that they find life financially tough. Meanwhile, Japan's Gini coefficient – a measure of relative economic equality – is higher than the OECD average; this was once one of the most equal societies in the world, an entire nation of middle-class people, but inequality is growing. The majority of Japanese parents believe their children will be financially worse off than they are.

Perhaps the single greatest contributor to that pessimism is the precarious employment market, which fuels economic insecurity and in turn makes people hold on to their money instead of spending it and stimulating the economy. Almost 40 per cent of workers are now on temporary contracts, which means they are less inclined to marry and have children and more vulnerable to being coerced into working long hours. According to a government report, 20 per cent of Japanese companies admit that their employees work more than 80 hours overtime per month; a working day of 20 hours is not unusual. As a consequence, there are roughly 200 official *karoshi* incidents every year – people working themselves to death – although some believe the true figure is in the thousands.

Over the next day, driving to Nara, the scenery tells the story of the rise and stalling of Japanese industry. I pass the Fuji Film factory, challenged by the arrival of digital cameras and the inexorable rise of the smartphone; the headquarters of Toshiba, which suffered a catastrophic accounting scandal in 2015; and beleaguered Toyota, which has recalled a record number of vehicles in recent years. I pass over the Nagoya plateau, one of the epicentres of Japan's incredible post-war industrial growth. Today it is a vision of the future as seen from 1975 – an endless concrete agglomeration of tower blocks, slag heaps, gas storage tanks and warehouses. There are forests of pylons and, down by the docks, rows and rows of gigantic red and white cranes. Most magnificent of all is the cat's cradle of flyovers which helps me to leapfrog the churning brown waters of the Ibigawa (Iba river), and a little further south I pass above the largest roller coaster I have ever seen.

Finally free of Nagoya's urban-industrial sprawl, the road climbs into green mountains, today shrouded by cloud. As I descend the other side, I come to Nara. This was briefly the capital of Japan in the eighth century and today is famous for its highly Instagrammable sika deer, which saunter like pampered concubines through the town centre's shrines, streets and parks. The sika are a pretty hazelnut colour with wonderful curving antlers and a scattering of lighter spots down their backs, like snowfall. They are tame to the point of being blasé as far as humans are concerned, and pose nonchalantly in front of the more picturesque pagodas. I stoop to take a selfie with one and only notice later, looking at the photograph, that the animal had started to eat the brim of my hat as I pressed the button.

Nara is a wistful, mystical kind of town which really comes into its own in the early evening when the day trippers have retreated back to Kyoto, the tightly topiaried hat-stand pine trees throw freaky join-the-dots shadows, and the narrow, maze-like backstreets are left to the town's four-legged inhabitants, lending it a vaguely post-apocalyptic mood. Instead of cockroaches, only the deer have survived.

But there was no apocalypse for the Japanese economy, not really, and these days its slow, manageable decline doesn't look all that bad from the outside. Whenever I think about Japan's economic stuation, I always come back to a quote in David Pilling's excellent book about Japan, *Bending Adversity: Japan and the Art of Survival*. Pilling, a former *Financial Times* Asia editor, reports a British member of parliament visiting Tokyo, staring up in wonder at the glitter of Ginza and saying, 'If this is a recession, I want one.'

Perhaps, Pilling writes, we need to readjust how we assess economies and their success. If you travel in Japan, you will experience a country which functions better than almost any other in the world on almost every level, from its low crime rates and exemplary public transport to extremely high levels of civic responsibility, not to mention the best service culture you will ever enjoy. It's still rich in real terms too – according to Bloomberg, Japan has more millionaires than Germany and China. Combined.

Looking back, the greatest blow to the Japanese may well have been to their pride. In 2010 China overtook Japan to become the world's second largest economy, restoring the ancient Confucian order of things with China as the Middle Kingdom, the centre of the world, the big brother.

With regard to China, there is one thing that the Japanese still have money for: their military, or rather the Self Defence Forces, as they are called. Military spending – largely incentivised by China's growing maritime power – has been rising for the last six years and is at a record high (5.19 trillion yen, £35 billion). The spending increases have been championed by the current prime minister, who is attempting to make other, more deep-reaching changes to Japan's military capability. He wants to revise its post-war pacifist constitution so that the military could one day be used for purposes elsewhere in the world other than providing humanitarian assistance. For some his proposals are seen as restoring the country's pride and independence, for others he is dragging Japan in a regressive direction with uncomfortable echoes of its imperial past, a past which Abe and his associates do not appear entirely to have rejected.

6

Kyoto

I get Kyoto wrong every time. I must have visited this ancient, unknowable, ugly-beautiful city a dozen or so times, yet still it catches me unawares.

The first occasion I came here, I had an idea I would somehow step off the bullet train into seventeenth-century feudal Japan but instead found myself marooned in the hostile concrete wasteland around the station. On another occasion I stayed in a hotel in the far north of the city, tumbleweed-miles from anywhere. Often I have walked for hours along soulless six-lane roads lined with anonymous office buildings and Starbucks coffee shops, keenly aware that richly textured time-warp backstreets were somewhere near. And I always overstuff my itinerary with UNESCO World Heritage sites – Kyoto has seventeen of them (Holland has ten) – and get shrine-blind by the end of the first day. My latest mistake: I arrive as cherry blossom season begins.

There is almost no low season in Kyoto, but in late March/early April the fabled *sakura* are unfurling their Hello Kitty charms, and as a result I have never seen the city – any city – as busy, or as pink. The Japanese government's post-bubble tourism drive has seen visitor figures soar from six million in 2011 to 28.6 million today. It has been a tonic for the economy and is expected to peak with the 2020 Olympics, but many feel it is destroying the essential nature of places like Kyoto.

I press on through the crowds to catch some of the *sakura* action. Contrary to expectations, far from being a seen-one-seen-them-all kind of deal, my first glimpse of a flowering cherry tree only makes me greedy for more, and I spend most of the rest of my first day in the city walking around taking photographs of the blooms in, frankly, a girlish rapture. I realise I am a lost cause when at one point a small child runs past me catching the blossoms as a gust of wind blows and I surreptitiously put out my hand to catch some too.

Auspiciously, not only is there an abundance of cherry blossom but on my first night in the city there is a full moon to boot. It is a meditation-on-the-fleeting-nature-of-existence double whammy, guaranteed to send the Japanese into a collective swoon. They softly chant 'sugoi' ('wonderful') and form orderly queues to stand in one particular spot for the perfect view of the trees overhanging the Kamo river, with the moon beaming up above. A man with a loudhailer kettles the crowd as we shuffle forward to take our photographs, get our billing and cooing over and done with, and move on.

Kyoto has an almost mystical significance for the Japanese, partly because it was the capital from AD 794 to the Meiji Restoration, including, crucially, the *sakoku* period. This was the era of unification and relative peace, the lotus-eating time when the samurai class indulged in ritualised tea ceremonies, calligraphy, poetry, elaborate multi-course meals and precision gardening. At least, this is the commonly held perception of Japan in the seventeenth, eighteenth and early nineteenth centuries.

'You do have to be careful about those preconceptions of Japan being isolated because it went through phases of profound engagement with Asia and the rest of the world,' explains Professor John Breen, who I meet for lunch the next day. Japan always maintained contact with the outside world, mostly via China from the western island of Kyushu and the Ryukyu Islands (modern-day Okinawa), he says, but also with Russia from eastern Japan; and in Nagasaki there was trade with Europe via the small Dutch presence there. Communication with Korea, just a short hop across the water from northern Kyushu, was fairly continuous too.

'Of course, Commodore Perry's arrival was profoundly important, but there were all sorts of things going on in Japan before that. There were serious internal social problems already in place,' says

Breen, an expert on the history of religious institutions in Japan. If it hadn't been the Americans, then the French, the Russians, the British or even the Germans would have attempted to open Japan, he adds. So much for my blame-the-Americans theory.

Breen is married to a Japanese woman with whom he has three grown-up children. He taught Japanese at London University for twenty years before moving to Kyoto ten years ago. He reminds me of a young John Berger with his unruly curly hair, heavily lined face and square jaw. He is exceptionally knowledgeable about Japan and its history. Even by the locals, Breen is recognised as an expert on the history of Shinto, the country's ancient religion. He is also remarkably well connected. During our talk he lets slip that he has met the emperor, empress and crown prince; the latter, he suspects, shares his father's unspoken liberal values. When we set up our lunch appointment, I noticed that the last four digits of his mobile phone number were 1868, the year of the Meiji Restoration.

Breen and I have met in a tofu restaurant beside the Kamo river in central Kyoto. I specifically want to talk about Shinto and the Yasukuni shrine, arguably the most controversial religious site in Asia.

Of all the niggling, needless sources of friction between Japan and its neighbours, the simplest one to fix, whose resolution would seem to me to bring disproportionate dividends for all parties, has to be the apparently deliberately provocative visits by Japanese ministers, prime ministers and other prominent figures to the Yasukuni shrine.

Located within walking distance of the Imperial Palace in central Tokyo, the shrine honours the approximately 2.3 million Japanese – mostly men, but also some women and even animals – who died fighting for their country up until 1945. No one is actually buried at Yasukuni; no ashes are interred there. The symbolic enshrinement of the spirits of the dead (their names are written on pieces of paper) is enacted in special night-time rites to the accompaniment of a wailing flute. Their spirits then reside in a special receptacle, the *Nainaijin*, which is housed in the *honden*, the main hall.

This ought not to be controversial. There are military memorials in virtually every country on earth; 400,000 soldiers are buried at Arlington Cemetery in Virginia for instance, and US presidents visit frequently without anyone making a fuss. The problem is that Yasukuni is inextricably linked to Japan's imperial past. Even more problematic is that in 1978 fourteen Class A Japanese war criminals (those guilty of committing 'crimes against peace') were secretly enshrined there – men found guilty of crimes against peace and humanity, those who orchestrated the war. No emperor has visited since, but fourteen prime ministers have, including a Christian (Ohira Masayoshi) and the current incumbent, Shinzo Abe. Some see the Japanese prime minister visiting Yasukuni is akin to Angela Merkel paying her respects at the site of Hitler's bunker. Abe stopped visiting in 2013, possibly at the request of President Obama.

Another point of controversy is that the spirits of around 50,000 Korean and Taiwanese soldiers are also enshrined in Yasukuni, legacy of a time when men from occupied lands were conscripted to fight for Japan. Rather like the Church of the Latter Day Saints, which post-baptises the dead, at Yasukuni they enshrine you whether you like it or not. Relatives have protested, including in Japanese courts, but to no avail. Yasukuni has a policy of never removing anyone once enshrined.

I first visited Yasukuni many years ago, by chance during the annual 15 August commemoration to mark the end of World War II. There was a large crowd of all ages, many carrying parasols to ward off the sun, but there was also a sizeable contingent of ultra-nationalists with loudhailers and their minivans parked on the street nearby. In the broad avenue leading up to the entrance of the shrine were gathered several men wearing colonial-era military uniforms. Some were young but others were old enough to be war veterans, including one man who I think was a kamikaze pilot. Another pilgrim stood in front of the main shrine building dressed in an all-white uniform, rigid as a clothes peg, holding a six-metre flagpole bearing the imperial Japanese flag.

'At the major occasions you do see these guys strutting around in imperial army uniforms, and there are even punch-ups between them and Japan-resident Koreans,' Breen tells me as we sit at the restaurant counter in Kyoto. Yasukuni literally means 'shrine of the land of peace' but Breen has described it as 'a place of violence'. 'The priests at Yasukuni shrine could refuse access to ultra-right-wing groups; they could request the police remove them ... The shrine does no such thing,' Breen has written. In recent years Yasukuni has also attracted foreign right-wing pariahs like Jean-Marie Le Pen and leaders of the British National Party.

Breen has visited Yasukuni with veterans, including surviving kamikaze, and once gave a lecture there. 'The kamikaze had survived because the weather had been bad the day they were supposed to fly, or their plane had had some faults and was force to return, or the war ended before they had a chance to complete their mission,' he recalls. 'The questions afterwards were really interesting. Someone asked me about this question of apologising and pointed out that, you know, coming from the world's first and greatest empire, don't you think it's time that Britain apologised if you are going to insist that Japan apologises. And I said that I agreed with him entirely!'

Even among the veterans there were different takes on the apology issue, which is another sensitive subject in relations with Korea and China. 'There are those who say the emperor should have apologised for the war, others who say leave the emperor out of it.' Some of the veterans were Buddhists, some Christians, some were even communists, but they all returned to Yasukuni to pray for the souls of their comrades. 'A lot of these guys felt they had been forced to sacrifice their lives in pointless ways and they felt a profound anger towards the senior officers who'd sent them there.' Some were former officers themselves, but they strongly opposed the enshrine-ment of the war criminals at Yasukuni. 'Those who led us into war should be treated differently from those who did not,' they told him.

As well as the veterans, Breen's Japan research group once invited a member of the Nippon Kaigi – the right-wing revisionist group which counts many leading Japanese politicians among its members – to talk. 'Afterwards, we went for a drink and I asked him about the emperor. He was really angry with him. He felt that the emperor should visit Yasukuni with pride – he used the Japanese word *dodoto*, which means "boldly" – and that that would have a profound impact on the morals of Japanese youth, that they would learn how to be patriotic Japanese.'

What does it mean to be a patriotic Japanese person? For many, it means facing up honestly to Japan's past, but for those on the right such self-reflection is considered 'masochistic' and detrimental to the morale of the nation.

During my travels in South Korea and China several people told me that the Japanese were 'special', and not in a good way. For them Yasukuni was a symptom of a deficiency of humanity, a lack of empathy. 'How can the people look so polite and rational but regard those criminals as their heroes?' one Chinese student asked me. 'Is there something more complex deep in their culture?' For the record, John Breen does not agree that the Japanese are different or somehow deficient, but in her 1946 book about Japanese culture, *The Chrysanthemum and the Sword*, Ruth Benedict, considered a great expert on Japan at the time, reflected that there were supposedly no moral absolutes in Japanese culture. Theirs was a shame culture, as opposed to our Western guilt culture, with its clearer (to us) moral landscape of right and wrong, guilty and innocent. In shame cultures one's choices are driven by preservation of reputation rather than a moral code: getting caught is the crime. These days many of Benedict's opinions are considered outdated, an aspect of the Orientalist 'othering' identified by Edward Said, but Martin Jacques, writing in his highly regarded book *When China Rules the World*, believes that in Asian societies it is 'how one is regarded by others, rather than one's own individual conscience, which is critical … A sense of guilt can be assuaged by an act of apology; shame, in contrast, is not nearly as easily assuaged.' Perhaps this explains some of the perceived inadequacies of Japanese apologies for their wartime behaviour: an apology is not really enough, can never be enough. The stain of shame will always linger.

With Shinto one of the unique aspects of Japanese culture and history, I had wondered whether it held some explanation for the perceived otherness of the Japanese by their neighbours. The first written records of Japan's ancient belief system date from the sixth century BC, but one can easily imagine its shamanistic, nature-focused belief that all natural things (and these days man-made objects too) are inhabited by gods might have existed in some form as long as humans have lived in Japan, or anywhere for that matter. Shinto has no founder or prophet, no creed or commandments, no sacred texts. More problematic from a contemporary perspective is that its role as a state religion was inextricably linked with the prosecution of Japan's imperial ambitions. The conversion of the Koreans and Taiwanese to Shinto was an important aspect of their assimilation into the Japanese empire, for instance, and the racial superiority which the imperialists believed was bestowed by the origins of the religion was used as a justification for their colonialism. This is why, when the Allies arrived in 1945, one of the key elements of the post-war constitution they drew up for Japan was the separation of state and religion, as laid out in Article 20. According to one story, General MacArthur even considered demolishing Yasukuni, but was persuaded against it.

Despite the hullabaloo over the visits by many prime ministers and senior politicians, Yasukuni is actually a private shrine, not a state site for mourning or worship, so ministerial visits are technically breaking Article 20 of the constitution. But the constitution also guarantees freedom of worship for everyone. To use the latter to circumvent the former, some prime ministers have visited as private individuals – the technicalities involved in this extend as far as making sure they don't travel to the shrine in government cars, or use their title when signing the visitors' book, and that gifts are not paid for from government funds. It gets quite silly at times: Prime Minister Nakasone insisted his visit was OK because he only bowed once at the shrine instead of twice. The ruling Liberal Democratic Party (LDP) has long wanted to revoke Article 20, partly in order to make Yasukuni a national place of commemoration and thus eligible for state patronage and funding.

Yasuhiro Nakasone, who had seen active service during the war as a naval officer, was the first prime minister to visit after the controversial enshrinement of the Class As. (A heads-up on Nakasone: he once declared that Japanese people were more intelligent than Americans because they had not had their average IQ diluted by 'blacks, Puerto Ricans and Mexicans'.) That was in 1985, the fortieth anniversary of Japan's surrender. At the time, Beijing had no problem with Nakasone paying his respects. Indeed, he had informed the Chinese government, then led by his friend, General Secretary Hu Yaobang, that he would be making the visit and Hu had agreed not to make a fuss about it. But shortly afterwards a delegation from the Japanese Socialist Party visited Beijing to pour poison in the Chinese leadership's ears. The Yasukuni visits were one step towards the militarisation of Japan, they told the Chinese, and soon there were anti-Japan protests on the streets of China.

It was over a decade before another prime minister dared to visit Yasukuni publicly, but Junichiro Koizumi (PM 2001–6) made it part of his election campaign, some say because he needed the support of the Japan Society for the War Bereaved (Nihon Izoku kai), and according to polls at the time 65 per cent of Japanese supported prime ministerial visits to Yasukuni. Interviewed recently by the *Financial Times*, Koizumi, now seventy-six, remained defiant on the issue: 'Regardless of whether there are Class A war criminals, three million Japanese citizens lost their lives, so why is it strange to visit Yasukuni, where so many of their spirits are enshrined?'

These days things have changed in terms of public opinion. Surveys tend to show the Japanese are marginally against prime ministerial visits; a recent poll showed 47 per cent against versus 43 per cent in favour, for example. This is perhaps one of the reasons why Shinzo Abe, though a pro-Yasukuni militarist, hasn't been since 2013. He does send ritual offerings though, such as money or small trees.

I asked Philip Seaton, an Englishman who is an associate professor in media and communications at Hokkaido University and who has written extensively about the country's relations with its former enemies, whether Abe's previous visits had been intended as a defiant gesture to foreign critics of Yasukuni. 'No, I think he is saying, "This is my belief system and if I don't go there, I am betraying myself,"' said Seaton. 'In order for his political and philosophical world to make sense, he has to go. I don't think he cares what the Chinese think; he would much rather they turned the other way and ignored him. That would make his life much easier. He is not trying to rile the Chinese.' Breen disagrees: 'I think it is very much an act of defiance.'

Do Yasukuni visits really enrage the Chinese? The reaction of the leadership of the Communist Party of China (CPC) seems to ebb and flow depending on the domestic situation. 'The Chinese problematisation of the issue has always intensified as domestic political issues have become graver' is how John Breen puts it. Yasukuni has, however, been the target of attacks by Korean and Chinese civilians. In 2011 a Chinese man set fire to one of the shrine's *tori* – red gates; in 2013 a Korean man threw paint-thinner inside the shrine, possibly as a prelude to setting fire to it; and in 2015 a Korean man blew up the toilets. (I don't think anyone is suggesting they were sent by their respective governments.)

What few mention in discussions about Yasukuni is that literally just down the road is Chidorigafuchi Cemetery, Japan's official state-funded non-religious national site of war remembrance which foreign dignitaries visit with prime ministers and the emperor on special occasions. In Chidorigafuchi Japan already has a place to memorialise the war, an uncontroversial site free from the spirits of war criminals and right-wing thugs. Also, every year on 15 August both the emperor and the prime minister of Japan attend a memorial service at the nearby Budokan stadium in central Tokyo, to express their sorrow for the devastation that Japan caused in the war. In 2018, in his final appearance at the ceremony as emperor before his abdication in 2019, and as he has done most years, the eighty-four-year-old Akihito again expressed 'deep remorse' on behalf of his people for the war waged in his father's name. Unfortunately, at the same time fifty members of the Diet, including Shinjiro Koizumi, son of the former prime minister and the man many tip as a future leader of Japan, were visiting Yasukuni.

*

Before I left Tokyo I had revisited Yasukuni. I had just read an opinion piece in the *Daily Telegraph* written by the Chinese ambassador to London, Liu Xiaoming, in which he likened the shrine to a horcrux, one of the seven vessels containing Harry Potter nemesis Voldemort's soul (apparently): 'If militarism is like the haunting Voldemort of Japan, the Yasukuni shrine in Tokyo is a kind of horcrux, representing the darkest parts of that nation's soul,' he wrote.

Japan has many ancient temples and shrines – eerie, majestic, unknowable places such as the Ise shrine and Izumo Taisha in Shimane prefecture, which are believed to be more than a thousand years old. Because of the fuss made about it and the reverence in which senior members of the government appear to hold it, I had always assumed that Yasukuni's roots must also go back centuries, and as I walked up the broad, paved approach lined with cherry trees, passing through the two large *tori* gateways to reach the *honden*, I tried to be more sympathetic to its role as a national focal point. Who was I as an outsider to judge the pre-medieval spiritual practices of the Japanese? Perhaps we should just tolerate them, as we tolerate other similarly offensive rituals and traditions, like the burning of a papal effigy in Lewes on Bonfire Night or the Black Peters which appear in Holland every December. Perhaps we should at the very least attempt to understand Yasukuni.

I had the shrine virtually to myself this time and explored the complex a little more, discovering that, tucked away around a corner from the main shrine, is a surprisingly large museum, the Yūshūkan. It was at this museum that I learned that, far from being an ancient shrine from a less enlightened time, Yasukuni was built in 1869 specifically to enshrine the memory of soldiers who had fought and died during the brief scrap which heralded the Meiji Restoration. That bombshell came later on in my visit; the first shocking moment came in the museum's atrium entrance hall, which featured a bold little ensemble of a kamikaze plane, a manned torpedo, a World War II-era Mitsubishi Zero fighter plane – whose blurb boasted of how it shot down 'nearly every one of the enemy planes' in its first battle and 'was the best carrier-based fighter in the world', a howitzer used in the defence of Okinawa against the US and a steam locomotive from the Thai–Burma Railway, otherwise known as the Death Railway.

On a plaque beside the train was inscribed: 'It was to be retired in 1977, but members of the southern forces field railroad squadron who were involved in the construction of the Thai–Burma Railroad contributed funds and bought it back from the Thai national railroad. In 1979 it was dedicated to Yasukuni Jinja (shrine)'. Around 13,000 Allied prisoners of war and 100,000 Asian forced labourers died building the railway, the story of which was depicted in the 1957 David Lean movie *The Bridge on the River Kwai*. Of those victims, there was no mention in the museum. As I stood back to look again at the locomotive, a small boy ran past yelling and laughing, waving a wooden sword.

Clearly, a great deal of money had been spent on the museum, but its running costs are presumably subsidised by the gift shop, where souvenirs on sale included models of imperial planes, tanks and warships, Yasukuni candy and glossy books about Japan's colonial era.

There were just a handful of other visitors taking in the parallel universe depicted in the museum's displays, in which Japan waged an entirely honourable war, completely free from atrocities, against the West's 'naked imperialistic demands' on Asia, all the Japanese soldiers were 'well-disciplined' and 'brave', and the Chinese were 'weak', positively welcoming Japan's intervention against the Western powers in the wake of the Boxer Rebellion. '[The Japanese soldiers] were respected and applauded by the residents of Beijing in contrast to the Western powers' soldiers, who looted wherever they went.' Japan had 'inspired other oppressed peoples' of Asia to rise against the colonialists, including the Indians, who apparently hadn't even considered the possibility of their own freedom until presented with Japan's shining example. The bad guys were clearly the Americans, who as the former supplier of 70 per cent of Japan's oil, steel, rubber and other raw materials, held the country to ransom and practically forced the Japanese to attack Pearl Harbor when they imposed their sanctions in the late 1930s. Japan's attempts to sue for peace were rejected by the Allies, and the war was eventually lost due to some unspecified clerical-type errors 'which brought unspeakable human miseries on the fate of Japanese soldiers'.

What to make of all this? There is an argument to be made that Japan did liberate a good part of Asia from Western colonial interference. It can also claim to have prevented a potential takeover of the Korean peninsula by the Russians or Chinese. But later on, when I was in Nanjing, the curator of a museum dedicated to the 1937 massacre there of as many as 200,000 Chinese troops and civilians by the Japanese imperial army offered this riposte to the Japan-as-saviour-of-Asia narrative: 'China was a sovereign country. It did not need the assistance of a foreign force, and even if it did, using the military methods that Japan used completely undermines their argument. Put it this way, imagine if today China invaded Japan on the pretext of liberating it from the Americans and their tens of thousands of armed forces stationed there. How would Japan feel?'

I continued my tour of the museum. There were some extraordinary artefacts including a rope made with hair donated by 10,000 Japanese women, which took a year to make, and photographs of young Japanese soldiers. In one a young kamikaze pilot is literally nuzzling a puppy. The kamikaze are the superstars of Yasukuni – it venerates these young men with an uncomplicated sentimentality – but critics usually point more to the fourteen Class A war criminals who are enshrined at Yasukuni, such as former prime minister Hideki Tojo and General Matsui, who was in charge in Nanjing during the massacre. I wondered about the Class B and C war criminals. They were hardly saints. Among them are soldiers who executed prisoners of war, for example, officers who ordered the suicide of Okinawans or were responsible for the starvation of soldiers in the catastrophic New Guinea campaign, men who resorted to cannibalism or decapitated innocent non-combatants in Nanjing. All are venerated indiscriminately as 'glorious spirits'. Not only that, but a link is clearly made between their 'sacrifice' and the post-war success of Japanese society. In the rhetoric of Yasukuni, that economic success was built upon the sacrifice of kamikaze, soldiers and, most of all, officers.

The Arlington Cemetery defence, which Shinzo Abe has used, argues that other countries pay respects to their war dead, so why can't Japan? It is true there may well be people who could be considered war criminals in American armed forces cemeteries; there are certainly Confederate generals at Arlington. General Samuel Koster, infamous for his role in the My Lai massacre in Vietnam in 1968, is buried at West Point Cemetery, and General Curtis LeMay is buried at the US Air Force Academy Cemetery in Colorado. LeMay was the man responsible for the 1945 firebombing of Tokyo, which killed 100,000 people and was arguably the worst individual instance of mass killing of non-combatants in military history. LeMay himself admitted, 'If I had lost the war, I would have been tried as a war criminal.' Meanwhile, in 1992 in London a statue was erected on Whitehall to Air Chief Marshal Sir Arthur 'Bomber' Harris, responsible for the bombing of civilians in Dresden in contravention of the 1922 Washington Treaty. Some consider Harris a war criminal too.

Then there is the 'victor's justice' criticism, which maintains that the trials of Japanese war criminals by the Allies in Tokyo in 1946 were fatally flawed. The Allies were arguably more concerned about the post-war order, and there were probably many men guilty of crimes, possibly Class A crimes, who were never prosecuted or were pardoned. Some even ended up running major Japanese corporations or, like Abe's grandfather Nobusuke Kishi, running the country. Kishi was categorised as a Class A war criminal for his role in overseeing slave labour in Manchuria in the late 1930s and early 1940s and was imprisoned for three years after the war. He was pardoned by the Americans and went on to become a notably hard-line right-wing prime minister of Japan in the late 1950s.

There is another argument in favour of Yasukuni – although perhaps not the museum. Part of the unspoken pact inherent in having armed forces – the deal between governments and the people they send to fight their wars – is that soldiers will be accorded respect and memorialised in the event of their deaths, otherwise how to maintain the nobility of the cause or any semblance of a military for that matter? 'If you think about it, what is the obligation of the government?' Philip Seaton asked me. 'It is to honour the troops that have served and died in its name. Every military needs its commemorative system, so that you can persuade ordinary men to volunteer to go off and fight and die. To do that, they need to believe that if they go off and sacrifice themselves they will be honoured. This is not just Japan, it's every country. It is just inconvenient that the Japanese lost. The actual process is precisely the same.' The prospect of enshrinement at Yasukuni could be likened to the seventy-two virgins promised by extremist imams to young Muslim men planning terrorist attacks. As a Japanese army veteran, Hajime Kondo told a BBC documentary crew in 2000, 'If you go to war and die in action then you become a god and are enshrined at the Yasukuni shrine and the emperor will kindly come and pray for you.' Not for nothing was the disastrous retreat by Japanese forces from Burma nicknamed by them the Road to Yasukuni.

As John Breen points out, the shrine is far from uncontroversial among the Japanese themselves. 'In Japanese it is rare to hear the word Yasukuni in isolation,' he tells me during our lunch in Kyoto. 'It is invariably paired with the noun *mondai*. That means "problem", as in "Yasukuni *mondai*" – Yasukuni problem.'

For now at least the problem has been parked in the name of better Sino-Japanese relations, much to the relief of all involved. It will probably remain that way unless Abe, or a successor, recommences those controversial 15 August visits.

7

Osaka

During the bubble years Japan spent some of its money on museums. Many of them are bafflingly specialised and built seemingly free from the burden of commerce. Often they are housed in flamboyant concrete buildings which reflect their theme – the horseshoe-crab-shaped Horseshoe Crab Museum in Kasaoka is one of my favourites. A more serious product of this late-80s spree is the sub-genre of museums to memorialise the suffering of specific cities or prefectures during the war, and the last of these to open, in 1991, just as the final gasps of air were draining from the Japanese economic balloon, was the Osaka International Peace Center in the grounds of Osaka Castle.

When it opened, the Peace Center was by all accounts quite progressive in the way it presented the context for the east Asian war, but following a campaign by local right-wingers, the tone of the museum has now changed. Despite the fact that the city is home to Japan's largest *Zainichi* population, Osaka's politicians have a reputation for 'outspokenness' regarding Japan's ethnic minorities. In 2013 a former mayor, Toru Hashimoto, caused outrage in South Korea, for instance, when he claimed that the comfort women system of military brothels had been a necessary component of Japan's imperial strategy. And the current mayor, Hirofumi Yoshimura, recently ended the city's sister relationship with San Francisco when a statue to the comfort women was erected in the American city's Chinatown.

I drive there the next morning from Kyoto – it only takes about forty minutes – and once inside the distinctive concrete and corrugated-iron building which houses the museum, it becomes apparent that the emphasis of the Peace Center today is mostly on the devastating US air raids in 1945, which claimed more than 10,000 lives, and on the suffering of the Osakans in general. One exhibit describes the Osakans as being 'victimised' by the raids. Another stresses the courage of the locals, who were able 'to cope with the air raids and tried to be excellent cooperative citizens'; there is even a bit on 'animals victimised by war' – the inhabitants of the zoo. There is little reference to *why* the bombing was ordered or to Japan's role in provoking it, instead the Peace Center gently nudges visitors elsewhere: 'Why did the US bomb densely populated Osaka so many times?'

By the early 1940s, Osaka had become 'the Manchester of the East', one of Japan's main industrial centres and the sixth largest munitions manufacturing city in the world. In the years beforehand, Japan had invaded several sovereign states, killed hundreds of thousands of their inhabitants, started a war with the USA when it bombed Pearl Harbor without warning and undermined the stability of the entire Pacific region, but I learn nothing about this in the museum. In terms of Japanese provocation for the American raids, the museum alludes only to 'rapidly increasing war dead' and 'people who Migrated to Manchuria'. But what was the nationality of those war dead? Why were Japanese people migrating to north-eastern China? All is obscure. One exhibit is labelled THE PEOPLE WAITING FOR LOVED ONES WHO WOULD NOT BE COMING HOME, again with no reference to why loved ones were abroad in the first place. 'We were full of intense patriotism, thinking that we must win. If we were to lose, Japan would no longer exist,' reads one testimony.

I leave the museum perplexed that a selective narrative like this could find a prominent place in Japan's second city, but in recent years this kind of historical revisionism, or flat-out denial of Japanese crimes, has moved into the mainstream, not just politically and in museums but also in the magazine and book-publishing worlds.

One of the highest-profile figures in the revisionist movement is Sonfa Oh, a Korean woman born on the island of Jeju, now in her early sixties. When I met her in Tokyo the previous week, she told me she had written as many as eighty books, many of which espoused her revisionist take on Japan's colonial era. Oh's works are part of the *kenchu-zokan* genre, meaning 'dislike China, hate South Korea', and big sellers in Japan in recent years. In 2013 three of the bestselling paperbacks in Japan were books attacking Korea, including the blockbuser *Bokanron* – 'Theory of Stupid Korea'. She had sold millions of copies, she said (according to my Japanese publisher, this is not the case).

One of Oh's books has been translated into English: *Getting Over it! Why Korea Needs to Stop Bashing Japan*, a borderline-unreadable litany of hair-splitting repetitious grudge-settling and tendentious allegations. Oh claims, for instance, that there are 120,000 North Korean spies in South Korea, but offers no evidence for this. She is on firmer ground when she asserts that the South Koreans have fabricated a story of colonial resistance which ignores the fact that their liberation was an 'incidental consequence' of the Allies' defeat of Japan; she is also right when she accuses Korean leaders of using anti-Japanese rhetoric for political gain.

This is the tricky thing about Oh and her ilk: there *were* Korean collaborators, many of them, but Japan ruled the peninsula for thirty-five years so it would be strange if there hadn't been cooperation. Korea benefited from Japanese occupation in terms of infrastructure and development, and much later, during the 1960s, Japan transferred funds and knowledge to Korea which helped to boost its manufacturing economy. And yes, Koreans have also done absolutely terrible things to each other since the war. Oh lists the postwar atrocities of South Korean dictators – the Gwangju and Jeju massacres, the imprisonment and murder of pro-democracy activists and so on – with relish, although oddly she excuses them all on the grounds of dictatorial necessity in the face of the threat of communism.

We met in the lobby of a smart Tokyo hotel. She brought along a female companion, who kindly acted as translator, and a young man who looked to be around twenty years old but who it later transpired was her publisher in the Philippines. We all sat rather awkwardly around a low coffee table.

Oh insisted that all the bad blood between the two nations was down to Korea and its outdated Confucian perspective of regional relations. 'Even before the occupation, Korea used to look down on Japan,' she told me. 'Even though the younger brother is much more successful than the elder brother, even though the younger brother is even richer and stronger, because he is the younger brother he needs to respect the elder brother. Korea thinks the younger brother doesn't respect it.'

Again there is a great deal of truth to this, as I would find out later in my journey, but to hear Oh describe Japan's colonial past you would think it was some kind of charitable outreach project. 'Japan tried to make Korea the same as Japan, at the same level of modernity.' As evidence she offered that the population went from 13 million to 25 million during Japanese rule; the rice harvest also doubled. In 1910 there were 100 schools in Korea. By the time the Japanese left there were 5,960 schools – in which, she added, Korean was taught for the first time. 'Before the Japanese they couldn't even read or write their own language! Well, only about 6 per cent of them. After 35 years [of Japanese occupation] that grew to 22 per cent.'

This echoed something Tom Gill, the Yokohama anthropologist, had told me: 'These far rightists think that actually Japan did a lot of bloody good things. You can find parallels with *Daily Telegraph* readers in Britain who think we brought civilisation to India, built the roads, the trains, the bridges and so on. It is exactly the same discourse about what Japan did to Korea.'

'No, the Japanese occupation was totally different from the British in India,' counters Oh. 'The Japanese didn't take anything, almost nothing, from Korea. There was no killing, no murdering or anything like that.' Yes, the Japanese were a bit harsh in the early years of their rule, she concedes, but they soon loosened up. 'The equation of colonialism with evil leaves no room for credit if people's standards of living actually improved,' she writes in her book, adding that people don't really care who rules them 'as long as their daily lives are not disturbed'.

What of the forced labourers who were taken to the coal mines of Hokkaido? They were 'recruited'. And the historians who claim otherwise? 'Not true. A lie.' Oh waved her coffee cup dismissively. Many more Korean men wanted to join the Japanese army than were permitted to because the recruiting criteria were so stringent. 'Only one in fifty [who applied] could go to war with the Japanese. To join the Japanese army was a very, very good thing for them. They really wanted to join. OK, towards the end of the war, let's say 1944, the Japanese government did say, "OK, let them work in the mines or a place like that." Kind of dangerous, but this job was well paid compared with other work.' She adds in passing that the Nanjing massacre was also 'a lie. Zero deaths. It didn't happen. Fake history.'

As we were parting, I asked Sonfa Oh if she felt her work in any way contributed *positively* to the relationship between Japan and Korea. She can no longer visit her homeland; in 2013 she was turned away at Incheon airport in Seoul, en route to her mother's funeral, and claims the Korean government has blocked publication of her works, so this seemed unlikely, but I was interested to hear what she would say.

'My books have very important contents for both Koreans and Japanese, and for the people in the rest of the world to know the truth. That's why I am publishing in English too. I will never stop writing this.' Yes, but might it help if she were occasionally a bit more critical about Japan, to balance things a little? 'It's not a question of being critical or not critical of Japan. Many foreigners accuse and criticise Japan by just looking at the surface phenomena.'

I persisted in search of some sign of conciliation. Wasn't there something that Japan could do to improve relations with Korea? Give them the disputed islands of Takeshima/Dokdo? Further compensation for the comfort women? Stop visiting Yasukuni? 'Takeshima belongs to Japan,' she said firmly. 'And the Yasukuni shrine has *nothing* to do with Koreans. The comfort women didn't exist. They were prostitutes. I found out the reality from history.'

So all the other historians around the world were simply wrong, or being paid by China or America? 'Yes, America made this history to be taught to the Japanese: "The Japanese are bad. We saved the Japanese from the war." Blah, blah, blah. Koreans are taught this anti-Japanese ideology. If you talk to Koreans who are over sixty years old, they are more friendly to Japan because they know the Japanese and remember the [colonial] time.' Growing up in Korea, she too had been indoctrinated to hate the Japanese, but when she moved to Japan, she could find no reason for this. She dismissed the black van protesters as 'only a few right-wingers. There are neo-Nazis in America or the UK – everywhere – but do you consider them normal Brits or normal Americans? No.' And she claimed never to have experienced even slight anti-Korean prejudice in her time in Japan.

Why would it be in America's interests to pit two allies in the region against each other? 'To make wars one day. This is how they can make money. Behind it, I think they want war between Japan and China.'

'And there are no clever Koreans who have worked out that they are being manipulated this way? You're the only Korean who knows this?'

'Not the only one,' she conceded. But one of very few.

Back in Osaka, after visiting the International Peace Center I make my way across the city to another late-80s relic, the Osaka Human Rights Museum.

Though housed in a rather more drab, municipal-style building than the prefab-modernist Peace Center, the Human Rights Museum presents a much more progressive, contemporary Japan, an inclusive, concerned, sensitive Japan keen to embrace every marginalised social group and support every cause, from gay rights (good) to nitrogen pollution (bad). There is an anti-bullying section, bits about LGBT rights and even information about the prejudice people on mechanical ventilators have to endure, of which I was not previously aware.

'Shouldn't society treat all life in the world as valuable?' asks a poster. Another suggests, 'Through the experience of wearing costumes and trying to play the musical instruments of various countries and regions, let's think about the benefits of learning about various cultures, customs and values and understand and respect each other.' The museum celebrates the diversity of the Korean community (around 100,000–150,000 *Zainichi* live in the city, out of a population of two million), which makes Osaka a place where 'you can enjoy learning many different cultures from the Korean peninsula that have taken root in society'.

It is easy to mock the museum's happy-clappy tone, but it is a reminder for me that, as noisy as the right-wing nationalists can be in Japan and as disturbing and insensitive as the rhetoric of its politicians and writers like Sonfa Oh is when it comes to reflecting upon the colonial era, ordinary Japanese people are just as likely to take a more tolerant, open and progressive approach to its ethnic minorities and its history. They are just as likely, if not more so, simply to be nice.

Of course, I realise a binary division like this is also reductive; 127 million people can't simply be divided between those on the right who deny Japanese imperial aggression and claim victim status, and those on the left who acknowledge Japan's war crimes and abhor the treatment of the *Zainichi*. English academic Philip Seaton argues that we shouldn't judge the Japanese by the nationalist tendencies of their political leaders; nor should we assume that, because Japanese school history textbooks give a perfunctory or ambivalent overview of Japanese colonialism, this equates to the view of the war held by most Japanese.

'The longer I live here, the more I realise that the stereotypes are unhelpful when it comes to explaining the diversity within Japan,' Seaton, who has lived in Japan for more than twenty years, told me. 'The default setting inevitably plonks them in the conservative bracket, but I spend a lot of time with civil society activists who spend their summer holidays up to their knees in mud digging up the bones of Korean forced labourers. Are they any less Japanese than the person screaming from a van, "Smelly Koreans get out of Japan"? No, they are equally Japanese.'

In his book *Japan's Contested War Memories* Seaton examines the common perception of outsiders about the Japanese approach to the war – that they are in denial, haven't said sorry, are misinformed about the reality of what was done in their name, and fail to hold their government to account – basically, that they need to fess up and be more like the Germans were after World War II. But these perceptions 'privilege the actions of officials over public opinion or cultural memory', he writes, which I take to mean that we shouldn't judge Japan by the fascist idiots who run it. He also makes the point that, more often than not, those idiots pay with their jobs when they say idiotic things about the war. There have been many such idiots, like Nagano Shigeto, a justice minister who in 1994 denied the accepted view of the Nanjing massacre. He was forced to resign. Or Seisuke Okuno, in 1988 a member of the cabinet, who publicly asked 'in what sense' Japan had been the aggressor in the war. Again, it was a stupid and provocative thing to say, and he was forced to resign. So there are usually consequences.

Conservatives in Japan might steer state-level discourse on the war, but Seaton believes the general public is probably more progressive and its 'views routinely exceed conservative and nationalistic views in opinion polls. Typically, 50 to 60 per cent of people characterise the war as "aggressive", while anything between 50 and 80 per cent, depending on the precise wording of questions, are either critical of the government's "inadequate" treatment of war responsibility issues (such as the level of compensation) or are supportive of additional compensation and initiatives acknowledging aggression.' It is also worth pointing out that generally the Japanese are better informed about the East Asian War than Americans or British people.

Just as there are different approaches to interpreting the war, in Japan there are different definitions of patriotism. 'If you are right wing, you think being patriotic, loving your country, means hating Koreans,' Seaton told me. 'But for progressives, loving their country means examining the past, learning from it and making sure they do something better next time. It's a different sort of love.'

Many organisations and individuals in Japan have worked tirelessly to discover the truth about the war, including the Violence Against Women in War – Network Japan, which organised the Women's International Tribunal on Japanese Military Sexual Slavery in Tokyo in 2000, which found Emperor Hirohito and the Japanese military guilty of crimes against humanity; and the Center for Research and Documentation on Japan's War Responsibility, a group of progressive academics. Various national groups regularly protest against prime ministerial visits to Yasukuni. As long ago as 1972, long before Korean or Chinese journalists had even begun to examine the history of the war in the public sphere, it was a Japanese journalist, Katsuichi Honda, who first brought to light Japan's World War II atrocities in his book *Journey to China*.

Honda is one of countless Japanese journalists who have unearthed evidence of Japan's war crimes over the years, their work often being published by *Asahi Shimbun*, Japan's second largest newspaper, which campaigned on behalf of the Korean comfort women when a Chuo University professor, Yoshimi Yoshiaki, found documents in the ministry of defence archives which incriminated the imperial government in organising the military brothel system. Meanwhile, in the 1980s the Chinese Returnees Association, a group of Japanese veterans who had spent time in Chinese prisons before being sent home, confessed to numerous horrendous war crimes. Other civic groups have worked to ameliorate the plight of the *Zainichi* and rallied to counter right-wing hate-speech groups. And in fiction and film Japanese artists have been confronting the horrors of their compatriots' actions since the epic and harrowing *The Human Condition*, a series of six novels by Junpei Gomikawa published in the late 1950s about the experiences of an idealistic Japanese soldier during and after the war, later turned into a film trilogy. The late Shigeru Mizuki's powerful autobiographical manga series *Showa* also explored the war era (and aftermath) with unsparing honesty from his perspective as a young recruit fighting in Papua New Guinea.

Just before we parted in Tokyo, Seaton, who I sensed felt a little exasperated about some of these misconceptions about his adopted homeland, had made the point that Japanese views on the war also vary depending on the region. In Hokkaido, where he lives, there is a stronger progressive movement because of the wartime presence of an unusually high number of forced labourers from Korea who came to work in the coal mines. And sometimes approaches to remembering the war can even differ *within* a region. 'If you go to Hiroshima, then the civil societies all revolve around the A-bomb, but even within Hiroshima Prefecture, if you go elsewhere to Okinoshima, it's all about the poison gas, because that's where all the chemical weapons used in China were produced. And the number of people killed by the atomic bomb in Hiroshima was fewer than the number killed [in China] by the poison gas manufactured in Hiroshima Prefecture. You also have the naval town Etajima, where the current Self Defence Force has a training base, which is still a highly conservative town. So, you see, even looking in just one prefecture, the picture is so mixed. It is very complicated.'

8

Hiroshima

As I drive west, first to Kobe to check out the thriving Chinatown there – and its exceptionally dull museum – then onwards to Hiroshima, the scenery grows more and more operatic. At a service stop the air is thick with dragonflies, and above, wheeling on the thermals, are eagles the size of hang-gliders. The weather adds its own drama. At one point, after catching a hallucinogenic glimpse of a full-scale replica of Neuschwanstein castle in the distance from a highway viaduct outside Tatsumo (I'm guessing another relic of the bubble era), I round a bend and go from blue sky and sunshine into a monstrous deluge. The road now transforms into a river. I can no longer see the end of the bonnet and effectively sail my way down through the mountains to the coast with occasional glimpses of the Inland Sea in the distance, its surface tiled with oyster farms between a threaded necklace of islets.

For no other reason than it looked nice online, I am spending the night at a curious Greek-themed (and -staffed) hotel. After checking in, with the rain now stopped I borrow a bicycle for a ride along the coast to decompress. I pass cats lazing on warm stone steps, and tiny crabs scuttle into the brickwork as I ride by. I come to a bathing beach, where, as the sun sets, families are lighting barbecues to cook their dinner and flying fish flash their scales out in the bay. The coast road narrows to a single lane as it weaves through depleted fishing communities with long-shuttered businesses and empty lots choked with knotweed. In some villages the only sign of commerce is a rusty vending machine. Unlike in the big cities, where I have spent most of my time so far, the impact of Japan's ageing population is very visible here.

Many of the houses along this part of the coast are built from wood which has been deliberately burned, a traditional technique known as *yaki sui-ita*. The charring is supposed to make the wood resistant to fire, and by neutralising the cellulose, less attractive to insects.

I think of these houses the next day in the Hiroshima Peace Memorial Park and Museum. At the entrance to the museum an entire wall is covered with a panorama of Hiroshima before the bomb, showing an elegant city of timber houses, waterways and bridges. This is contrasted with a photo of the city a short time after 8.15 a.m. on 6 August 1945, the moment the first atomic bomb, Little Boy, was detonated 600 metres above Shima Hospital, causing a 'beautiful flash of light'. The city was incinerated. Tens of thousands of people were killed instantly; an estimated 146,000 died in the subsequent days and weeks. After the mushroom cloud dispersed, black rain fell. In 2000 a BBC documentary crew interviewed Hiroshima survivors, one of whom recalled looking down at her legs and realising the water had dissolved her skin: 'I saw many victims, their arms held out in front of them and their skin all peeled off … There was another man whose upper body had lost all of its skin and all we could see was the red raw flesh.'

The museum has many sobering relics – clothing, the charred frame of a child's tricycle, and so on. I read how one survivor had to carry his schoolmate because the soles of the boy's feet had burned off. Witnesses recalled the cherry trees ablaze.

Hiroshima was selected as the first target for the US's new weapon partly because it was a busy military port, but also because the surrounding hills would concentrate the blast of the bomb – as was also the case in Nagasaki. The bomb dropped on Hiroshima used uranium, the larger bomb which fell on Nagasaki used plutonium.

As I walk around the museum, I notice a member of staff wearing a badge which indicates she is available to answer questions. Her name is Miko Ikeda. She tells me that her father, now in his early nineties, was born in Hiroshima. He was living in Kyoto when the bomb dropped and arrived back in the city, hoping to help, ten days later. He had lost many of his family members in the blast so was astonished to see that his wooden house still stood, albeit minus its roof. His abiding memory, she said, was of the terrible smell which hung over the city.

We talk about the necessity or otherwise of the atomic bombs. Miko is very much of the opinion that the Americans deployed the weapons to send a message to the Russians and to justify the cost of the Manhattan Project, but she concedes that there were many military bases in Hiroshima and in that sense it was a fair target; she also says she has heard that the Japanese were working on their own atomic bomb, which theoretically could have been dropped on Los Angeles. A couple of years ago, a retired professor from Kyoto University unearthed blueprints for this bomb, along with other drawings for a centrifuge for the processing of uranium. It was due to be finished in August 1945 but the Japanese didn't have enough uranium – a Nazi submarine en route to Japan with 1,200 pounds of uranium oxide had been captured by the Americans in May 1945.

The museum describes Japan in 1945 as being in 'an extremely weak position' and points out that the Potsdam Declaration, issued in July 1945 by the US, Britain and China and demanding Japan's surrender, made no mention of the existence of atomic weapons. The implication is that, had they known about the bombs, the Japanese would have surrendered without the need for their deployment, but this is very unlikely. Records show that Emperor Hirohito persisted in his belief that the Americans might still sue for peace on terms favourable to Japan even *after* the bombing of Hiroshima. Incredibly, he wanted his people to continue fighting. The decision to surrender was eventually his, but through it all he seems to have been entirely preoccupied with the preservation of the monarchy, even at the expense of hundreds of thousands of his subjects' lives, although he went as far as to claim in his surrender speech that he was sacrificing himself to prevent the extinction of mankind. After he renounced his divinity, the emperor was very careful to minimise his role in the conflict. 'Dissembling until the end' was how his American biographer Herbert Bix puts it.

The Allies, General Douglas MacArthur in particular, were perfectly willing to help Hirohito cover his tracks. They needed Japan back on its feet to face the threat of the Soviets and, finding the post-surrender Japanese remarkably cooperative, believed there was little to be gained by bringing the emperor to justice. 'He is a symbol which unites all Japan,' concluded MacArthur. 'Destroy him and the nation will disintegrate.' The Allies were also aware of the effects the swingeing terms of the Treaty of Versailles had had upon Germany following World War I. A war guilt aspect had been included in the terms which helped foster the economic and social conditions in which Nazism incubated so virulently. But Hirohito's immunity from prosecution in the Tokyo Trials of 1946 (against the protests of the Australian delegates, among others) is still used by the Koreans and Chinese as evidence that the Japanese never fully acknowledged their culpability. The man in whose name the war was waged and who was not only fully informed of what was happening but often encouraged Japan's imperialist expansion, was never tried, never confessed, and died of natural causes forty-four years after the war ended.

As with the Osaka Peace Center, the Hiroshima museum offers little of this kind of context. There are a couple of sentences about how the First Sino-Japanese War of 1894–5 helped turn Hiroshima into an important military base, and it is clearly stated that Japan started the Pacific War against the Americans, but when it comes to Japan's broader actions in Asia, the language is often strangely passive. 'The Manchurian Incident of 1931 escalated to a full-scale war with China in 1937,' it tells us. It also refers to 'the incident known as the "Nanjing Massacre" [in which] the Chinese sacrifice included soldiers, POWs, civilians and even children', which is a curious way to describe the most notorious crime of the war. The reference to Korean slave labour is similarly opaque, stating merely that Koreans were 'conscripted to serve the war. Many were assigned to factories in Hiroshima.' Around 30,000 Koreans died in the two blasts in Hiroshima and Nagasaki, while another 100,000 died as a result of war-related service as military conscripts and so forth.

As I left Hiroshima that evening, my mind was reeling from the horrors of which I had been reminded, but I was also trying to understand the city's approach to the subject of the war and Japan's role in it. The people who run the Hiroshima Peace Memorial Park and Museum argue that its purpose is to memorialise the dead, not to explore the context of the war or to apportion blame. The focus is thus on the child victims and the elderly; the epicentre of the blast, one plaque tells us, was mostly temples, where turtles and carp swam in ponds and which were popular playground areas (so not munitions factories). But it is this kind of emphasis on the civilian suffering that has led one commentator to refer to the Peace Memorial Park as Japan's 'national shrine of victimhood'.

There is no question that the Japanese people *were* victims. They were victims of an out-of-control military elite which brutalised young recruits and led three million to their deaths. After the war, the country was shocked by the plight of the half-million Japanese prisoners captured in northern China by Soviet forces and held for years in Siberian labour camps. They too were victims.

Philip Seaton told me that this victim narrative is dominant in the mainstream media in Japan and often 'avoids explicit reference to Japanese war responsibility'. He cites the Hiroshima Peace Park as complicit in this, and mentions the country's most popular TV series about the war, *Oshin* (1982), and most popular war movie, *The Burmese Harp* (1985), both of which emphasise the Japanese-as-victims aspect.

Japan's victim status has been further burnished with a kind of unimpeachable piety thanks to the strict post-war pacifism as laid out in Article 9 of its constitution, imposed by the Allied occupying force in 1946. This continues to stipulate that the Japanese people 'for ever renounce war as a sovereign right' and that 'land, sea and air forces, as well as other war potential, will never be maintained'. Pacifism does seem to be deeply ingrained in the character of contemporary Japanese people, hence those two-fingered peace signs every single Japanese person makes every single time they are photographed.

Many in Japan are justifiably proud of their non-militarism. 'Renouncing war, not killing people, not being killed – this may be an ideal, but this may be the greatest thing that Japan has achieved,' Koichi Yasuda, the news reporter I had met in the Korean quarter of Tokyo, told me. 'This beautiful Article 9. We have made automobiles and electronic products, we have created many things, but to the extent that I am a proud patriot, it is because of Article 9.' He would, he said, protect it with his very being.

It was one of the most moving sentiments, and the best defence of Japan's pacifist constitution, that I have heard. His views are far from unusual. Polls tend to show Japan pretty evenly divided on revising the constitution and turning the Self Defence Forces into a military capable of 'belligerence', perhaps one day even equipped with nuclear weapons. Usually there is a slight majority against changing the constitution (51 per cent in the most recent poll), and only around 30 per cent actively want change. Pretty remarkable, given that Kim Jong-un keeps firing missiles in Japan's direction.

The Japanese are also the least patriotic people, not only of all Asian nations, but possibly in the world. The World Values Survey of 2010 revealed that Japan has the lowest percentage of people proud of their country (24 per cent) of all the nationalities polled, with only 16 per cent willing to fight for it. Similarly, an Asia Barometer survey revealed that only 27 per cent of Japanese were 'proud of their own nationality' compared to 46 per cent of Chinese.

As Brad Glosserman and Scott Snyder put it in their book *The Japan–South Korea Identity Clash*, '[Shinzo] Abe may hanker for a more conservative Japan, but the public is not likely to follow him.' Despite this apparent lack of a mandate from the people, his government recently passed bills allowing for 'proactive pacifism', and in May 2017 gave the deadline of the Tokyo Olympics in 2020 on repealing Article 9 and giving the prime minister an additional role as the commander-in-chief. Japan already has a larger navy than

Britain and France combined, as well as 1,600 aircraft and 250,000 military personnel, and in April 2018 the country took another step towards militarisation when its first unit of marines since the war was activated in Sasebo, near Nagasaki, specifically to counter fears of Chinese attacks on Japanese islands.

So why is Japan's government so gung-ho while its people are more equivocal? Like the rest of us, the Japanese often have to accept ugly or contrary opinions in their elected representatives: indeed a 2017 poll revealed that 65 per cent of Japanese people support no political party. Tom Gill, the Yokohama-based anthropologist, believes that Abe is in power largely because of the promises he made to shore up the Japanese economy. 'Yes, you've got this racist right-wing prime minister who has won two big elections, but it's not because people agree with him that Japan should return to some sort of pre-war, emperor-centred military state. To that I would say, first of all, it is only eight years ago that Japan elected a much more progressively minded political party with a landslide. Are we supposed to think that the Japanese suddenly became first very right-wing, then very left, then very right again? Obviously not. It's still the same Japanese people. It's just that they get pissed off with crappy politicians and boot them out.'

'Really, people don't vote for Abe, but they vote for his party,' one Japanese friend explained to me. 'The opposition is also very weak.'

It is true, from what I've seen of them, that Japan's opposition parties do seem uncommonly prone to implosion at inopportune moments – usually a couple of weeks before a general election. I would almost say it was intentional – if I believed in conspiracy theories ...

9

Fukuoka

I have two reasons for coming to Fukuoka. First, this is the only way to get to South Korea without flying, and I have a romantic idea that I must do this journey the slow way. A ferry departs daily from Hakata Port (Fukuoka and Hakata are two cities conjoined into one) for Busan, South Korea's second largest city, on the south-east tip of the country. Second, Fukuoka is the home of one of Japan's most popular far-right YouTubers, Yoko Mada, better known as Random Yoko.

This tall slim thirty-two-year-old had recently popped up on the international media's radar on account of her pro-Trump videos, recorded in English as many of her videos are, in her customary chatty, light-hearted style. It seemed an odd phenomenon: a young Japanese woman falling for a seventy-year-old orange demagogue, but Yoko obviously sympathised with Trump's distrust of international political orthodoxy and his hatred of mainstream media. Those who explored her YouTube channel further will also have discovered, among other things, a young woman with a unique musical talent. Yoko has recorded countless synth ballads of her own composing, featuring energetic keyboard playing and her distinctive vocal style.

She was born in Fukuoka in 1985, but went to university in Osaka, which as we have heard has the largest Korean population in Japan. These days she is vehemently anti-Korea, indeed she has written various offensive songs about Korean comfort women and the colonial period. Though these are not obvious subjects for power ballads, Yoko makes her lyrics fit the form in much the same way as a toddler wedges wrong shapes into wrong holes.

In her song about the colonial 'benevolence' of Japan towards Korea she sings about how the Japanese gave them "massive railways, clean streets, water and sewer services", also managing to shoehorn in references to "libraries, factories, including nitrogen fertiliser factories".

I don't imagine many songs have referenced nitrogen fertiliser factories, at least not since since the collapse of the Soviet Union.

Yoko posted her first YouTube video in 2006. In 2011 she won the inaugural YouTube NextUp newcomers award. Her channel has had more than 6.5 million views. Her 'Comfort Women Rap' (sample lyric: 'Slaves don't get paid, do they even smile./ Where were Korean men when they were supposed to be crying?') has had 650,000 views. And she is fast making her name on Japanese TV as a right-wing commentator.

I meet Yoko in Fukuoka station and we adjourn to a nearby café, where she explains her beginnings as an Internet star. It all began four years ago when she quit her office job. 'I was going through a rough time with my body, like, I had to go to the cancer centre,' she tells me. She didn't have cancer, but 'something that had to be tested, and I was going there, and I was overthinking, and things were not good, so I got mentally tired'. Yoko talks in a garbled rush, her face very expressive. 'At the same time, in 2012, in the fall I believe, I started to get interested in politics, because I got time to think as I kind of broke up with my boyfriend.' He was an American. I infer that he dumped her, although it would be wrong to speculate that this precipitated some kind of breakdown.

It was around this time that the dispute between Japan and China over the ownership of the Senkaku Islands flared up with those violent anti-Japanese protests in Beijing.[6]

---

[6] The five Senkaku Islands are roughly midway between Taiwan and Okinawa, but because the Chinese claim Taiwan as their territory, they also claim the Diaoyu Islands, as they are known in China. Chinese fishermen and naval vessels regularly traverse their waters, and Beijing claims they have been Chinese territory since the time of the Ming dynasty. The islands are important strategically because of their location. The Japanese gained the Senkakus along with Taiwan at the Treaty of Shimonoseki in 1895, after the First Sino-Japanese War. After 1945 they were administered by the Americans, but returned to Japan in 1971.

'At the time I didn't know anything about politics and I was, like, "Why are they so angry and smashing up their stuff?" and so I asked my father about it.' Yoko describes her father, a teacher of English, as a conservative, not politically active but with lots of books on politics, which she began to devour. 'I used to hate politics because I could study maths or physics and I know that I could master it, but when it comes to politics I thought that's never something that I will ever understand.' I take this acceptance of the lack of absolutes in politics as a positive sign. I am wrong.

'I used to hate my own country before I got interested in politics because I was taught that Japan was the bad guy in history. So I start to read my father's books and I discover what really happened in the past, and how the disputes [with China and Korea] were fabricated, based on the strategy of the Chinese Communist Party without *any evidence.*' Heads are now turning in the coffee shop. 'Basically, the big idea is, they want to speak badly about Japanese people so that the American people lose trust in us and start fighting against us.'

This, then, is why the Koreans and Chinese are apparently taught from school age that, as Yoko puts it, 'Japanese are evil.' It is all part of a conspiracy between the CPC and socialist teachers in the USA. After the war, Yoko says, traditional Japanese family values were destroyed because the Americans encouraged the building of small apartments, isolating people and severing family bonds, and implementing unnatural gender equality. (This is a particularly laughable claim for anyone who knows anything about contemporary Japan.)

'Men and women are different. A lot of females are stupid.'

'So are a lot of men,' I venture.

'But, like, in a different way.'

'So you wouldn't describe yourself as a feminist?'

'I am a true feminist. And men are weak. What I mean is, females are good at talking and interrupting, or playing with kids and that kind of stuff. But they are not really good with mathematics.'

I should stress that Yoko imbues these kinds of statements with a good deal of humour, but I do think she means it. She admits that she does get into trouble sometimes with her family for the things she says. Her brother, a banker, was told by his boss not to talk about his sister in front of clients.

What, I wondered, were some of the other untruths she was taught at school?

'That we did the Nanjing massacre. We had to write about it in exams, so I was really shocked when I learned that it was actually a fabrication.'

'OK, so that's *not* a fabrication, Yoko.'

'Well, there was a Nanjing *incident*, but it was *not* a massacre. Only, like, fifty something people [were killed].'

'Fifty thousand?'

'No. Fifty.'

I ask for her evidence. She says it is hard to show evidence for something that didn't happen, which I suppose has a kind of twisted logic. Except that, though we will probably never know the exact death toll which resulted from the Japanese army's occupation in 1937 of the then capital of China, there is plenty of evidence that many tens of thousands, perhaps hundreds of thousands, of Chinese were killed by the Japanese in Nanjing. Yoko disputes this, citing the pictures of happy crowds welcoming the Japanese invaders, holding babies and so on, which you can see on right-wing websites. The diaries written by Western witnesses to the atrocities which are also cited by historians as evidence have been tampered with, she says. Japan was not the aggressor in World War II. The Japanese were fighting communism, just as the US continued to do in the post-war years. As for Korea, it was not colonised by Japan because there was no oppression of the Koreans, and many Koreans were in charge of things. 'We taught them their own language, we gave so much, we could have destroyed everything when we left. We only wanted Korea strong. And in China that place wasn't Chinese territory, it was like a blank area.' She is talking about Manchuria, original home of the Qing dynasty, which had ruled China for over two centuries.

I ask her how she is able to deny generally accepted historical evidence with such confidence. 'Mmm, it's like, for example, if you're in school and the majority of your classmates are bashing one kid, but this one kid is saying the truth.'

'That's not really a good analogy, Yoko, because they are not experts who have studied bashing kids all their lives and have degrees in it – you know what I mean?'

'But they're bashing.'

'But what about the experts who have studied this thing, made it their life's work?'

We continue like this for some time, me arguing the experts' case, Yoko telling me the experts are in the pay of the communists who want to divide Asia and America. 'Experts,' she exhales at one point. 'They couldn't even see that Trump was gonna be president. Some people go online, but they get the wrong information, with no evidence.'

In one of Yoko's lighter videos she complains about the appropriation of Japanese culture by the South Koreans, claiming that their tourist information films include references to sumo wrestling and sushi, implying they were Korean inventions. I ask her what her source is for this. Was it actually an *official* South Korean tourist board promotion? She isn't too sure, she says. But if she isn't sure about the source, how can she accuse the Koreans of appropriating Japanese culture? And, besides, didn't the Japanese do precisely this in the 1960s, and the 1890s come to that, when they visited the West to learn the secrets of its industry?

'But that was technology; the Koreans are stealing our culture, like the martial arts and that kind of stuff, and saying they are the origin, and that's just wrong.' The Koreans could be happy, enjoy their success and have harmonious relations with Japan, she says, but they choose to be angry, they choose to perpetuate disputes over colonial atrocities, useless islands, slave labour, comfort women and so on.

I wonder how Yoko feels about the booming Chinese and Korean tourist trade in her home town of Fukuoka. Surely it is a good thing – both economically, and in terms of providing the Japanese and their neighbours with first-hand experience of each other?

'There are Chinese and Koreans everywhere.' Yoko shakes her head. 'Yeah, the money is good, and we have encouraged them, and it is good that, though they have been taught that the Japanese are evil, they can see us for themselves, that Japan is actually a great country, and they can take back that knowledge with them to their home country and spread it. It's not all bad. But I feel like this city has been taken over.'

Back when she was at university in Osaka, Yoko used to have several foreign and *Zainichi* friends. Not any more. 'My foreign friends started to attack me, to call me stupid and racist.' After she posted her most watched film to date, 'Comfort Women Rap', she even started to receive death threats. She ignores them, she says. Her new fame will protect her. 'If I die or something they're gonna be in trouble.' And, she says, she has won new Japanese friends to replace the foreigners.

Based on the lyrics to her pro-Yasukuni song ('The winners hanged those men for fighting for us'), I had assumed that Yoko was a Shinzo Abe voter. But this is not the case. She votes for the Nippon Kokoro, an anti-immigration party originally founded by a former governor of Tokyo, Shintaro Ishihara, who in an interview with *Playboy* in 1990 claimed the Nanjing massacre was a fabrication by the Chinese. He has also described the occupation of Korea as being justified, and once said that 'old women who live after they have lost their reproductive function are useless and are committing a sin'. There's more, but you get the gist.

'People think we are extreme right or whatever,' Yoko tells me. 'But though it looks like we are on the right, it's the rest of the world that's on the left.' That includes Prime Minister Abe, the man who wants to re-arm Japan. The man who pays his respects to war criminals. The man whose deputy prime minister, Taro Aso, once asked, 'Why don't we learn how to do constitutional reform from the Nazis?' But Yoko feels Abe is compromising too much with Japan's neighbours.

As our time together draws to a close I ask about her future plans. There's not much money to be made from YouTube, she says. 'What

I have learned from Trump is, I need to be rich.' She intends to achieve this by being a motivational speaker. As for a move into mainstream politics, that would be too restricting. 'You have to always choose your words.'

Yoko and I say goodbye. She is heading back home to her parents' house, where she still lives (she has since married and now goes by the name Yoko Ishii). Just before we part, she tells me she suffered from depression for a long time. Now she has the same complaint that forced Shinzo Abe to terminate his first stint as prime minister in 2007: irritable bowel syndrome. 'I have so much power, but I try not to hurt people. I get hurt, and it goes to my gut.'

I leave Japan on the ferry to Busan troubled by Yoko's blithe historical revisionism and xenophobia, and also worried for her and her country. If she does represent the views of anything like the number of people who watch her videos, then Japan does seem to be heading down a very dark path indeed.

THE REPUBLIC OF KOREA

10

Busan

In the months prior to my arrival, events in Korea have dominated global news headlines. All eyes are on the peninsula. I feel like I am setting sail for the centre of the world.

It had all begun in late 2016 when South Korea's president at the time, Park Geun-hye, daughter of the country's late military dictator, Park Chung-hee, embroiled herself in a picaresque scandal involving a mystical guru, Danish equestrians and millions in bribes from Samsung. Hundreds of thousands of Koreans took to the streets of Seoul in protest, the crisis eventually ending in an impeachment which didn't seem to follow any kind of conventional legal process but nevertheless resulted in Park going to prison, which seemed to make everyone happy.

In the meantime, America had installed its Terminal High Altitude Area Defence system (THAAD) on a golf course south of Seoul. The system was ostensibly to protect against North Korean missiles, but the Chinese interpreted it as also directed at them, and promptly imposed unofficial sanctions on South Korea. The result was an almost instant and drastic fall in tourism and trade between China and South Korea. And North Korea had recently mounted long-range missile tests in the direction of Japan (and in theory the USA), prompting excitable conjectures that World War III was about to break out.

As I arrive in the Republic of Korea, to give South Korea its proper name, the election is about to take place to choose Park's successor, prompting yet more international news headlines. The hot favourite is Moon Jae-in of the Democratic Party. He is promising a more conciliatory approach to North Korea and to revive the country's vulnerable economy, which many feel is being fatally undermined by the all-powerful *chaebol*, South Korea's family-run conglomerates, which include Samsung and Hyundai.

All of this has pushed relations with Korea's former colonial ruler, Japan, slightly down the agenda, but the old resentments – the 1910–45 occupation and slave labour, including the comfort women; the Dokdo/Takeshima dispute; Japanese school history textbooks; and Yasukuni – are never far from the surface. I want to get a sense of how the Koreans regard these issues on a day-to-day basis, away from the headlines and political posturing, and to better understand the historical relationship of these two countries in general. Above all, I just want to see as much of Korea, and meet as many Koreans, as possible.

For all the noise it generates, and though it is home to over 51 million people, South Korea is surprisingly small. I could drive straight to Seoul, the capital in the north of the country, in about four hours, but I plan to spend a couple of days in Busan here on the south coast, before heading west to Mokpo and Gwangju, then driving up the west coast. After an initial visit to Seoul, I am going to head over to the east coast, and then north to the Demilitarised Zone (DMZ) and the border with North Korea, before returning to spend some more time in the capital.

Already, as I wait in the departure terminal at Fukuoka port, I note some key differences between Koreans and Japanese. The latter stand in line long before embarkation time, but the Koreans can't be doing with that. They have a nifty method for avoiding the tedium of queuing: they simply let their luggage do it for them, placing their suitcases in front of, or behind, the Japanese while they pop off for some last-minute duty-free shopping. This seems to suggest a unique combination of high social trust and blithe entitlement. Interesting.

Three hours later, having arrived in Busan (formerly Pusan), following a ferry ride which passes in my usual anti-seasickness-medicine-induced anaesthetic fug, the contrasts between the two near-neighbours are thrown into starker relief by the taxi to my hotel.

Japanese taxi drivers are courteous, efficient, law-abiding and careful; often they wear white gloves for that extra *Driving Miss Daisy* vibe. They always know the way or stop to ask people if not. My first Korean taxi driver is different. He shoots off from the ferry terminal as if he has just heard that the North is invading. Though I am staying in a large and prominent hotel right on the seafront, he has not the faintest clue where it is and looks at the map on my phone as if seeing hieroglyphics for the first time. Korea is said to boast a 99 per cent literacy rate, the highest in the world (this is where moveable print type was invented by the way, two hundred years before Gutenberg), and their teenagers are the most literate and numerate in the OECD.

Eventually, I am deposited at my lodgings, but the bracing introduction to Korean service culture continues at the restaurant in Eel Alley, where I dine that evening. The waitress, a tiny scowling woman in a flowery pinny, brings me a laminated picture menu featuring many intriguing-looking dishes. I mull over my options and choose a dish, but the waitress snatches the menu from me, opens it at a different page and jabs her finger at one of the pictures while looking away over her shoulder and talking to another member of staff. Apparently, this – a bowl of something red – is what I will be eating this evening. I try to point at something on a different page – call me quirky, I fancy some eel – but she closes it on my hand.

It is now, as I wait for my bowl of red, that I notice for the first time the most striking quotidian difference between Korea and Japan: in Korea they use metal chopsticks. I have never once encountered metal chopsticks in Japan but in South Korea they are the norm; wooden chopsticks are very rare. Metal ones are much heavier and more slippery, though. They render my chopstick skills, honed to average over decades, virtually void, which is confusing and humiliating. Sharing food from a communal pot or hotplate is a major feature of Korean dining – some would say of the Koreans' collective emotional landscape – so there is nowhere to hide if you can't handle your chopsticks properly. What's more, your fumbles involve other people's food as well as your own. The chopsticks also make my right hand ache. I will grow to hate them during my time in South Korea and ponder this schism a good deal. The main reason cited by Koreans for metal sticks is their cost-effectiveness. They can be washed and reused while wooden chopsticks must be disposed of. After the Korean War the country was broken economically and almost completely deforested, making wood scarce, but Japan had a fairly rough time economically in the late 1940s too, and South Korea's economy has developed at an unprecedented rate in the last few decades. Why still the metal chopsticks? Perhaps people find it reassuring to have a potentially lethal weapon close at hand.

Busan is ranged around a series of bays, harbours and crescent-shaped beaches, a bit like Rio de Janeiro. It also feels a tad Brazilian or at least less uptight than Japan. This is both good (I worry less about being a clumsy oaf as I do constantly in Japan) but also not so good. I am trying to be diplomatic here, but aesthetics, at least in the public sphere, do not seem to be so much of a priority for the people of South Korea's second city. The rash of cheap laser-printed signage on shops and businesses makes everything look like a Streatham fried chicken joint, for instance. And everywhere cranes scratch at the skyline, adding to the forest of forty-storey tower blocks, none of which appear to have detained an architect at a drawing board for very long.

I take in a panorama of the city the next morning from the United Nations Memorial Cemetery, a rare green oasis up on a plateau. The cemetery contains the remains of a few hundred of the 37,000 United Nations soldiers who died during the 1950–3 Korean War. As we've heard, the war was a result of the vacuum left when the Japanese left the Korean peninsula following their defeat in 1945, but let's rewind a little: how had Korea become so weak that it was unable to repel the Japanese in the first place?

From the late fourteenth century up until the Japanese annexation of Korea in 1910, it was governed by the descendants of a single dynasty, founded by the ruling family that had kicked the Mongolians out. Not all of these monarchs were wise, just and fair – in fact several seem to have been borderline insane – and towards the end of the 1800s the country was being run by 'incompetent aristocrats and corrupt rulers who lost their nation to thieves', as *Pachinko* author Min Jin Lee puts it.

Japan invaded Korea twice in the late 1590s (more on that in a moment), but by the nineteenth century it was fear of Western colonial powers that had turned it into the so-called Hermit Kingdom, closed to the world as Japan had been. Following the Meiji Restoration and Japan's military and technological rise, Korea added its next-door neighbour to the list of dangers, and when in 1875 the Japanese imposed an unequal treaty upon the Koreans just as the Americans had done to them, it marked the beginning of a stealthy annexation of the entire peninsula via trade-related infrastructure investments – a port reclamation here, a railroad there, and so on.

The Qing Chinese, upset at seeing its vassal state invaded, responded by sending in troops. The subsequent First Sino-Japanese War was not much more than a skirmish but ended in 1895 with Japan victorious and annexing Taiwan along with the Liaodong Peninsula, a strategically crucial piece of territory jutting down from China into the Yellow Sea to the west of Korea. Japan's 1905 defeat of Russia – a war also fought in part for control of Korea – was a more seismic shock from a global perspective. After that, Japan eased itself into full control of Korea as if slowly lowering itself into a hot bath.

The Japanese spun their 1910 annexation of Korea as the beginning of the Greater East Asia Co-Prosperity Sphere, a supposedly mutually beneficial pan-regional project to modernise and drive the Western powers from the continent. Many years later Sun Yat-sen, China's first republican president, would give credence to the scheme: 'We regarded that Russian defeat [in 1905] by Japan as the defeat of the West by the East. We regarded the Japanese victory as our own victory.' Today many Japanese still defend their actions in these terms. Korea was unstable and vulnerable to Russia or China, with Britain, the US and even France ready to pounce. As one German military tactician put it at the time, Korea was 'like a dagger pointed at the heart of Japan' – ominous geographical feng shui which Tokyo felt needed addressing.

During the 1930s the Korean peninsula would become a vital source of food, minerals and manpower for the expanding Japanese empire; by 1944, more than 15 per cent of the population of Korea was living in Japan, and at the outbreak of the Second Sino-Japanese War in 1937 Japan's colonial grasp of Korea tightened further. The teaching of its language and history was replaced by Japan's, in order 'to annihilate the Korean spirit', as the history museum I visit in Busan puts it. The Japanese built hundreds of Shinto shrines, closed Korean-language newspapers and made it a requirement (though some Japanese argue it was voluntary) for all Koreans to take Japanese names, an especially bitter pill because of Korea's strong culture of clan names. Whether forced or not, by the end of the war, 84 per cent of Koreans had done so.

Many Koreans volunteered for the Japanese armed forces not least because, if you wanted to be sure of a full belly, you had to fight.[7] Initially, most volunteers were rejected; that began to change when Japan declared war on China in 1937, but it was only in the last year of World War II that the Japanese military, desperate for manpower to fight off the Americans, initiated forced conscription of Koreans.

Later in my trip, in Seoul, I asked British journalist Michael Breen, who has lived in Korea for decades and is the author of *The New Koreans*, one of the best – and the most enjoyable – books about post-war Korea, how the Japanese occupation was perceived these days. He told me the Koreans were still taught that they were brutally exploited, their farmland was seized, rice stolen, that 'everything Japanese was bad . . . the assimilation policy was a form of genocide'.

[7] Apologists for the occupation will point out that rice production grew under the Japanese, but most of the crop was exported. According to Andrew Grajdanzev's book *Modern Korea*, consumption of rice by Koreans decreased from 0.707 bushels per person in 1915–19 to 0.396 in 1934–8.

But he also pointed out that 'the Japanese did not interrupt any development plans when they took over'. In his experience, older Koreans, those who had lived through the occupation, were not as virulently anti-Japanese as the current generation.

This was odd, because the younger Koreans I spoke to on my travels generally accused the *older* generation of perpetuating the hatred. Younger Koreans loved Japan, visited it as often as they could and wanted Korea to become, if anything, more Japanese. Which all rather begged the question: do the Koreans really hate Japan? And if it's not the younger generation nor the older folks, which Koreans are we talking about?

11

Mokpo

I leave Busan after a couple of days spent visiting museums and being told what to eat by waitresses, and head west to Mokpo, just over three hours' drive away.

It is mildly discombobulating to go from a right-hand-drive car in Japan to a left-hand-drive one here, and my fellow road users appear to have little patience with my attempts to adjust. Korean drivers are noticeably pushier, less inclined to use signals or really just give a shit than their peers in Japan. I had read in an online guide that on Korean roads larger, more expensive cars take precedence, but this does not seem to apply to me even though I am driving a Kia Stinger, a dressy new four-door saloon, which I have been assured is the epitome of South Korean technological advancement.

At my hotel I take a few minutes to acquaint myself with the Stinger's features. It has many, including eight gears, which is three too many. As the journey progresses, I will discover it has other marvels, including a wireless phone-charging system, which is something I only thought existed in TED Talks, and 'smart cruise control', which maintains a safe distance between me and the car in front, although Korean road users tend to disagree with what constitutes safe and force their way into whatever gap the car leaves. But the biggest eye-opener is that the Kia is self-driving. I had no idea this already existed, and for the first hundred miles of highway I do my best to ignore the strange tugging sensation which I occasionally feel through the steering wheel until, finally, in a moment of reckless abandon, I let go of the steering while doing about 70 miles per hour on a bend and, eerily, the car guides itself. This is very exciting, but after a few seconds a warning sign lights up: 'Driver's grasp not detected'. I retake the wheel, but over time this feature does come in extremely useful for the opening of packets of snacks while on the move, specifically chocolate peanut *mochi* cakes, which have a nasty habit of exploding melty pieces of chocolate all over me and thus require both hands free.

On the outskirts of Busan, driving in the shadow of serried ranks of numbered pastel-pink tower blocks, I am jolted from my thoughts (which go something like *Why do I find those numbers so soul-crushing? Ordinary houses have numbers, why should I feel differently about forty-storey apartment blocks? The Orwellian-ness, I guess. The fact that you would need to number something so colossal which by dint of its sheer scale should be easy to identify, yet in the presence of so many others of a similar size is rendered quotidian to the point of anonymity ... As if you might lose it. Some have names though. I see Happy Suwon and Joy Family; is that to convince the residents they are homes rather than housing; places people might choose to live?*) by a piercing alarm. At first I assume something is drastically wrong with the car, but all systems seem to be functioning. I realise that the noise is coming from my phone. I let the car take over for a moment as I take a look. It seems to be some kind of text alert but it is in Korean. To what is it alerting me? Nuclear war? Invasion? Earthquake? Chocolate crumbs? I have no idea. I stop at a petrol station in the hope of finding an answer.

Not to go on ... but in Japanese service stations, almost before your car comes to a halt, a team of men will descend upon you, pulling the windscreen wipers away, sponging down the spotless glass regardless and filling the tank with fuel before saluting you on your way and refusing any offer of a gratuity. In Korea things are a little different. The pump attendant might grudgingly saunter over in his grubby overalls and eventually get round to filling your car up and then wait for a tip. This one asks me what kind of fuel I want, and I have to confess that I have no idea. Dilithium crystals? He gives me a withering look and fills it up with whatever. I give him some coins as a tip and mime-ask what the message on my phone means. He glances at it and tells me it is warning me of the ambient temperature, which has exceeded safety levels.

The heat – the kind that makes the air wobble – presumably explains the ghost-town feel of the streets of Mokpo, a port at the far south-western corner of South Korea where I am to spend the night. There is not a single pedestrian to be seen.

I had read that Mokpo is one of the few places which has kept its Japanese colonial-era architecture, and over the course of the afternoon track down a few of the sturdy, Western-style Meiji buildings – former banks, mostly. They are not difficult to spot. Everything else in Mokpo looks as if it has been built down to a price, and again the commercial signage smothers business front-ages in a screaming jumble of dayglo acrylic, like architectural psoriasis.

I walk up Yudal Mountain, a hill in the centre of the town and the location of the main attraction as far as old Japanese buildings go. Originally the Japanese consulate, when they left this large red-brick villa, built in 1897, became the town hall and is now its museum. It paints a fairly balanced picture of the colonial era, making it clear that the Japanese stole land and exploited workers, but also pointing out that they built the first hospital in the city and that the popula-tion of Mokpo increased during the colonial era. It even admits that the town was 'flourishing' in the 1930s with major urbanisation projects and a railway, although it does say that this was in order to help the 'plundering' of rice for the Japanese market.

Returning outside to the baking heat, I follow signs to an air-raid shelter dug into the side of the mountain by Korean slave labourers during Japanese rule. Inside the cool subterranean tunnels, the labourers are represented by eerie white statues of skinny men in loincloths being beaten by Japanese soldiers with batons.

I walk further up the hillside to take in the view of Mokpo harbour and the outlying islands. At the top of the hill is a statue of the sixteenth-century admiral, Yi Sun-shin, clad in armadillo-like armour. The monument is a reminder that, long before the twentieth-century occupation, these waters had witnessed an epochal battle between the Koreans and the Japanese when Toyotomi Hideyoshi's army attempted two invasions of the peninsula in 1592 and 1597, collectively known as the Imjin Wars.

Toyotomi Hideyoshi had unified Japan, rid the country of its troublesome Christians and now had his sights set on an empire. What better way to foster a spirit of national unity than to attack the neighbours? China was his ultimate goal, but he began by invading Korea, reaching Seoul and destroying a great deal of the city. This was quite a shock to the Koreans, who until that point had very much seen themselves as the superior culture in the Confucian hierarchy, with the barbarian Japanese at the bottom. The Imjin Wars are largely remembered in Japan for the skilled Korean craftsmen among the 50,000 or so prisoners taken to Japan during the conflicts. Kyushu, the main island closest to Korea, is still famed for its Arita and Satsuma pottery, made using techniques introduced by Korean prisoners. The Koreans cite this as evidence that they were the superior race at the time.

The Imjin Wars were a huge conflict, yet globally are almost unknown. Over a million Koreans, almost a third of the population, are believed to have died during the fighting, making the wars the most devastating event in the country's history until the 1950–3 civil war. 'Hell cannot be in some other place apart from this,' wrote a Japanese Buddhist monk who witnessed a massacre at Namwon in Jeolla Province in south-western Korea during the Second Imjin War. He saw children slaughtered, their mothers killed, and the able-bodied taken off as slaves, secured in bamboo collars. To this day the atrocities are considered by some Koreans to be indicative of the latent barbarity of the Japanese, of that essential inhumanity: this is what they do when given the opportunity.

Although the final defeat of the Japanese was mostly thanks to the help of Chinese forces and the (un)timely death of Hideyoshi in 1598, the Koreans prefer to emphasise the exploits of Admiral Yi, the greatest hero in their military history. Even beyond Korea, among those who know about this kind of thing he is considered one of the greatest naval tacticians of all time. Yi took on the

Japanese in over twenty-three battles, all of which he won. Up here on the hill above Mokpo, legend has it that Yi fooled the advancing Japanese navy into believing he and his men had a far greater stock of weapons than they really had by covering some rocks at the top with straw. The Japanese withdrew believing the rocks were piles of weapons.

Admiral Yi's many similar against-all-the-odds exploits are still regularly recalled in Korean movies and TV dramas. He also features on the hundred-won coin. His life is a rip-roarer. At the height of his military success, Yi was imprisoned and tortured on the orders of the Korean king (he had disobeyed some flawed orders) and demoted to the rank of infantryman. But, just as the Japanese were on the verge of winning, he was reinstated. Retaking command of the thirteen remaining Korean ships and using all his famed cunning, he defeated a Japanese fleet of over three hundred craft at the Battle of Myeongnyang. He died during the final battle against the Japanese, at Noryang in 1598.

Every war museum I visit in South Korea has a replica of one of Yi's famous turtle ships – the armoured rowing boats he used to defeat the Japanese. Whenever I see one of these replicas, I try to think of an equivalent figure from British history, a military leader who is still regarded with such respect. Does Francis Drake figure prominently, or at all, in the consciousness of teenage Brits? I think not. Then again, perhaps he would if the Spanish had landed and done the things to the English that the Japanese did to the poor Koreans ...

12

Puan

The next morning I head north from Mokpo in search of some severed noses. I have very little to go on, not least as the noses I seek are over four hundred years old and have travelled very far.

In Hideyoshi's day it was normal practice for the Japanese to sever the heads of their enemies after a battle to obtain the bounty for each one killed, but so many Koreans were slaughtered during his army's invasions of Korea in 1592 and 1597 that shipping their heads back to Japan proved a logistical challenge. The ingenious Japanese came up with a solution: as a contemporary observer put it, 'Men and women, down to newborn infants, all were wiped out, none was left alive. Their noses were sliced off and pickled in salt.'

The Japanese kept meticulous records which show that they took the noses of over 214,000 Koreans and Chinese, mostly in the southern and western Korean provinces of Gyeongsang, Chungcheong and here, where I am, in Jeolla. The noses were preserved in barrels of salt for the journey to Japan and, once there, displayed as a warning to anyone else who might have been planning to cause trouble, before being buried in specially built tombs. The main nose tomb was dedicated on 28 September 1597 in Kyoto, then the capital of Japan.

To add confusion to an already distressing story, over the years, as they lay beneath their grass-covered hillock in Kyoto close to a temple later dedicated to Hideyoshi himself, the noses were referred to instead as ears. One theory is that, over the centuries, the Japanese became a little self-conscious about what they'd done, and to them cutting off ears sounded slightly less cruel than severing noses. In the 1960s a plaque offering a little historical context was installed by the mound. It read: 'One cannot say that cutting off noses was so atrocious by the standard of the time.' Indeed, Japanese right-wingers still defend the taking of these grisly trophies by pointing out that similar incidents have been committed by victorious soldiers throughout history, by American troops during the Vietnam War, for instance. The Japanese also claimed that the nose tombs were a symbol of their respect for the deceased spirits of their adversaries, but the tombs continue to cause deep resentment among many Koreans, who quite reasonably don't care a fig for historical context.

The plaque is no longer there but the nose mound is. I took a look at it when I was in Kyoto earlier in my trip and, as per Hideyoshi's wishes, found it well tended. Apparently, it is popular with school trips from Hiroshima, presumably because of their heightened awareness of the horrors of war, but most Japanese are unaware of its existence. Korean tourists still come to pay their respects though. It was larger than I expected, a grassy hill supported by a hexagonal stone wall dwarfing the surrounding houses. There were fresh flowers at the top of some steps leading to a kind of altar and a stone monument, along with some random shrubbery. Close by was a playground; electricity cables criss-crossed above. There was a community noticeboard on one of the walls. Someone was growing plants up another.

Kyoto is not the only resting place of Imjin noses in Japan. In 1983 another long-rumoured tomb, the Thousand Nose Mound, was unearthed in Bizen in Okayama Prefecture, west of Osaka. Its discovery revived the subject of the noses in Korea, and in 1990 a Korean Buddhist monk, Pak Sam-jung, started a campaign to bring them back. He finally got permission from the Japanese in 1992, but excavations revealed that sadly there was nothing left of the noses themselves. Unperturbed, the Koreans took some symbolic soil back to a temple in south-west Korea, where it was interred amid great ceremony.

I thought I would try and find the noses' new burial place and pay my respects. I didn't have much to go on other than a reference to a temple in Buan, a county on the south-west coast of South

Korea. In a guidebook I find Naesosa Temple, a few miles from the town of Buan, capital of the county, in the Byeonsanbando National Park. If I were looking to rebury the noses of ancestors who had died defending the honour of my country, I thought as I set the Kia's GPS, I would want to put them somewhere appropriately grand and ancient. Naesosa was built in the seventh century and is the largest and most important Buddhist temple in the region. Also, 'Naesosa' sounds a bit like 'nose'.

I takes about an hour to reach the temple, driving through a gorgeous lush landscape with distant rocky mountains, the vista only partly marred by the Koreans' affection for polytunnels, which turn every field into a sea of plastic corrugation. The temple complex is set in a steep cove, like the crook of an arm. A couple of gnarled old geezers are manning the ticket booth at the entrance. I ask them if this is the 'nose place'. They don't speak any English so I attempt a mime, but that only serves to confuse matters further. Fortunately, a family with teenage daughters arrives. The younger generation in Japan tends to have better English than the older, and thus it proves with the Koreans too. Mine is a singular quest though, so I have to write it down and add some helpful diagrams.

The two young women convey my query to the men at the gate, who discuss it for a while before offering the name of another temple a short drive away. Here, they assure me confidently, I will find the noses I seek. At this stage of my journey in South Korea, I still take directions offered to me by Koreans at face value. Later, following many, many wrong turns and unnecessary detours, I come to realise that, just as many Japanese are often unable to say no to foreigners but will instead tilt their head equivocally to one side, Koreans are incapable of admitting that they don't know where something is, the loss of face being apparently unbearable.

Anyway, I head off excitedly towards the temple, driving higher up into the forested hills along a winding mountain road lined with flowering trees, tea bushes and densely packed pines. At the entrance to the second temple are several massive statues of warriors carved from wood with mad painted eyes as if they are absolutely furious about something – noses perhaps? Surely this, the Gaeamsa Temple, also seventh century, must be the place. A brief climb in fierce heat brings me to two rows of wooden guest huts. They seem empty, but after a few moments a young, round-faced woman with spectacles emerges. No, she hasn't heard anything about repatriated noses, but she kindly offers to ring the local park ranger, who might know, handing me the phone when he answers. The ranger's English is almost completely unintelligible, and my Korean has temporarily deserted me. He does, however, furnish me with a phone number which, I intuit, will connect me with some distant office in Buan city hall, but when I call, no one answers. By now severely dehydrated, and running behind schedule, I give up and begin to drive out of the national park, but then I pass a sign: RANGER STATION. I assume this is the workplace of the man to whom I have just been speaking. My quest now hangs by the most tenuous of threads. I decide it is worth one final effort.

Inside the ranger station I find a young man in a green and grey nylon uniform with a patch sewn on his shoulder depicting a big brown bear. A ranger! My ranger? Yes! He admits a little warily that he is the man I have just been speaking to. His name is Kang Gong-hyeop. He will turn out to be a living Korean hero.

It requires some more miming and diagrams, but eventually I persuade Mr Kang to google, 'Japan noses Buan'. As the page loads, his eyes light up. He springs into action, picks up his phone and excitedly rings a contact. A heated conversation ensues, and when he hangs up Kang looks at me with a triumphant smile. 'Now I am going to tell you a story,' he says. 'My forefathers were made slaves by the Japanese, and they had their noses cut off and buried in Japan.'

'Yes,' I say. 'I know. You see, that's why I—'

'And then a monk went there to get the noses, but the noses had ...'

He pauses, trying to find the right word.

'Decayed! They had decayed so much that he just took some soil instead. I know where the soil is!' Would I like to see the place?

Yes, I very much would.

'You can follow me,' he says, gesturing towards the door.

He climbs into his little pick-up truck filled with logs, and I follow him in my car out of the forest, back down the mountain and out onto the main road to Buan. After a couple of miles we turn down a dirt path into some fields where there stands what looks like a recently built wooden temple painted in the traditional Korean blue-green, red and yellow pattern, with a roof of heavy grey ceramic tiles.

The temple was built on the site of a great battle which took place in 1897. Unfortunately, it is closed today, but this is where the monk entombed the soil from Japan, says Kang. I thank him profusely. He has gone far beyond the call of duty, leading a confused foreigner on a cockamamie quest for some decomposed noses. We both take photos to commemorate the moment, then stand around for a while wondering what to do next before saying our awkward goodbyes.

13

Gwangju

The next morning, heading back south towards Gwangju, I stop for breakfast at a motorway service station – a bowl of spicy noodles costing not much more than a pound. I elect to accompany it with an onion-flavoured soft drink. This is a mainstream product, on sale alongside the Cokes and Sprites, and not as bad as it sounds. Korea has a few of these unusual savoury soft drinks. After a period of trial and error, I conclude that sweetcorn is the best.

At the urinal afterwards the man next to me answers his phone as he pees with predictable consequences. Walking back through the car park to the Kia, I pass another man going in the other direction towards the shop. He is alone and dressed as Superman. It is at this point that I realise I must stop comparing everything to Japan. I am in Korea now. Things are different here.

Gwangju, a city of one and a half million, is perhaps best known outside Korea for the brutal crackdown on a pro-democracy uprising – considered by some to be the country's Tiananmen Square – which took place here in May 1980 against the recently installed government of General Chun Doo-hwan. His chum President Park Chung-hee had been assassinated by the head of the Korean equivalent of the CIA the previous October. There had been a brief period of hope for democratic reform in the country, but Chun had taken power in a military coup on 17 May, imposing martial law and ordering mass arrests of politicians and other civic leaders. The next day more than 200,000 people took to the streets of Gwangju. On 21 May the army fired on protesters gathered in front of the city's local government offices, and for the next six days continued to attack demonstrators, killing 165 and injuring 1,600. These are the official figures; witnesses and relatives of those still missing put the figures much higher. General Chun claimed the pro-democracy protests were a North Korean plot. Reportedly, he was prepared at one point to send in jets to bomb the entire city.

Many hundreds of protesters ended up in Seodaemun Prison in Seoul, where they were subjected to interrogation and torture. Later in my trip I visited Seodaemun, which these days is a museum offering an evocative insight into how awful it has been to be Korean during pretty much the entire twentieth century. The prison was originally built in 1908 to house Korean resistance fighters as Japan tightened its grip on the peninsula prior to full occupation. After the Japanese left, it was used by successive South Korean military regimes up until its closure in 1987. At one time it was the country's largest prison, and thousands were incarcerated there.

The cells were as they had been when the prison closed, apart from some ghoulish exhibits including a full-scale anatomical diagram depicting torture points on the human body. In the 'underground torture chamber' I spent time trying to decipher a waxwork diorama of a Japanese-era interrogation scene with one fellow suspended by the ankles and next to him a smartly dressed man wielding a kettle. 'Narrow room torture' sounded especially awful – the prisoner was confined in a space so small there was not enough room to sit down or stand – but 'airplane torture' – in which victims' arms were tied behind their backs and then used to hoist them into the air – was simply beyond imagining.

A volunteer at the museum had experienced the airplane personally. 'I was tortured like you wouldn't believe,' he recalled. 'I thought I was going to die.' Philip (many Koreans have an alternative English name) was only seventeen when he was arrested during the Gwangju Uprising. He had been imprisoned here, hundreds of miles away from his family, for four months. He still has problems with his neck and shoulders as a result of the torture, he said pointing stiffly.

The emphasis of the exhibits at the museum was very much on the Japanese era: on how its colonial rulers had turned Korea into a 'state of slavery and frantically attempted to liquidate Korean culture and language', as one caption put it, and how 'In spite of the Japanese forcible annexation of Korea in 1910, the Korean people were never frustrated about the annexation but actively launched independent movements. From 1910 to 1945, they strongly fought against the Japanese rulers with various methods to recover their country.'

Generally the museum evaded the issue of the Korean military's role in carrying out the dirty work of its dictators in the decades after the Japanese left. In terms of the Gwangju Uprising the military were, one caption explained, 'possessed by demons', which is why they 'gave up their humanity ... turned into senseless and mindless beasts'. I suppose that's one explanation for bayoneting demonstrators in coffee shops and using flamethrowers on peaceful civilian protesters, but I was curious as to how Philip felt about the fact that his own countrymen had been responsible for his imprisonment and torture. Not a problem, he told me. After democracy came to South Korea in the late 1980s, the military apologised to him and he held no grudge against them. Anyway, he blames the Americans for Gwangju: 'They could have stopped it.' The United States did give tacit and sometimes concrete support to Chun and other South Korean military dictators. Washington had stood by as the junta murdered thousands of their own citizens, not just during President Jimmy Carter's administration at the time of Gwangju, but on many occasions prior to that, and even afterwards, all in the name of holding communism at bay.

One of the first things Moon Jae-in did after he was elected in 2017 was to commission a government investigation into the massacre. This will be the fourth such inquiry. During the first one the military experienced a strange collective amnesia. After another investigation, in 1997, Chun and his successor and ally Roh Tae-woo were sentenced to life and seventeen years respectively, only for both to be pardoned by the then president, Kim Young-sam. A 2007 investigation could find no military documents relating to the uprising whatsoever.

I had read that there was a museum about the uprising in Gwangju itself, and after a lengthy tour of what seems a strangely centre-less city, I finally find it in a municipal building, the May 18 Memorial Culture Center. The place is mostly empty, but in a dark corner on the first floor of the entrance atrium there is a small temporary-looking cluster of information stands recalling the brutality of the military at the time – at one point going as far as to describe their actions as 'genocide' – recounting how soldiers ransacked houses and carried off young protesters like Philip. Nearby, I find some people working in an office. This is the International Affairs Department, with a staff of twenty. A polite young woman appears from behind a bookcase. Her name is Lee Dasom, and she is the assistant coordinator. The Center's activities range from organising a winter school for young human rights defenders to running a cultural and educational department, and helping with the ongoing research into the events of May 1980, she says. Wasn't everything known already? I ask.

'Actually we are not really aware who the perpetrator who ordered the shooting of people was,' Lee tells me. Candidates range from the former president to various army officers. How involved were the Americans? Lee didn't think any orders came directly from Washington, but it was more a question of them turning a blind eye to the brutality of the Chun regime. 'We aren't sure. It's a long, tricky question. For me American responsibility is because they allowed the troops to move to Gwangju. They knew it was happening, and they didn't stop it.'

A new film about the Uprising, *A Taxi Driver*, has just been released in Korea. Based on a true story, it focuses on Jürgen Hinzpeter, a German TV reporter nicknamed the Witness with Blue Eyes by the Koreans who covered the protests, and a local taxi driver who helped him sneak through a military cordon into the city at the height of the fighting. Hinzpeter's photos led to global condemnation of the Korean junta's crackdown, with protests by Korean-Americans in the US and even hunger strikes in support of the Koreans by Germans. Hinzpeter, who died only recently, is revered as a hero by the Koreans, and there is a memorial to him in Gwangju. The film had gone straight to number one in Korea with six million tickets sold in the first nine days.[8]

The success of the film, which is now among the ten most popular in South Korea history, prompted a concerted effort to trace the taxi driver, who had been called Kim Sa-bok. It became one of the most searched-for names on Korean Google that month. Eventually, a man came forward with evidence that his father was the cabbie. Sadly, he had died in 1984.

[8] The Chinese authorities swiftly banned it, presumably not wishing to encourage anything even remotely redolent of the Tiananmen Square protests.

14

Seoul I

The closer I come to Seoul the more cataclysmic grows the pollution. An hour outside the capital and I can't really see the countryside, just a rusty haze. In the queue on the highway I edge past a beaten-up old pick-up truck loaded with about twenty caged dogs, not the kind sold as pets. It feels like I am in the opening pages of some Ballardian anthropocene dystopia.

How do people live with this pollution? Apparently, they don't. The government quotes a figure of 12,000 deaths per year due to airborne particulates, so presumably the real toll is much higher. According to the OECD, South Korea has the worst air quality of its member nations. Later, I heard that the air improved during the Winter Olympics because factories were ordered to close for a few weeks, which rather undermines the often-heard claim of the Korean administration that the pollution is 'all the fault of the Chinese'.

From what little I can see beyond the bonnet, the South Korean capital doesn't appear to have suburbs. It goes from forested valleys and those now-familiar polytunnel fields straight to dense thickets of tower blocks which continue unbroken until I reach the River Han. It all looks like it was thrown up in a hurry some time around 1983 with a broken promise to sort it out later when there's more time; as Monument Valley was sculpted by the wind, Seoul looks to have been shaped by the cyclone of cash which has engulfed it for the last few decades, unhindered by regulations, planning or taste.

Half of the population of South Korea lives within the metropolitan region, and it would appear every single one of them drinks coffee at least once a day. As estate agents are to London and pharmacies are to Paris, so are coffee shops to Seoul. They are everywhere – 18,316 of them to be precise – with two or three hundred opening every month. The average South Korean over the age of twenty drinks 413 cups of coffee a year. The country spends a bewildering $5.68 billion a year on the stuff, and consumption is still increasing. At one point I count three coffee shops next to one another. This city makes Seattle look like Harrogate.

I dump the car at my hotel in Itaewon, a rather sleazy expat district of tacky bars and sticky pavements, and head out to explore. I take the Seoul Metropolitan Subway to Gangnam. Koreans, it seems, actually talk on trains, sometimes to each other but mostly into their phones, loudly and constantly. In Japan no one ever does this.

The South Koreans are the biggest users of smartphones in the world. We are all struggling with screen addiction, I know, but these people put the 'vice' in 'device'. Based on what I saw, I would estimate that at any given time around 80 per cent of Koreans are glued to their phones. I lost count of the people I saw holding their screens in front of their faces, earphones plugged in, watching films as they walked or blocked escalators, elbows splayed. In my entire time in the city, over three visits, I saw not a single person reading an actual physical newspaper or book. Not one. I recently read that Elon Musk has a company, Neuralink, which is working on a brain–machine interface, a physical connection between the human mind and technology. Forget it, Elon. The Koreans have beaten you to it. They have mind-melded with their Samsung Galaxies.

The second shock is that people spit with abandon here. And spitting is not the only customarily private bodily function which the Koreans perform in public. I hear my first uninhibited fart on my second day, at the National War Museum. Public flatulence is apparently no biggie in South Korea, but the first couple of times it happens within earshot I am still startled. One time I literally jump. Older Korean men are always the culprits. As for younger Korean males, they seem completely preoccupied with their appearance. They have the look of people who spend far too long in front of the bathroom cabinet. The large full-length mirrors hanging close to the ticket barriers at many Seoul Subway stations are utilised equally by both genders.[9] Then again, if I looked as good as they do, I would want to admire myself too. Korean men clearly spend a lot of time down the gym; they are buff and trim, although, having lavished so much time on their physiques and faces, it seems strange that they are content to dress so uniformly in a style I came to think of as high-street hipster. There is a particular dearth of imagination when it comes to glasses, which either have thick flat-fronted black frames like Psy's of 'Gangnam Style' fame, or thin round black frames with a gold bridge. It was literally a binary choice.

Other Japan–Korea differences. In Japan tattoos are frowned upon because they had to be the preserve of the yakuza – having one will get you banned from the *onsen* (communal baths) – but in Seoul they are employed to a near-Scandinavian degree by both men and women. As for the quantities of 'product' they use in their hair and on their skin, Korean men make Cher look like Sister Wendy. According to a 2018 BBC report, they use more cosmetics per capita than any other men anywhere in the world, a fifth of the world's supply. In Japan the Metro stations and the walkways connecting them are filled with cake, sweet and ice-cream stands, in Seoul they have replaced the confectionery with make-up and beauty products. South Korea's largest health and beauty chain is Olive Young. Its flagship store, here in Gangnam, Seoul's glitziest district, offers 15,000 products. I take one look at the placenta masks, double-eyelid tape and snail-extract repair creams and retreat, bewildered.

At one point on the Subway a group of university students enters my carriage. Of the three boys in the group, two are sporting full make-up – foundation, mascara, eyeliner, pale lipstick. They have

[9] A few years back, they started installing full-length mirrors on some Metro platforms in Japan too, except these were an anti-suicide measure, the idea being that potential jumpers would see themselves and reconsider.

done it extremely well and look great, but the point is, this is an everyday thing for them. They aren't on their way to a party or a club, but a classroom.

Cosmetics adverts are everywhere, from vast roadside billboards erected apparently without restriction, to the smaller ads which plaster every available space on trains, and they address themselves as much to males as to females. Though the city authorities have promised to phase out plastic-surgery ads on the Subway, the message has not yet reached Gangnam station, which is wall-to-wall with posters promising that you too could become a blemish-free symmetrically faced replicant. The adverts always feature the same type of shiny-skinned anodyne-androgynous young people. The focus is on skin whitening and tightening, the aim apparently being to turn one's face into Chopin's death mask. No target audience is too young.

Around 1.2 million plastic-surgery procedures are carried out in South Korea every year, the highest number per capita in the world. One report I read claimed that half of Korean women in their twenties have had surgery, a third of all women in Seoul. One of the most popular procedures is double-eyelid surgery, a component of the so-called Gangnam look, which, again based on empirical observation, requires having an almond-shaped face with a pointy chin, a synchronised-swimmer's nose and a forehead like a billiard table.

Why has physical appearance been raised to such a pitch of fetishised neurosis in South Korea? Why the desperate need to conform to such a narrow bandwidth of physical conventions? Is this somehow a symptom of Korea's terrible century of occupation, war and military dictatorship – a giddy, liberated release? Or is it a symptom of the constant threat of annihilation looming from the North? In one newspaper report on the industry I read a quote by a Gangnam plastic surgeon: 'Koreans react strongly to power, privilege and status because of a certain survival mentality.' Perhaps beauty is a power play. Up until a few years ago job applicants in South Korea were required to pin a photograph of themselves to their CV; it is not hard to imagine how this might put pressure on the young to look a certain way too. Maybe the Koreans value personal beauty because their urban environment is so dispiriting? They can do little about where they live, but they can at least control how they look. One thing is certain: if there was such a thing as a psycho-anthropologist, they would have a field day diagnosing the South Koreans. There was only one way I could find out the truth. I would have to go and have some plastic surgery done on myself.[10]

I ring my wife to tell her I am about to get 'some surgery done'. She doesn't ask what I am having done, which on reflection is probably not a good sign.

Actually, my plan is not particularly ambitious. For some years now I have had two small red lumps on the side of my nose. I had them checked by my doctor, who offered the same shrug she reserves for the many other age-related ailments with which I regularly regale her. They were harmless, she said. She may actually have tutted as I left the surgery. But here I was in the global capital of cosmetic surgery. What better opportunity would I have to fight back against the ageing process, resist the march of time, to laugh in the face of ... well, I guess, my own face?

I take the Subway to Apgujeong, close to Gangnam, and home of the largest concentration of surgeries in the city – the capital of the capital of cosmetic surgery, if you like. Again, the train carriage is full of adverts for surgeons, without exception really quite ugly middle-aged men, posing alongside blemish-free models like something from the Tyrell Corporation catalogue. There are ads for breast surgery, jaw-sculpting and 'nose control measures'. One entices with 'surgical facial rejuvenation for the North East Asians', another promotes 'round faced lifts'. Another claims to be able to

[10] Neither of these statements is in any way accurate. I had been looking for an excuse to get something done for ages, and I gained no new insights from the experience other than discovering how burning flesh smells.

cure bandy legs. At Apgujeong station a billboard quotes Audrey Hepburn: 'Happy girls are the prettiest.'

Outside the station I survey my options. I can see a good half-dozen plastic surgeons; some buildings house four floors of clinics, including one called the Second Coming. Nearby is a kind of cosmetic surgery tourist visitors' centre, displaying the brochures of many of the practices and with open consultation rooms. Here I read one clinic's advert, which boasts that it was responsible for the world record amount of fat extracted from one person via lipo-suction: 21,500 cubic centimetres. 'Turn the 102kg body into S Line,' it offers. According to OECD 2015 figures, the Koreans have the second lowest rates of adult obesity (around 5 per cent) in the developed world, beaten only by the Japanese. Where are they finding all this fat to suck up?

A little way down the street I come to another clinic. It meets my main criterion for a plastic surgery (it does not have a biblical refer-ence in its name), so I enter and explain to the Stepford receptionists what I am hoping to get done. They call the surgeon, a short round man in his late fifties. I notice immediately that he has a slightly squiffy left eye, not your full Marty Feldman, but enough so I don't know which one to look at when talking to him. I make my excuses and try another surgeon a little further down the street. This one's eyes are facing in the right direction. I agree to the operation.

I am shown to a basement waiting area next to a door marked LASER ROOM. A pretty young man dabs some anaesthetic cream on my nose and instructs me to wait twenty minutes for it to take effect. I note that the clinic sells bridal wear as well as a range of cosmetic products, among them Skinbolic, with its patented 'skin injecting' technology.

Finally, the time has come for my operation. In the laser room I recline on a dentist's chair. The pretty young man holds the end of a vacuum cleaner tube to the side of my face. Odd. The surgeon arrives trailing an air of brisk efficiency but has, I only now notice, quite trembly hands. He double-checks what exactly it is I want removed. 'Is it this?' he asks, pointing to a completely different part of my face with which, up until now, I have been reasonably happy.

'No, here – these things on my nose.' I gesture.

Unperturbed, the surgeon goes to work on my red nose-lumps with his laser pen. It takes less than half a minute, but the pain is excruciating, and despite the vacuum cleaner going full blast the room is filled with the smell of burning flesh, as if someone is spit-roasting a pig.

At the end of it all I am shown a mirror and see that, in place of the red lumps, I now have two red sores. I am assured by the surgeon that they will heal in a week or so. As long as I purchase some Skinbolic and apply twice daily.

15

Seoul II

It is another baking-hot day, which is good because it means that the Namsangol Hanok Village ('Village of Traditional Houses in the Namsan Valley') in central Seoul is mostly empty. This is a relief, as my lesson is to be a public affair, taking place in an open-sided rectangular pavilion, its roof painted minty green, orange and mauve, a traditional Korean decorative style called *Dancheong*.

I sign a release form and am given some white pyjamas to change into, removing my shoes and socks. Up in the pavilion I meet my instructor, Mr Kang, who is a good six foot three tall, handsome, and a black belt. We are joined by the only other person mad enough to sign up for a public tae kwon do lesson in forty-degree heat, a small Japanese woman called Sue, from Nagoya.

The pavilion overlooks an ornamental pond. Mr Kang explains that the pond acts as an air conditioner, cooling the hot air as it moves across its surface, but I am not feeling it. As he speaks, he eyes me up and down and suggests we begin with some basic stretching exercises. Within just a few moments I am sweating profusely and have pulled two muscles I did not know I had. Tae kwon do is South Korea's national sport, Mr Kang says. He is doing a talky bit to give me time to recover, I suspect. This martial art is over 2,300 years old. Its name means 'the way of the foot and the fist'.

Back to the action: he shows us how to block an opponent's blows by lifting our forearms up above our head, then down below our waist. We practise this. It feels a bit like a Village People routine. Mr Kang now demonstrates a more complex punching-while-stamping-forward-then-kicking sequence, which ends with an aggressive exhalation: 'Huh!' Our index and middle fingers are connected through a line to our forearms, he explains, but we must keep our little fingers tucked in. Apparently, the pinkie is crucial in supporting the power of the punch.

Another pause. Mr Kang looks concerned as I bend over to catch my breath. He invites us to consider the Korean flag, with its central yin and yang symbol. See how it resembles the way the little finger supports a punch? And look how the four groups of three lines in each corner of the flag are like the four blocking points we've just practised. The other key to a tae kwon do punch is to twist your fist at the moment of impact. Sue performs this annoyingly well but later admits to having studied tae kwon do for three years in Japan, which is downright devious. When it is my turn I feel as though I beat her in terms of sheer commitment.

Next, Kang picks up some P-shaped padded bats which we must attempt to hit in a special sequence, a kind of whack-a-mole routine. I am quite good at this too and am actually beginning to enjoy tae kwon do, but then I catch sight of a group of teenagers sitting in the corner of the hall watching us and imagine how I look from their position. It is too late for a midlife crisis of confidence though as we have arrived at the grand finale: breaking a piece of wood in half with a single punch.

'If you hit it in the middle, you only need a force of about five to ten kilos,' says Kang. 'But if you hit the edge, it is about a ton.' On my first attempt I miss the board completely and hit his forearm, the blow glancing off as if I am striking an overinflated bouncy castle. I don't think he even notices. At the second attempt my aim is still a bit skew-whiff, but I break the board. I pick up the pieces proudly. Looking more closely, I think they might be balsa wood.

The session ends with a short lecture from Mr Kang about tae kwon do and its role in recent Korean history. After the devastation of the Korean War, South Korea was helped in its recovery by sixteen different nations, and sixteen tae kwon do masters were sent to each of them by way of thanks. So, long before K-pop, Korean movies and TV dramas were being devoured by a grateful international public, tae kwon do was the country's first post-war attempt at cultural branding, at defining who the Koreans were in foreign eyes. It occurs to me then that tae kwon do is the forerunner of *Hallyu*, the Korean wave of popular culture which went international in the 1990s, the watershed year being 2002, when the country co-hosted the World Cup with Japan, the K-pop singer BoA had a number-one hit in Japan and the TV series *Winter Sonata* debuted.

These days South Korea's image abroad is almost entirely founded on these popular entertainments. Some feel this is a shame because the country has so much more traditional culture and art to offer, going back centuries, but most Koreans I speak to are proud and grateful that their country has any kind of international cultural profile at all, that it's not all missile tests and demilitarised zones. *Hallyu* has worked particularly well in the country's close neighbours China and Japan. In a 2018 poll of Japanese people, an 'interest in South Korean drama, music, or culture' was cited as the number one reason for 'having a good impression' of South Koreans by just over half of respondents.

Jonathan Kim is more qualified than most to talk about *Hallyu*. He is one of the most successful South Korean film producers of the past two decades, responsible for five of the country's fifty top grossing films. I meet the dapper fifty-seven-year-old later that morning after my tae kwon do efforts in his offices above a coffee shop (what else?) in Itaewon.

'I get that question all the time from people everywhere. Why not a Japan wave or a China wave? Why Korea?' Kim says as we begin to talk. He is sitting behind a big movie mogul's desk and, I am pleased to see, is wearing one of those multi-pocketed safari waistcoats just like film people are supposed to. I sit in a director's chair. 'Finally, it dawned on me. I looked at the history of our country, which was once three countries or kingdoms. For thousands of years it had this stability. Not like China – you know, every forty-five years everything changes. When you are stable like Korea, basically you have nothing problematic, so what do you do? You party!'

It's an interesting theory. After all, Japan's own period of stability, in the seventeenth and eighteenth centuries, resulted in its own great cultural flowering; but then again didn't *Hallyu* follow straight after Korea's century of oppression, war and destitution? Kim has an answer: the suffering helped make Korean art universal. That, and the invention of VHS.

'In the 1980s we were making all the VHS machines, but we didn't have much domestic content,' he says. Porn was – and remains – illegal in South Korea, so that avenue was unavailable for the new VHS industry. Fortunately, a new generation of directors and producers emerged to meet the demands of the new format, and the *chaebol* – the Korean conglomerates manufacturing the VHS recorders – had the money to back them. Another boost to the industry came in 1997 when South Korea finally got rid of censorship.

One of the first movies to take advantage of this was a North–South Korean romantic comedy called *Shiri*, starring Yunjin Kim, who later appeared in the US TV series *Lost*. *Shiri* was part-funded by Samsung. At the time the average budget for a South Korean movie was about half a million pounds. *Shiri* cost over two million, but it went on to beat *Titanic*'s record box office receipts.

'*Shiri* is the name of a Korean fish, so we say that was the fish which sank the *Titanic*,' chuckles Kim. He has enjoyed his own *Hallyu* successes. In 2003 his company produced *Silmido*, an action movie about death row prisoners training for a mission to assassinate the North Korean leader. It was the first film to break the 10 million ticket sales barrier in South Korea, partly because its release coincided with the opening of the country's first multiplexes. *Shiri*'s success in Japan and Hong Kong alerted the South Korean government to a potential export stream, and it made tens of million of pounds available as seed money for Korean films. The government continues to fund roughly 40 per cent of the domestic industry. There is, though, still some debate about what role the South Korean government has played in the global success of *Hallyu*.

In her 2014 book *The Birth of Korean Cool* Euny Hong attributes much of the success to the direct involvement of the South Korean culture ministry, but British expat journalist Andrew Salmon disagrees. '[Hong] went with the whole top-down thing, which, to be fair, is how everything else is in Korea – the economic revolution, the high-tech revolution in the early 1990s – but the only thing we've really had from the bottom up is *Hallyu*,' he told me. Another British journalist who witnessed the *Hallyu* phenomenon, Michael Breen, believes it happened *in spite of* the Korean government's meddling. In his book *The New Koreans* Breen writes that its attempts to jump on the *Hallyu* bandwagon 'have all the style of your dad leaping up and doing his Mick Jagger moves at a teenage party'.

Whether the government was behind their success or not, Korean films took the world by storm. Probably the best known director to emerge from the first wave was Park Chan-wook. His first overseas hit, the utterly bonkers revenge movie *Oldboy*, was released in 2004. It is not for the squeamish, or octopus lovers. One of the strengths of contemporary Korean movie-making is that directors like Park often write their own scripts and enjoy greater levels of autonomy than their peers in Hollywood. The result is highly idiosyncratic films with a raw, some might argue specifically Korean, emotionalism, plus lots of inventively graphic violence.

Another explanation for the success of Korean films in China in particular is that they show widely recognisable traditional aspects of Asian society, but combine them with cool modern lifestyles. 'They see on the television or movie screen a modernised society filled with capitalistic commodities like modern buildings, cars, restaurants and fancy clothes. At the same time, however, they observe behavioural patterns that accord with Confucian traditions, including emphasis on the family, male dominance, patriarchy, strong hierarchy, spirit of self-sacrifice among males and female obedience,' writes anthropologist Jang Soo-hyun of Kwangwoon University.

Korean television series have been just as popular. As with the film industry, the rise of Korean TV dramas also features a new technology in search of content, in this case the arrival of cable TV in Taiwan and Hong Kong. Korean dramas were cheaper than their rivals from Japan. 'The people kind of look the same –' Kim laughs '– so all you have to do is dub, and they don't know the difference.'

South Korean TV enjoyed several massive international hits such as *Dae Jang Geum* (*Jewel in the Palace*), a fifteenth-century royal epic which sold to ninety countries. The Chinese loved it, including reportedly Premier Hu Jintao. The Japanese preferred *Winter Sonata*, a love saga first shown there in 2003. Its male lead, Bae Yong-joon, inspired hordes of female Japanese fans to visit the Korean locations where the series had been filmed. Both dramas were also successful in the Philippines, Vietnam and further afield in Iran and South America.

I hesitate at this point to turn the conversation to K-pop because I find its appeal elusive. It's not that I have especially refined musical tastes – I don't – but then perhaps synthetic auto-tuned pop emoted by winsome teenagers with all the vocal nuances of a faulty car alarm is not supposed to appeal to middle-aged men. I don't even really understand what it is. For example, this is a quote from an article I read about one current K-pop band in the *New Yorker*: 'They dabbled in the golden era sounds of G-funk, boom-bap, and turntablism, alongside the residual nu-metal and overloaded trap bangers then commonplace among Korean boy bands. Few made it out of those years without a dubstep breakdown.' Answers on a postcard.

Jonathan Kim tells me that K-pop is where the term *Hallyu* originates. 'We had a singing group called H.O.T., and they became very, very big in China. When they performed in China, we would see people waving Korean flags in the audience – that was where the Korean wave thing came from – a Chinese DJ called it that.' In 2000 H.O.T. was the first Korean band to perform in Beijing. In 2006 BoA (the queen of Korean pop, real name Kwon Bo-ah) became the first Korean act to reach number one in the Japanese charts. Actor-singer Rain followed in 2007, and from 2009 to 2014 Korean music exports grew by almost 60 per cent a year.

Then came the fat man with the horse-riding dance, and the Western mainstream media went all-in too. Despite being entirely unintelligible to Western audiences, once seen, the video for 'Gangnam Style' could never be forgotten. The South Koreans found Psy's 2012 success as a *Hallyu* act odd as he is a portly fellow and K-pop acts are preternaturally slim and trim, and the two comedians who appeared with him in the video were much more famous than he was in South Korea.

In the last couple of years *Hallyu* has begun to decline in China. Concerned about the impact of cultural imports, the Chinese authorities have made concerted efforts to generate their own domestic TV dramas and films, and Chinese pop has undergone something of a boom too. The THAAD missile defence system business further damaged South Korea's cultural exports to China. 'We were completely banned [in China]. Cinema, TV, music, everything. We can't even use our own name as a company so I had to create a Hong Kong company,' says Kim. 'It was like the [Chinese] animosity moved from the Japanese to the Koreans. I have had six contracts "delayed", but really they have been cancelled.'

I asked Youngruk Cheong, an economist I met at Seoul national University who has focused on relations with China for many years, how these kinds of sanctions worked.

'It is very ambiguous. There is no strict clear policy, no sanctions; it is indirect patriotism. About 88 million Chinese are members of the Communist Party, which is huge, and you know SMS is very prevalent in China.' In other words, the message goes out almost subliminally: *We are not happy that Korea is allowing this*, and suddenly the Chinese stop going on holiday to Korea and go to Thailand or Indonesia instead. Within a year, tourism from China to Korea declined from five million to two million; K-pop stars found their visa applications to China refused; thousands of Hyundais and Kias were left standing in the ports. Something similar had happened a few years earlier in Japan – the Japanese market turned against *Hallyu* when South Korea and Japan clashed over the Dokdo/Takeshima Islands. Cultural exports are, it seems, the first thing to suffer when relations deteriorate between the east Asian siblings.

Jonathan Kim is now turning his attention elsewhere. 'When I look at South East Asia it reminds me of South Korea in the early 90s. They don't make enough movies themselves, and major American companies are dominating.' It is an opportunity Chinese films could never take advantage of, he says; their cultural output is just too Chinese, too specific. 'The jokes they use, the references, other countries, even Chinese-speaking countries, don't understand them. The mentality and trends in China are very different right now, and because of the censorship it's not edgy enough for audiences here. Chinese movies are too predictable.'

According to Kim, a typical Chinese box office hit resembles a 1990s Korean rom-com. 'It is always the son of a rich man, filthy rich, who is the main star. Everything has to be flamboyant, with big houses.' He once pitched a movie to the Chinese about a working-class boy who falls in love with a girl who has terminal cancer. 'She says, "Don't worry, we will meet in heaven," but in China heaven has too many religious connotations. You can't have ghosts either. No ghosts. And no cops. That's how bad it is.' He leans back in his chair and throws his arms up in exasperation. In the end he had to change the protagonist into a rich man. 'Chinese people want to see rich people on the screen instead of themselves. The final word is always "This is China. This is different."'

Happily, the rest of the world has yet to reach *Hallyu* saturation point. In June 2018 the Korean boy band BTS became the first K-pop group to top the Billboard 200, America's album chart, and with a song in Korean to boot. Some say this was a direct result of the Chinese sanctions; the Koreans had instead focused their efforts on the American market. Whether true or not, the Koreans are definitely back, and the next waves of *Hallyu* are already gaining momentum: the South Korean e-sports industry is huge, having doubled since 2009 to the point where it accounts for almost 15 per cent of the global market. Playing computer games for money is Korea's new unofficial national sport. Many predict the next wave will be the Korean cosmetics and plastic-surgery industry – K-beauty. Korean skincare and make-up trends are increasingly popular throughout Asia.

Sometimes these *Hallyu* categories cross over, as happened in 2017 with the K-pop band Six Bomb, who released a song, 'Becoming Pretty', extolling the virtues of plastic surgery. They didn't stop there. Each of the four female group members underwent various procedures – breast implants, cheekbones shaved, nose jobs, etc., and in the video they danced in the operating theatre with their bandages on as they sang, 'Everyone follows me, they know I'm pretty.'

In other words, reports of the demise of *Hallyu* soft power have been greatly exaggerated. Consider yourself warned.

16

Daecheon Beach, Boryeong

I meet the Mormons at the mud festival bus stop. The two young men are being loudly harassed by a group of other young Americans, drunk spring-break types in gaudy nylon wife-beaters, baseball caps and cargo shorts, who are inviting the Mormons to join them for a drink. I don't interfere because I am a coward, but wait until the drunks have moved on like a whoop of baboons in the direction of a nearby bar and sidle up to the two young evangelists, with their buzzcuts, narrow ties and short-sleeved shirts. What on earth are they doing here?

'I'm based here for two years,' the taller of the two says cheerfully. He introduces himself as Elder Dustin. He looks like a young, goofy Robert Redford. 'We're learning the language, being missionaries,' says Elder Burt, the darker haired of the two. The Koreans here in Daecheon on the west coast of Korea, two hours south of Seoul, have been very receptive to their message, apparently.

The first Christian to come to Korea accompanied the Japanese invaders during the Imjin Wars in the late sixteenth century. Since then Koreans have generally been receptive to Western religions and have even come up with a few versions of their own. Today almost a third of South Koreans are Christians, compared to about 1 per cent of Japanese and perhaps 2 or 3 per cent in China. The majority of Korean Christians are Protestants; conversions boomed after the Americans arrived in 1945.

Seoul now boasts the largest Christian congregation in the world, the Full Gospel Church, as well as a few wilder spin-offs, most famously the Unification Church, or Moonies, founded in 1954 by the late Sun Myung Moon, noted tax felon/messiah. Christianity in all its forms is big business. I was surprised to see an ATM built into the wall of one church I passed in central Seoul, but by all accounts Korean churches are intensely relaxed about money – members typically donate around 10 per cent of their income, and many churches are extremely wealthy as a consequence. Korea expert Daniel Tudor noted: 'Protestantism is seen as the pro-capitalist religion ... 42 per cent of CEOs of large Korean firms are Protestant. Large Protestant churches are criticised by some as places where business networking and deal-making take place.'

Back at the bus stop, I wonder aloud why Mormons always travel in twos. 'We help each other avoid temptation,' says Burt. There is certainly plenty of that here at Daecheon Beach in Boryeong on the Yellow Sea coast. This is the home of an annual mud festival, which looks from what I've seen of it to be an excuse for scantily clad hedonistic excess (should you need an excuse). Each summer this seaside resort town with its long wide sandy beach fronted by an ugly rash of 1990s-built hotels and restaurants draws around 400,000 people to wallow and play in what is, essentially, a gigantic mud bath.

The mud festival has been going for twenty years, and Daecheon has embraced the theme. The accommodation has names like Mudbeach Hotel and Hotel Mudrin (which I *think* is a play on 'Mandarin Oriental'); there are mud-themed statues and monuments along the seafront; and a Mud Museum, a glorified cosmetics boutique. The main action takes place in a giant mud-filled pen featuring all manner of obstacle-course amusements. People can fire water cannons at each other, wrestle, slide, whatever. There is a separate children's zone, and around the mud pit are various other mud-related activities such as body-painting ... Actually, that's about it. Just the body painting. The rest of the stalls mostly focus on selling pissy Korean beer.

I had assumed the mud was a naturally occurring phenomenon as the coast here boasts one of the world's five largest tidelands, but the truth is slightly more prosaic, as I discover when I get chatting to one of the festival organisers, Chang Woo-hoi.

'Oh no,' admits Woo-hoi cheerfully. 'We ship the mud in from a cosmetics factory – 250 kilotons in powder form – and then we add water. The powder is the base for all their cosmetics.' So, basically, all the people in front of us are wallowing in a very expensive beauty product? 'Exactly!' Total revenue from the festival last year was 70,000,000,000 Korean won (£47 million). Daecheon lives off this messy knees-up for the entire year.

Woo-hoi, a biology graduate, is a volunteer. He speaks with a distinctive Estuary English accent, which he says he picked up from playing computer games. He tells me that one positive by-product of the fact that people walk around for most of the day slathered from head to toe in grey mud as if they've just been rescued from some kind of quicksand-related mishap is that it neutralises their ethnicity. 'When you are covered in mud, people don't care about your skin colour, what you do, where you are from – that is no problem,' says Woo-hoi, who was born here in Daecheon. 'Everyone just wants to enjoy themselves or do something fun. It makes everyone the same – that's the spirit of the mud festival.'

I ask if many Japanese people come to the mud festival. 'Actually, the Japanese mind is a little different. They don't like to be covered with mud, so we get very few Japanese.' The event is much more popular with Americans and Europeans, especially students. '*So many English*,' he adds a little too wearily. I ask about safety issues. Thousands of drunk teenagers and a big slippery surface look like a recipe for very busy A & E waiting rooms. 'Of course, there are so many accidents, especially with American military. I have been threatened by a drunk American soldier once. He wanted a fight.'

There are currently 28,500 US military personnel in South Korea, many of them living in the Yongsan base right in the centre of Seoul. When Camp Humphreys, forty miles south of the capital, is completed in 2020 it will be the largest overseas US military base in the world, home to 42,000 personnel. The mud festival attracts so many soldiers – and so many fights – that the army sends along military police to patrol the event. I try to imagine other sovereign nations tolerating that kind of thing, but for now my thoughts are with the Japanese and their reluctance to get muddy. I share their reticence but, very much contrary to all my natural instincts, I am now going to change into some different clothes – a K-pop band T-shirt I picked up from a nearby store and some garish shorts – which I am prepared to say goodbye to at the end of the day. I store my other things in a locker and venture forth into the mud zone.

Well, I have to tell you, my natural instincts don't know what they are talking about. This is 'hella' fun, as I believe the current youth argot has it. Jousting on muddy inflatable mattresses turns out to be completely brilliant and a task at which I excel, at least right up until a very large Korean woman takes her turn and sends me skittling off into the muddy pool with one (lucky) thrust.

After spending some time flushing rapidly drying grainy mud from my crevices, I retreat to the beach, where a massive stage and lighting rig has been erected. A heavily tattooed young Korean man with dreadlocks has just finished doing whatever it is he does on stage, and the audience of bodybuilders and Korean girl gangs is buzzing. Later, Psy of 'Gangnam Style' fame will perform, although I will be long gone by then.

As for the magic mud, that lingers for some days afterwards, but the Mud Museum, which I visit the next morning, claims the goo can 'restrain stress' and 'promote breathing of skin cells'. It can also make people fall in love with you, and if you rub it on your forehead, you will pass your exams. Word of its magic properties has spread: Boryeong has begun exporting the mud to the New Zealand town of Rotorua, which is planning to hold its own mud festival.

It seems sensible for the mud zone to close at 6 p.m. as by then people are beginning to seem a little the worse for wear. Mud and booze, not to mention vomit and impaired coordination, make for a potent cocktail. I retire to one of the open-air restaurants where people sit around grills built into the tables, cooking fantastic shellfish – scallops, mussels, clams.

In *The New Koreans* Michael Breen describes the typical Korean holiday as sunbathing on a crowded beach and then 'dinner at one of a line of identical restaurants that sell only seafood and don't have a view of the sea, lots of drink and noise, a lurch to the beach to set off fireworks, the karaoke, more noise, and then the motel'. This is pretty much what I experience that night in Daecheon, but Breen explains that until recently there was no indigenous tourism in South Korea. People worked too hard to take time off, and there were few resources to preserve historic towns or prettify existing ones: 'you'd be hard-pressed to find a nice-looking town'.

This reminds one that judging South Korea by the same criteria as you might other developed nations doesn't really work. In 1945, when the peninsula was partitioned by the USA and the Soviet Union, the south was even poorer than the north, which had seen the larger share of the colonial-era industrial development – it had 80 per cent of the power stations, for instance. The south was one of the poorest places in the world, with virtually no natural resources, not even enough agricultural output to feed itself. The return of the Koreans who had been working in Japan put further pressure on resources, and then came the civil war, in which more than three million were killed or starved to death. Hardly a town was unaffected by bombing, barely a tree was left standing, to the extent that MacArthur predicted it would take at least a century to rebuild the country.

The recovery of the following decades is referred to as the Miracle on the Han – after the river which flows through the centre of Seoul – but the miracle took a while to kick off. After the war around a third of the population of South Korea was homeless, and for the first few years the country subsisted on US handouts. Land reforms, which redistributed farmland to tenants, and massive improvements in education, began to pave the way for recovery, but in 1961 the country's GDP was still 101st in the world, on a par with Haiti's. Throughout the 1950s and 60s South Koreans grew accustomed to the *Borit-gogae* ('Barley Hump'), the spring famine which preceded the barley harvest, during which people would be forced to forage for roots, wild herbs, even tree bark.

Under Park Chung-hee's leadership, which began in 1963, agricultural advances including the creation of a new strain of rice

(Unification Rice) by Seoul National University, meant the end of these famines. Nevertheless, unemployment in South Korea was so dire in the mid-60s that nearly 8,000 men emigrated to West Germany to work in the coal mines and over 10,000 women went there to work as nurses. In 1963 there were 46,000 Korean applications for 500 German mining jobs, which paid seven times what a government worker might earn in Korea. There are still large Korean communities in parts of Germany because of this exodus.

The miraculous economic growth which eventually materialised – averaging almost 9 per cent during most of the late 1960s – was largely due to the form of state-controlled, planned private enterprise that Park introduced and closely guided. The Vietnam War boosted the South Korean economy immensely too, as did slowly thawing relations with Japan in the late 1960s, which brought cash investments. Japan also provided an economic role model, which one Korean commentator said led them to 'do what the Japanese have done, but cheaper and faster', predominantly in steel, shipbuilding, electronics and cars. Today the South Korean economy is the twelfth largest in absolute terms in the world, and it is the seventh largest exporter.

In 1953 it would have been unthinkable that South Korea would one day be in a position to export TV programmes and pop songs to a grateful world; that the people of Seoul would be so awash with cash that they would spend it injecting their foreheads with monkey gland extract or going on holiday to Japan of all places; or that the country would host the Olympics and a World Cup. And play in the semi-final.

When I find myself recoiling at the ugliness of Korea's urban landscapes, I try to remember this. To reach the point where they can let rip in a giant mud bath without feeling guilty about it, the South Koreans had to suffer under a murderous regime, work like drones in the worst conditions for the lowest of wages and longest of hours, and basically just suck it up for forty long years.

17

Seoul III

I arrive back in Seoul on the evening before the general election and take a walk through Meong-dong, one of Seoul's main shopping and nightlife districts. One of the presidential candidates, a small round man with hair like a Playmobil figure, is holding a rally. Clearly not a front-runner, he has wisely chosen to set up his stage in a narrow shopping street where there isn't much space for supporters, thus averting the risk of Trump Inauguration Syndrome. His followers wave Korean flags and chant slogans. Many are waving American flags too, suggesting this is one of the more conservative candidates. Shoppers go about their business without giving him a second glance.

A little later outside the city hall I come across a small but persistent band of pro-Park protesters who have pitched camp and are trying to convince passers-by that the ex-president's impeachment is a sham. 'It is a subversive conspiracy promoted by the press, the prosecution and the national assembly. Dear fellow citizens, let's fight tooth and nail!' reads one of their banners, with a picture of Park Geun-hye wearing a lovely-canary yellow *hanbok*, the Korean traditional dress with its distinctive high-waisted A-line dress. The protesters are huddled under a plastic gazebo drinking coffee. They are all quite elderly and initially try to brush off my questions by claiming that they cannot speak English.

I start to walk away, and one of their number, a gentleman in a gardening hat and fishing waistcoat, gestures grudgingly as if he might be able to help. I ask who is behind the ousting of Park. 'North Korea,' the man says. 'They want Park to go. She has been strong against them.' There are pro-Trump banners nearby and one poster of the then US secretary of state. Someone has labelled the poster 'Sir Rex Tillerson'. As he enjoys his forced retirement, I hope Rex will take comfort from his knighthood.

There is a core of voters in South Korea, generally of the older generation, who are prepared to ignore or deny the deeds of the dictator's daughter and her brazen cronies in the name of maintaining a strong line against the North and appeasing the Americans. Can they pull off a surprise victory tomorrow night? (Obviously, we all know they didn't: Moon won with a landslide, but allow me a little suspense.)

The next evening is election night. I spend most of it among the surprisingly sparse crowds on Sejongno, the broad avenue through the centre of the city where protests form and from where the major TV stations are now broadcasting live. Searchlights streak the sky; cameras mounted on booms swoop overhead, and news anchors pace brightly lit shiny floors. Beside the stages, massive Samsung screens show live broadcasts of what the assembled crowds are seeing in real life just in front of them. But the mood is subdued. At one point there is an attempt to get a Moon Jae-in chant going, but the response is lacklustre. There is a much bigger cheer when a goofy kid from the crowd is pulled up on the stage to give his view on proceedings.

I get chatting to a younger couple standing just in front of me but make the mistake of asking who they voted for. The young woman puts her finger to her lips and says, 'Secret.' It is all quite a contrast to the crowds which had formed right here just a few months earlier and ended up toppling what was, for all its obvious faults, still a democratically elected government. Those demonstrations had begun in late 2016 with candlelit rallies containing an unusually broad spectrum of society, famously including mothers pushing prams, and had continued every Saturday for several weeks, growing in size and organisational efficiency, acquiring stages, Portaloos, clean-up teams, musical performances, fireworks and street food. The organisers were a coalition of 1,500 civic organisations under the umbrella name the Emergency Action for Park's

Resignation. By 26 November the gatherings calling for her impeachment were numbering millions.

'I was there at the beginning,' student journalist Stephanie Sehoi-Park told me. 'It all started on social media – that there was going to be this big happening. Maybe fewer than a hundred people turned up, but eventually we ended up with a third of the population of the country.' Stephanie is in her mid-twenties, studying political science at Yeonsung University and working as an intern at an online newspaper. We met by Gangnam station a couple of days before the election and adjourned to a nearby coffee shop, an airy, spacious place with floor-to-ceiling windows and complicated muffins.

Stephanie explained that the original protests had coalesced around half a dozen different issues. People were unhappy with President Park, very unhappy at the *chaebol* and corruption, and extremely unhappy about the April 2014 *Sewol* ferry tragedy in which nearly 304 people, mostly high-school students, had perished. But then one particular issue, out of left field, began to gather momentum.

An applicant for the highly prestigious Ewha Womans University in eastern Seoul, a young woman called Chung Yoo-ra, had got herself onto a course despite not having the requisite exam results. Clearly, someone had pulled some strings. The other students – most of whom had worked excessively hard and made painful sacrifices to achieve their grades – organised a protest. This was picked up by a journalist from JTBC, a media company which, surprisingly given what transpired, belonged to a pro-Park newspaper group. The journalist realised that the rogue student was the daughter of Choi Soon-sil, lifelong friend, guru and fashion adviser to the president.

'The students didn't know the big picture. They were just focused on "Come on! She got in without proper tests!" so they were mad about that,' explained Stephanie. 'Then people realised she had ties to Samsung, ties to the president.'

Eventually the rest of the media couldn't ignore the story. Dominoes began to teeter. Choi Soon-sil was discovered to have acted as a go-between in the transfer of many billions of won (equivalent to millions of pounds) from Samsung and other organisations, including the Korean National Intelligence Service, which had been delivered in cash to Park's aides in car parks or quiet back alleys close to the Blue House – the South Korean presidential residence – in return for the passing of legislation helpful to their owners. The money had been funnelled through various foundations and 'charities', one of which was keeping Choi's daughter supplied with expensive dressage horses.

Choi was eventually tried and sentenced to twenty years in prison. Her daughter was arrested in Denmark, where she had reportedly been buying a dressage horse with Samsung money, at the request of the South Korean authorities. For some weeks the Danes refused to allow Chung Yoo-ra's extradition out of concern for her one-year-old child. When she finally returned to South Korea she described events as 'unfair' and denied all knowledge of the affair. She did however admit that she 'didn't even know my major' when she was admitted to the university and had preferred to concentrate on her dressage practice. This did little to endear her further to the Korean public; neither did her other public comments such as, 'Money is a kind of ability. If you're poor, blame your parents.'

President Park Geun-hye was arrested in March 2017 but denied the accusations. The prosecutors held her in custody on the pretext of wanting to prevent her from destroying evidence, but many people wanted Park behind bars as soon as possible. Her approval rating had plunged to 9 per cent. Later, with Park in prison, the media gleefully reported that the dictator's daughter, who had lived in luxury all her life, was now doing her own washing and eating cheap dinners at a detention centre in Uiwang.

Park's aloofness had always aroused the suspicion of the gregarious, demonstrative Koreans, who seemed to consider her a bit of a queer fish. She was nicknamed the Notebook Princess because of her inability to make speeches off the cuff, and she didn't hold a press conference for the first ten months of her presidency.

'I would describe Mrs Park as a rare species of South Korean. I would almost call her autistic, very self-enclosed,' Tei Tai-Kin, the

Zainichi academic I had met in Tokyo, told me. 'Generally, South Korean people like to be with lots of people and have friends around them, but she seems to have had no friends. And that kind of an isolated mindset is peculiar.'

Stephanie Sehoi Park said something similar – that President Park was an oddball, doomed somehow: 'Even before she was elected everyone knew there was something shady about her because she wasn't a political figure other than the fact that she was the daughter of the dictator Park Chung-hee.'

The impeachment of Park didn't seem to follow any kind of normal legal procedure. It was almost as if she went from the Blue House to a prison cell by sheer force of public will. 'It is true, her defenders have said that this is not a legal judgment, more of a political judgment,' said Stephanie Sehoi Park. 'But they [the police, judiciary and media] were too afraid to go against the people. People are sick and tired of this happening over and over again ... It was like a compilation of everything that has been going on for the last ten years. If you have power, you just get away with it. If you have money, people will find a way to get out. It has happened so many times.'

The hasty impeachment of Park was partly motivated by lingering resentment towards her conduct after the *Sewol* ferry tragedy. She had taken hours to respond to the 2014 disaster; some even blamed her directly for the ferry sinking. Andrew Salmon explained to me that the downside to running a government which appeared to have magically created an economy from scratch – as Park's father's had done – was that when things went wrong the populace was notably unforgiving. 'There was the feeling that, "Well, if the government can do magic, the fact that they didn't save those kids [meant it] must have been deliberate." I remember one reporter saying that if the president's daughter had been on the *Sewol*, those kids would have been rescued. That's the kind of shit they believe. They have a very high emotional IQ, so you can say all sorts of shit when you're angry and emotional, and no one is going to hold you to account for it later.'

I had heard this characterisation of Koreans from Japanese acquaintances many times before: that they were emotional, impetuous, unstable, drawn to the comfort of the crowd and collective expressions of feeling. It had seemed borderline racist to me, but when I asked Koreans about this, every single one happily agreed. They *were* an emotional people. They *do* have an unusual propensity to want to gather together in large numbers.

Tei Tai-Kin described the Koreans as having 'a kind of herd mentality'. He used a word, skinship, which I had never heard before. 'It's a Japanese-English word. It refers to very close bodily contact, physical contact to show that there is an emotional friendship. When people like to be close to each other in a crowd. When that happens, they are easily manipulated by propaganda.' There is actually a Korean word which is close to this – *chung*, meaning 'group consciousness' or 'loyalty' – but it has a moral aspect: collectivity is good. Standing together benefits the country as a whole.

'I would definitely agree with the Japanese people,' Stephanie Sehoi Park said. 'We are very emotional. We have a lot of love, lots of feelings. Everything is so intense. I think everyone would agree that we're emotional. But I think we are the friendliest out of all the east Asian countries.' She mentioned the Korean word *simjeong* – 'mind evidence' or 'gut feeling', which can lead to perhaps questionable justice but will also, she believes, one day lead to Park being pardoned before completing her sentence.

Jang Han-la, an anthropology student I also met while I was in Seoul, placed the Koreans in the middle of a sliding scale of Far Eastern emotionality. 'Of course Koreans are more emotional than Japanese, but maybe a little less than Chinese. That seems to be using "emotional" negatively, but I think rationality is not always the number-one priority. Emotion was the key to driving people to get to know more about the situation in the case of the former President Park.' Jang argued the impeachment was nevertheless still 'the democratic will of the people, a proper democratic process'.

Shimpei Ota, a Japanese anthropologist I spoke to who has taught in Korea, had a different take. He believes that the Japanese are every bit as emotional as the Koreans, 'and think about it – which country invented karaoke?' He has a point. The Japanese are pretty big on emotional public demonstrations too. Whenever I visit Tokyo there is always a crowd protesting outside one or other of the ministries or the Diet. What's more, the most openly emotional and demonstrative people you see on the streets of Japan are the far-right protesters, like the ones who had driven past me in Yokohama or who shout and scream outside *Zainichi* schools or Korean restaurants. It is quite an irony that the anti-Koreans are the most Korean of all the Japanese.

When I suggested to Yoko Mada, the right-wing YouTuber I'd met in Fukuoka, that Japan's rather constipated political life could learn a great deal from the peaceful democratic mass protests in Seoul against the corrupt rule of Park Guen-hye, she had brushed me aside: 'That's what happens all the time in Korea. Every president gets assassinated or put in jail. They are so extreme, they go by emotions. We're like, "Oh, again?" That's just Korean culture to get rid of a bad guy.' Unfortunately, she is kind of right. What was happening with Park was a fairly typical course of events for the Koreans. Impeachment, scandal, corruption, imprisonment: these are as much a regular feature of the Korean political landscape as MPs being caught cruising Clapham Common is of British political life. Two former South Korean presidents are currently behind bars, and that's not even unusual. Here is a list of South Korea's post-war leaders and what became of them.

Syngman Rhee (in power 1948–60). First president after the war, installed by the Americans. An authoritarian accused of vote-rigging. Fled to Hawaii following public protests, where he died.

Park Chung-hee (1963–79). Brutal military dictator. Assassinated by his security chief.

Chun Doo-hwan (1980–8). Responsible for the Gwangju massacre. Tried for treason and mutiny; sentenced to life; pardoned.

Roh Tae-woo (1988–93). Associate of Chun. Tried for treason, sedition and mutiny. Sentenced to twenty-two years; pardoned.

Kim Young-sam (1993–8). First democratically elected president and first of a trio of largely admired presidents. Career ended with the Asian financial crisis and a humiliating IMF loan. Not charged with anything himself, but his son was jailed for corruption.

Kim Dae-jung (1998–2003). First president from an opposition party. His government made massive secret payments to North Korea to secure a summit (and earn him a Nobel prize). Not charged with any crime, but two of his sons were jailed for bribery.

Roh Moo-hyun (2003–8). Impeached in 2004 but carried on in office. Later committed suicide by jumping from a cliff amid – comparatively minor – allegations of corruption.

Lee Myung-bak (2008–13). Former mayor of Seoul and CEO of Hyundai. In October 2018 found guilty on charges related to multi-million-dollar corruption, bribery and secret slush funds (some of this involving, yet again, Samsung) and sentenced to fifteen years in prison

Park Geun-hye (2013–17). Sentenced to twenty-five years on corruption charges in 2018.

Will Moon Jae-in, the new president and architect of a sensational rapprochement with North Korea, buck the trend and retire on a high? 'He's going to be impeached, or there will be an attempt,' Michael Breen said without hesitation when I asked him about the president's prospects. 'Every Korean president, every single one, is disgraced or a lame duck by their fourth year in office.'

Back on election night in the centre of Seoul the small crowd and I wait watching the show on the lawns of Sejongno. Korean TV news is famed for its use of computer graphics, and one of the channels has superimposed the heads of the presidential candidates on the bodies of battling *Game of Thrones* characters. Finally, the news comes in that, with Park's party split, as expected Moon Jae-in has breasted the tape with 41 per cent of the vote. The next day, several of the *chaebol* have full-page adverts in the national newspapers congratulating him on his win.

Breen's prediction seemed ridiculous at the time, but some months later, as I write, and despite the progress in negotiations with the North, Moon's approval rating has dropped to a low of 49 per cent from a high of 78 just a few months ago. His fate would seem very much to depend on the caprices and motives of Kim Jong-un, not to mention Donald Trump. Watch this space.

18

Seoul IV

I think we can all sympathise with Cho Hyun-ah. We've all been there. In December 2014 the poor unsuspecting woman was sitting in her Korean Air Lines business-class seat waiting for her trans-atlantic flight from JFK to Seoul to take off, oblivious to the drama which was about to unfold, when suddenly she found herself embroiled in a simply horrific incident.

One of the flight attendants – through oversight or quite delib-erately, we may never know – served Cho some macadamia nuts, not on a plate but *in a bag*. And then acted as if he had done nothing wrong. As any right-thinking person would, Cho took grave offence, remonstrating with the witless attendant, ordering him – well, *screaming* at him really – to kneel before her and beg forgiveness, and insisting the flight return to the gate. This delayed its departure and the subsequent journey home for Christmas for the hundreds of other passengers on board, but that couldn't be helped. One must take a stand. She also fired the cabin crew chief on the spot.

You would think that a measured response to poor service such as this would be applauded, so it must have been quite a shock for Cho, who was head of cabin service for all Korean Air flights at the time, when she was charged with breaking aviation laws and given a suspended sentence.

By all accounts, Cho's siblings are similarly conscientious strivers for corporate excellence. Her younger sister, Cho Hyun-min, hit the headlines in 2018 for a glass-throwing tantrum when an employee of an advertising company contracted to Korean Air displeased her during a meeting. She was charged with assault and questioned by police for fifteen hours. She did scream, she admitted, but denied assault, saying that the glass she had thrown was empty and aimed at a wall, not a person. And the other glass she threw, the one full of plum juice, that was just an accident. She apologised for the incident and the charges against her were eventually dropped. There is also a brother, Cho Won-tae. A few years earlier, he had come under scrutiny following allegations that he pushed a seventy-seven-year-old woman in a road rage incident. He was later reported to have ordered the pilot of a Korean Air flight to stop his announcements because they disturbed the computer game he was playing (I think we can all sympathise with that one too).

The three Cho siblings sound nice, don't they? Their mother is a peach as well. She has been questioned by police in the past regarding allegations that she abused employees verbally and physically – she did not recall the incidents – and in the end, the court denied a request from prosecutors to arrest her. The patriarch of this wonderful family was Cho Yang-ho, the second-generation chairman of Korean Air Lines, part of a family-run conglomerate, the Hanjin Group, founded by his father, Cho Choong-hoon.

'As chairman of Korean Air, as well as a father, I feel terrible about the immature actions of my daughters,' Mr Cho said in a statement after their various conniptions were made public. 'Everything is my fault and my wrongdoing. I apologise to the people.' But Mr Cho, who died in April 2019, was being rather coy about his own achievements. He had previously been convicted of tax evasion, and had been summoned for questioning on further charges of embezzlement. His three children had all been fast-tracked to executive positions in the company, doubtless based entirely on their own personal merits and abilities. Cho Hyun-ah, or the 'nut rage heiress' as she was quite unfairly dubbed, returned to work in the company managing their hotels.

The Hanjin Group is a so-called *chaebol*, a type of family-owned conglomerate these days unique to South Korea. The behaviour of Hanjin's scions is not unusual and part of why the *chaebol* are considered a major problem for the nation.

The *chaebol*'s origins go back to Japanese rule, when the occupiers embarked on massive government-controlled industrial expansion using their own conglomerate model, the *zaibatsu* (*chaebol* and *zaibatsu* both translate as 'wealth clan'). However, in Japan the American occupiers helped dismantle the monopolies of the *zaibatsu* within two years of the end of the war because they were seen as anti-democratic. Ironically, many *chaebol* were founded in Korea using assets taken from these Japanese companies after 1945, and from the 1960s to the 80s their activities were closely 'guided' by the president. Park Chung-hee decided which industries would be favoured with beneficial trade terms, domestic monopolies and cheap loans from state-controlled banks. He also selected which sectors of the economy they should focus on – starting with the 'white product' industries of cotton, flour and sugar (and, weirdly, wigs, which were a big export in the early days), before progressing to cement, chemicals, textiles and fertilisers.

Park would say, 'Steel!' the *chaebol* would say, 'How much?' and, bingo, South Korea had the world's largest steel production plant. Park was very much in control: on one occasion he forced businessmen who had displeased him to walk through the streets bearing placards which read I AM A CORRUPT SWINE. He decided South Korea should move into shipbuilding, and the country eventually became the world's largest shipbuilder. Automotive and electronics industries followed. Japan's own post-war manufacturing growth was the model and the motivation. In the early 1960s, there were poster campaigns exhorting the South Koreans to 'Beat Japan'. South Korea's 'industrial soldiers' responded, helping to increase exports by 1,340 per cent during the decade, compared to 200 per cent in Japan. At times South Korea's economy very much resembled the centrally planned communist model used in the North, except for the fact that the workers never got a sniff of owning the means of production – although, neither did the proletariat in the North.

Some assumed that the Asian economic crisis of 1997 would see the end of the *chaebol*; the South Korean won lost half its value and the IMF imposed new corporate governance rules as a condition of its bailout loans. Many *chaebol* did indeed go bust, including the fifth largest, Daewoo, but the *chaebol* endured, and by 2011 the country had bounced back, recording its first ever trillion-dollar year of overseas trade. Today forty-five *chaebol* remain. The five largest – Samsung, Hyundai, LG, SK and Lotte – account for over half of South Korea's annual GDP.

There are numerous reasons Moon Jae-in wants to reform the *chaebol*, not least because many are predicting that their practices will bring about South Korea's economic doom. The problems are twofold: structural and cultural. Structurally, cross-shareholding practices mean that a family might on paper only own 2 per cent of a company but still in fact have a controlling majority share and treat it essentially as a private entity, milking it for funds. Lotte – a *chaebol* with interests in everything from construction to confectionery, whose ninety-five-year-old founder was recently sentenced to four years in prison for embezzlement (he avoided cell time on health grounds) – is particularly notorious for this practise, which is also known as tunnelling. In the case of Samsung, tunnelling meant that the family's third-generation heir, Lee Jae-yong, was able to take a £4 million loan from his dad and transform it into the controlling stake in a company worth about £5 billion. Tunnelling also means that the ruling families often behave like emperors, but avoid responsibility when things go wrong. It is not necessarily illegal, but the optics aren't good.

Many of the *chaebol* are also now suffering from the curse of the third generation – 'the spoiled children' as economist Young Ruk-chuk put it to me. Usually *chaebol* heirs are careful about conspicuous displays of wealth, privilege or tantrums, at least while they are at home in Korea; they prefer to let rip while at their Malibu beach houses or Knightsbridge duplexes. Sometimes, though, as with the Chos, they can't control themselves. One of the most badly behaved is Kim Dong-seon, the third son of the Hanwha Group chairman, who has an unfortunate tendency to get drunk and belligerent. Visiting a Gangnam bar with company lawyers in 2017, he demanded they call him 'Mr Shareholder' and slapped one of them on the cheek. He also grabbed a female employee by the hair. 'From now on treat me with respect,' he was reported to have slurred. Earlier in the year he had been arrested in another bar for hitting two waiters. He apologised for the Gangnam incident, and the police dropped the charges.

Which brings us to the second reason most agree reform is needed: the way the *chaebol* treat their employees. Many operate rigid, top-down hierarchies. Employees often progress according to seniority and longevity, rather than merit or intelligence. The *chaebol* tend not to reward initiative, but rather punish failure. This fosters risk-averse working environments in which employees and entire departments do their best simply to remain unnoticed, treating other departments as the enemy. The way employees address each other mimics traditional Confucian family hierarchy titles, which can be quite demeaning: managers will call executives 'older brother', for instance. Bosses at many *chaebol* have been known to bully, beat and berate those beneath them. Stories of abuse are legion.

President Moon has increased the minimum wage and brought down the maximum permitted working week from 68 to 52 hours, but South Koreans are still among the hardest working people in the world – labouring on average 2,113 hours per annum, compared to 1,681 in the UK and 1,790 in the USA – although productivity per capita is low, $33 per hour for Korea in 2016, compared with $63 for the US.[11] One other lamentable aspect of Korean corporate culture is gender inequality: women make up less than 3 per cent of company board members (Japan is barely better with 4 per cent, compared to 24 per cent in the UK and 17 per cent in the USA), and South Korea comes bottom of the OECD's gender pay equality ranking, with Japan third from bottom.

Eric Surdej, a Frenchman who worked as a director of LG Electronics in Seoul, recently published a tell-all book called *Koreans Are Crazy* about his decade with the *chaebol*. He revealed a torrid,

[11] OECD figures.

cult-like working environment in which executives screamed at underlings and threw things. Surdej once saw a company president hurl a pile of documents at an employee's head. It took him a while to adjust to Korea's corporate drinking culture too: 'I had to drink for four hours, sitting outside in the bone-chilling cold. The drinking session led to pledges of allegiance to LG. It reminded me of a pagan ritual.' On another occasion one of his colleagues collapsed and was rushed to hospital, where he had to undergo an operation. As soon as the man woke from the surgery, he asked how soon he might return to work. 'It was a sad self-portrait of Koreans who ... take it for granted to sacrifice themselves for the organisation they belong to.' I haven't seen any record of LG responding to Surdej's claims. Perhaps they deny them completely, but they do ring true to many who are familiar with how the *chaebol* function.

All recent South Korean presidents have come to power pledging to rein in the *chaebol* families. In 2014 President Park did introduce some restrictions on cross-shareholding, and over the years the chairman of Hyundai, Chung Mong-Koo; the chairman of SK Corporation, Chey Tae-won; the chairman of Lotte, Shin Dong-bin, and Lee Jae-yong of Samsung have all been convicted of various crimes, but then pardoned. It doesn't help that the South Korean media is extremely cautious about challenging the *chaebol* simply because they depend on their advertising budgets and other funds for their survival. One Korean economist told me that if the tenth largest *chaebol* pulled its advertisements from a particular Korean newspaper, that newspaper would not be able to survive. Hardly surprising then that in a 2017 Pew Research Center survey only 36 per cent of Koreans felt that their newspapers were reporting the news accurately, compared to 65 per cent in Japan. Evidence of the incestuous relationship between the South Korean media and the *chaebol* came recently when text messages and emails from journalists to an executive at Samsung were revealed. These asked for help in getting their children jobs or increases in sponsorship money. 'We'll reward you with good articles,' one wrote with shameless candour (it is not believed the Samsung executive responded to the requests in this case).

So why are the *chaebol* tolerated? Because the South Korean economy is unusually dependent on exports (78 per cent compared to the OECD average of 56 per cent) and relies on their continuing success. 'They have brilliant synergies,' Andrew Salmon told me. 'And they've globalised extremely successfully, with great marketing these days, great branding, pretty good pricing, good products. They're really good. They've got it all apart from the governance issue – that is their Achilles heel.'

The strength of the *chaebol* has been that it only takes one man to make a decision and it will be implemented. In the 1990s, for instance, Samsung's chairman took a gamble on semiconductors which has earned the company over six billion dollars in profits. Samsung, which started off as a sugar producer during the Japanese colonial era, now makes components not just for its own products but for arch-rivals like Apple (the iPhone X uses Samsung displays and memory chips). The company is now the world's largest maker of semiconductors and has a virtual monopoly on organic light-emitting diodes – super-thin screens. Famously, South Koreans can live in a Samsung apartment, be treated at a Samsung hospital, have fun at a Samsung amusement park, and shop for goods shipped by Samsung container ships to a Samsung-owned retailer. They can buy a Samsung car (made with Renault) with money borrowed through a Samsung credit scheme, and use Samsung-refined petrol to fuel it. They can even buy a Samsung smartphone.

Today Samsung encompasses around sixty different commercial entities which together constitute around 28 per cent of the value of the Korean stock market, but since 2014 it has experienced a few hiccups. In 2014 Lee Kun-hee, the chairman and son of the company's founder, suffered a heart attack. He has been hidden away in a Samsung-owned hospital ever since, and, echoing the North Korean playbook, there are rumours that his death is being kept secret because of issues relating to the succession of the company – South Korea has an inheritance tax rate of 50 per cent. Samsung has also been found guilty of bribery and price fixing, and fined hundreds of millions of dollars in the US and Europe; it has faced legal action for allegedly ripping off designs from, among others, Kodak (digital technology), Sharp (flatscreen TVs) and of course Apple (iPhones and iPads); and then came 2016's Galaxy Note 7 debacle, when the tablets started bursting into flames and were banned by many airlines. Millions of the product were recalled at a cost of about £3 billion. It is hard to imagine another company surviving its products being the focus of a safety warning at the commencement of every single commercial flight on earth for several months, but Samsung has flourished.

Even the conviction in 2017 of Lee Kun-hee's son and presumed heir Lee Jae-yong (aka Jay Y. Lee) for bribery and corruption in connection with the impeachment of President Park and his sentencing to five years in prison has had no impact on the company's fortunes. Indeed, Samsung's share price rose 65 per cent, hitting a record high, and it posted record operating profits of $14.1 billion for the last three months of 2017, up 63 per cent on the previous year. Meanwhile, the new Galaxy 8 sold 270,000 units in its first weekend in South Korea, compared to 160,000 for the Galaxy 7. As a result, Samsung went from tenth to seventh on Forbes' 2018 list of the world's most valuable brands.

Such is the company's domination of its home market that it wasn't until January 2018 that Apple opened its first store in South Korea. The shop opened in Gangnam, not far from Samsung's headquarters, a towering stack of malevolent black glass cubes. Outside it, when I visit the HQ, is a permanent-looking protest camp built from scaffolding and black tarpaulins, with generators, a PA system and kitchen area. Inside the tent (with shoes left neatly outside) I chat with some of the protesters. These are former employees who claim that the company is responsible for the death of seventy-nine of its workers. There have been unaccountable clusters of leukaemia, multiple sclerosis and brain tumours among workers at Samsung plants, but the company will not even talk to representatives of the relatives, one of the protesters tells me. 'What has Lee Jae-yong done for Samsung workers? NOTHING,' reads one of their banners.[12] Afterwards, I visit Samsung's d'Light show-room, as it is called, in the basement of the headquarters building.

The only Samsung product in my house is an infuriatingly slow and overly complex television of whose functions I have a very limited grasp; I often have to call for a child to help start it. But I entered the showroom with an open mind and I was excited to sample virtual reality for the first time in my life. In the middle of the showroom, in a small fenced-off area, were two car seats mounted on plinths in which visitors could sit like the targets in a fairground dunk tank wearing what looked like snorkelling masks.

I sat down, put on a mask and watched a film shot from the point of view of someone on a rollercoaster. It wasn't very good really. I felt mildly nauseous. I was similarly nonplussed by another interac-tive 'experience', which involved me answering questions on a touch screen in order to divine something or other about my personality. This resulted in a photo which the machine had grabbed of me – squinting unedifyingly at its screen – being displayed on a much larger screen across one wall of the store along with the message: 'Hi Michael. You are thoughtful, calm and insightful. If you follow your heart, you can find out what you're really capable of.'

The next day I follow my heart to Professor Park Sangin, a vocal advocate of *chaebol* reform. We meet at his office in Seoul University's economics department, part of a vast and beautiful campus sprawling over a hillside densely planted with lush greenery and huge, rambling flowering bushes.

Sangin believes that if the Moon government fails to reform the *chaebol*, the country could end up like Venezuela or Argentina. 'Korea will follow that vicious cycle of Latin America because, first of all,

---

[12] This protest had been going on for eleven years, but was finally resolved at the end of the year, with Samsung paying about a hundred thousand pounds to each of the victims.

the economy is not as big as Japan's so we cannot have long-standing stagnation,' he tells me. South Korea is too dependent on manufacturing and exports. 'The economy is very vulnerable to a concerted effort by the nationalised industries in China to price Korean goods out of entire sectors. It happened with shipbuilding over the last decade, and the impact is exaggerated by the structure of the *chaebol*.' The third-generation owners are well aware of the destructive potential of what they are doing but are afraid of losing everything. They are hindering the economy from moving away from industries in which the Chinese are expanding aggressively – cars, electronics, ships, steel, construction and petrochemicals – thanks to their advantages of cheap labour, bottomless government funds and centralised planning. South Korea is still exporting high-tech components to China, but that will not last for much longer.

Many of the *chaebol* also have a habit of stealing others' ideas, he believes. 'There is a huge problem with small companies coming up with good ideas and then the *chaebol* taking away their intellectual property,' says Park. 'Legally it is very difficult to fight them. The patent system doesn't work here. If someone steals an idea or intellectual property, even if the business sues and wins in court, they will receive a very small portion of the money.'

Stephanie Sehoi Park, the young journalist I talked to about the anti-Park demonstrations, also spoke of the difficulties that small companies face: 'If there is a small company with a great idea, Samsung can just buy either the company itself or the building they are in. The conglomerates take up everything.' In 2016 the OECD reported that, as a result of this kind of thing, only 0.01 per cent of South Korean small start-ups become mid-sized companies.

The *chaebol* have huge influence in the legal and political systems too. According to a 2018 Real Meter survey, 89 per cent of South Koreans believe their state prosecutors are corrupt in one way or another, and it is not unheard of, Park Sangin tells me, for draft legislation to be leaked to the relevant *chaebol* before it goes beyond committee level. And, as in Japan, lawmakers and government bureaucrats apparently often move on to board positions or consultancies with the *chaebol* after they retire as a reward for assisting them.

'You know that if you do something helpful for the *chaebol*, especially Samsung, Samsung will take care of your retirement. Your life will be much easier,' says Park Sangin. He wasn't convinced by Samsung heir Lee Jae-yong's conviction for bribery in the President Park scandal and predicted that he would soon be free. 'Many of the *chaebol* owners have committed serious economic crimes and go to jail once or twice, and they don't serve the full time – they are all pardoned. In Korea we say that if you have money, you are not guilty, if you have no money, you are guilty.'

Though he reportedly had to endure watching an LG television in his cell, and despite his case having originally been described as 'the epitome of collusion between business and government', Lee Jae-yong, South Korea's third richest man, was indeed freed from jail in early 2018 on his first appeal, having never even given up his vice chairmanship of Samsung. Afterwards, *Chosun Ilbo*, South Korea's bestselling newspaper, ran an editorial warning against attacking the *chaebol* and defending Lee – essentially saying that the president had asked him for money, and if he hadn't given it, Samsung would have suffered. And we wouldn't want that, would we?

Lee's release was timed to coincide with the start of the Winter Olympics in South Korea, and the story was soon engulfed by coverage of the largest sporting event held in the country since the World Cup. The last time I saw Lee on the news, in late 2018, he was attending a state dinner in Pyongyang, sitting just a couple of metres from the presidents of both North and South Korea.

19

Seoul V

Whether the *chaebol* are entirely to blame or not, one thing we do know for sure is that the South Koreans are deeply unhappy. According to the 2018 United Nations World Happiness report, they rank 57th out of 106 countries and do even worse when happiness is adjusted for wealth.[13] South Korea has the highest suicide rate in Asia and is usually among the top five suicide nations globally.

Eunkook Mark Suh is a Korean psychologist who specialises in happiness. His research has encompassed topics such as 'Does physical attractiveness buy happiness?' and 'Does Honorific Raise Your Positive Mood: Interrelation Between Language Form and Affect Valence' – in other words, do the Koreans' strict age- and social status-related forms of address make them miserable? I went along to meet Dr Eunkook in his narrow book-filled office in the Department of Psychology and Social Psychology at Yonsei University, a rather imposing ivy-clad building with a crenellated clock tower.

I am fortunate enough to live in Denmark, which is usually among the five happiest countries in the world, according to the U.N. Superficially, the Danes are actually quite a grumpy, suspicious bunch, but I can imagine how they might feel themselves to be 'content' or 'satisfied' with their life. I wondered if the problem might be that different nations interpret the notion of happiness in different ways. Is that why the Koreans, who are so rich and free compared to most nations, do so badly on these lists?

[13] Japan was not much better at 54th and the Chinese were a woeful 86th; the US and UK were at 18th and 19th, and Taiwan a creditable 26th.

'Ultimately, what Koreans or Danes or what all these people are trying to establish in their lives is strikingly similar,' Dr Eunkook, a slight fellow dressed as if for a day's yachting in jeans and deck shoes, begins. 'They want to be powerful, they want to be recognised as an important figure. The only difference – the tricky part – is how we need to play a different cultural game to reach those desires.' In my experience, being powerful and recognised as important were not priorities for the Danes. Did Koreans place greater importance on status, perhaps because of their Confucian heritage?

'I don't believe there's any person, whether you are a member of an African tribe or whatnot, who desires to be considered as a loser in the group, but yes, there are differences. One cultural variable that is very much related to happiness across nations is individualism, and the essence of individualism is you're kind of trained mentally to live your life and not care too much about how other people evaluate your life. That mentality is very beneficial for maintaining a high sense of happiness because you don't need validation from other people. It's none of their business.' The opposite is the case in most Asian cultures, especially Korea, and according to Dr Eunkook this was perhaps their greatest source of stress and unhappiness.

'Everybody meddles in your life here. It is always someone else calling the shots. You're supposed to do this, you're wrong if you do that, and so you get very much sensitised to how others constantly value you. Sometimes my valuations may not be consistent with how other people see me. I may think things are fine, but others think I am living a lousy life.

'Koreans have this very strong need for social approval. You need to *demonstrate* your success, not for yourself but for your family. A lot of east Asians care more about how they are evaluated by other people. I think this may be in part Confucianism.'

The Confucian pressure to live up to other's opinions and values and then precision-place yourself within the social hierarchy according to your status and age must be exhausting. The rampant individualism of Western cultures leads to all sorts of other psychological pressures, but at least there is the option for individuals to interpret their 'success' on their own terms. We can say, 'Fuck it!' and opt out of having to be rich, beautiful and successful yet still put on a fairly convincing show of being happy, but in Asian cultures, as Eunkook puts it, 'There are going to be very few winners, by definition. A lot of people will feel relatively inferior.' Michael Breen believes South Koreans have 'an extreme sensitivity to the views of others ... there in every waking moment'. This is perhaps part of the explanation for the South Korean suicide rate.

Eunkook offers the example of golfers as an explanation for how pressure to achieve demonstrable success can have fatal consequences. Around a third of the top one hundred female golfers in the world are South Korean 'because their families have completely devoted their whole lives, since these girls were, like, six years old, to their golfing careers. The dad quits his job. That's an enormous pressure, right? The lucky story is she becomes a famous player, fine, everybody's happy, but that's a fairy tale; for most people it's not going to work out that way, and sometimes, if everything clicks in the wrong way, those people's final decision might well be to take their lives.'

One aspect of presenting yourself as a success to the world is avoiding a loss of face, Eunkook says. It is an Orientalist cliché to say that Asians place greater emphasis on this than Westerners, but it is one of those clichés which does seem to be true. I had already experienced one tiny aspect of this: Koreans' pathological inability to say 'I don't know' when asked for directions. Asking for directions to Dr Eunkook's office, a student had pointed at a nearby building with complete conviction but hadn't been even close. But the best example of this – one which, now some time has passed, I quite cherish actually – was a woman from whom I asked directions on the street in Seoul a few days earlier. I wanted to know the way to the nearest Subway station. She had pointed with great authority and said, 'So, you see down there? Go down there, OK?'

I nodded, following her gesture.

'OK, so, like, walk down there, turn left and –' she paused as if about to offer the final direction '– ask someone else.'

And with that she bustled off in the opposite direction, the direction in which, about half an hour later, I found the station.

A couple of years ago a South Korean Zen Buddhist monk, Haemin Sunim, began offering pearls of wisdom on social media to help people deal with the pressures of modern life. He built up such a following that his aphorisms were turned into one of those books with lots of white space and fifty words per page which I often think I should get into writing. *The Things You Can See Only When You Slow Down*, published in Korea in 2012, stayed at number one on the bestseller list for almost a year.

In particular, Haemin seems to recognise the pressure of others' expectations on Koreans, writing several individualistic entreaties about choosing your own religion and life partner, including: 'Do not select your career based on what others will think of your choice. The truth is that other people do not really think about you that much.' And: 'Above all, please understand that what makes you feel tense and awkward is ... the pressure from your family to conform.'

Refreshingly, Dr Eunkook has little time for Haemin. In fact he has little time for happiness as a life goal at all. 'Actually, I just wrote a book criticising all this happiness business, the positive-psychology bandwagon. I think it's crap because, sadly, we're not designed to be happy. *Homo sapiens*, we're like birds or animals, and they're not designed to be happy, right? From an evolutionary perspective, happiness is just a tool, a sort of signal to direct you to seek resources which were essential for your survival. When do we feel happy? When we eat or have sex. That's just a signal that you are a functioning human being.'

You cannot discuss happiness in Korea without mentioning the concept of *han*. I have seen *han* described variously as a suppressed grudge, helpless rage, unrequited resentment or a brooding sense of grievance, preferably remaining unresolved. *Han* is to Koreans as *hygge* is to Danes – omnipresent, intangible, understood by all, accepted as an intrinsic part of being Korean. And like the Danes with *hygge*, the Koreans like to make out that *han* is untranslatable.

Stephanie Sehoi Park described *han* as 'melancholy and bitterness. It is anger not expressed, directed at the world and at yourself; there is no specific target. No one knows where it came from. No one knows *why* it came here. No one knows how to resolve it, but yet ... it's there. It's not supposed to get a resolution. It's always been there and it will always be there.'

Jonathan Kim, the film producer, disagreed entirely: 'People say, "We can not explain *han*, because it only exists in Korea." That is bullshit. It is just a grudge, it's having a grudge!'

Song Sokze, a South Korean poet and novelist I met one day for lunch in Seoul, also believed that *han* is universal. 'It is something that accumulates within you when you are under some stress or when you go through a lot of hardship, like an internal wound. It can be expressed in all sorts of different art forms – dance, literature, singing – or some people cry and groan about the pain that they have within them, but I don't think this is something that just Koreans feel. Everybody in the world can relate to *han*.'

Dr Eunkook was similarly sceptical. 'I don't think Koreans have any special brand of misery. It's a kind of hopelessness or depression which exists in all cultures, right? Maybe we made a big deal out of it because of our recent history, and it was used by the regimes to motivate people. I'm not saying it doesn't exist, but it's like *kimchi*. We make out that's something special, but other cultures do have pickles, you know.'

Was *han* – if it exists at all – a symptom of a kind of victim mentality, a legacy of Japanese colonial rule? I wondered. In which case, might it even be described (quietly, without any Koreans over-hearing) as an inadvertent *gift* from the Japanese – the avenging fuel which has fired Koreans to post-war economic glory? In Tokyo I had spoken with the *Zainichi* academic Tei 'Tai-Kin about this. 'Colonial rule by Japan was a negative experience,' he told me. 'But after the war the sense of humiliation was the stimulant that caused them to think that if Japan can do it, why not Korea?'

Stephanie Sehoi Park disagreed. 'It started long before colonisation. It might come from being a tributary state of China, but it has reached a point where we have started enjoying it. We're miserable and proud of it.' I am sure Korea's centuries-long history of social oppression, poverty, invasion and sexual discrimination must be a factor. In Korea, everyone knew their place and stayed in it; for centuries women were not allowed to dine with men, there were curfews at night, and all Koreans had to wear ID tags – made of ivory for the elite, deer horn for the middle class, poplar wood for lower-ranking bureaucrats and ordinary wood for the common people. 'In a Western sense, Koreans did not exist as individuals,' writes one Korean expert.

Han-la Jang is an anthropology student at Seoul University currently specialising in gender studies. I met this softly spoken but enjoyably opinionated twenty-six-year-old in the park beside the National Assembly building. She didn't go for my hypothesis that *han* had gained impetus from the Japanese occupation. 'I think it has a kind of low, deep root from a long, long history. When we refer to *han*, it is rather like a sadness with a little bit of anger, but it's different from that drive to compete with the Japanese, it's different from an eagerness to be successful. There's nothing positive about it.'

Sonfa Oh, the Korean-born pro-Japanese author I had met in Tokyo, had contrasted *han* with Japan's *mono no aware*, a kind of wistfulness at the passing of time. 'The Japanese just put everything in the water and let it flow,' she said, implying, I think, that the Japanese are better at accepting what fate brings and better at forgiving and forgetting. Koreans, on the other hand, brood endlessly on both real and perceived injustices and work themselves up into what my grandmother would have termed 'a right old lather'. 'Koreans make a lament to themselves – they moan. Japanese don't usually show the emotion, but that doesn't mean they don't have emotions,' Oh said.

It does seem likely that *han* – or at least straightforward Korean misery – is perpetuated by South Korea's high-pressure education system. According to the most recent international school assessment rankings, South Korean students rank seventh in maths and reading, and eleventh in science, which is decent, albeit below China, Japan, Hong Kong and Taiwan. But when it comes to students' well-being, young Koreans score very badly indeed. Only half reported that they were 'satisfied' or 'very satisfied' with their lives, compared to the average of 71 per cent, and 22 per cent classified their lives as 'low' in terms of satisfaction against an average of 12 per cent. They all put huge pressure on themselves – 82 per cent said they wanted to be top of their class, compared to the average of 59 per cent.[14]

Clearly something is amiss here. It may well be the infamous *hagwon*, the after-school crammers which many – perhaps the majority of – Korean children attend, often until late at night. The government has introduced legislation limiting the hours they can operate; they are not supposed to teach between 10 p.m. and 5 a.m. (Can you imagine having to *legislate* against that?) But *hagwon* are big business: according to one estimate, in 2009 they made more money than Samsung. There also seems to be something dispiriting about the way South Korean schools teach, with a Confucian emphasis on rote learning and students' unquestioning acceptance of what they are taught. And *hagwon* tuition costs a fortune, so only wealthier parents can afford it, which means their children tend to do better in exams, get to the better universities and get the best jobs, thus exacerbating South Korea's rapidly growing economic inequality.

I noticed that late at night the Seoul Subway was nearly always full of kids. One evening I sat next to a boy in his mid-teens. He was obviously on his way to or from one of the thousands of *hagwon* in the city and was engrossed in a mathematics textbook, rocking gently backwards and forwards in his seat, thumping his calf muscle with his free hand. Maybe this was some kind of memory technique to help him to better cling to some facts in

[14] OECD Programme for International Student Assessment (PISA), 2015.

order to regurgitate them at an exam, or maybe he was just slowly losing his mind.[15]

The most important school exam is the *Suneung*, the all-or-nothing university entrance test held every November. Flights are redirected and roads closed to give the students peace when they sit the examination, which decides whether or not they get into the four or five most prestigious universities, the top one being Seoul National University. A place in one of these is considered essential for a job in the *chaebol*. Failure condemns a young Korean not just to a second-tier university but to a second-tier life, or at least that is the perception.

China has had a similar all-or-nothing college entrance examination system – the *Gaokao* – for hundreds of years. Schools there have been known to set students up with energy-boosting amino acid saline drips when they sit the exam. A first-year university student I met later on my trip in Beijing told me how he had studied from six in the morning until late at night every day for three years in preparation for the two-day test, which takes place every 7 and 8 June. He was a good student, expected to do well, he told me, but hadn't lived up to his expectations. His score of 584 out of a possible total of 750 had not been enough for him to study languages at either one of the top universities – Peking or Tsinghua – as he had hoped, so he had just started a business and economics degree at a second-tier university.

What would a top score have meant to him?

'You learn from the best lecturers and you get the opportunity to go and study abroad afterwards, that is the big aim.' Despite his experience he believed the system worked well and in a country with such an enormous population that this kind of filtering was brutal but necessary. 'It makes you tough,' he told me. 'If you can't

---

[15] Jonathan Kim told me that the 2014 US film *Whiplash*, about a sadistic hard-driving jazz drum teacher and his long-suffering pupil, was much more successful in South Korea than in any other country in the world, which is rather revealing, I think.

do well in that, then maybe you don't deserve to do well in life.' However, another Chinese college student I spoke to told me his schooling had been so tough that he had suffered from post-traumatic stress disorder. 'Every night nightmares, teachers torturing me. The pressure was intolerable,' he recalled.

Han-la, the South Korean anthropology student I met in Seoul, felt that because of the enormous cost of getting a good education and competition in the *chaebol*-dominated job market post-graduation, young Koreans were increasingly conservative when it came to planning their futures. She narrowed it down to just four choices for those coming to the end of their education: try for one of the rare and precious jobs-for-life at the *chaebol*; keep studying, for which you needed to be relatively wealthy; go to law school (lawyers always do well in Korea); or take the exams for a government job. For the majority, entrepreneurship or travelling were fantasies. When I mention the creative sector, which the previous president had emphasised as a priority for Korea's future, Han-la laughed scornfully. 'That's kind of empty rhetoric.'

There was however a fifth option which many young Koreans were choosing, she said: 'To marry someone and raise kids costs so much, and it's so risky, so many are just choosing not to take the risk. They have seen how harsh it is to be a child here and how tough it is to give your child a proper education. So they give up. Give up on marriage, give up on love, give up on having kids.'

20

Seoul VI

A hundred or so high-school children are sitting cross-legged on the pavement in a business district of Seoul. Each holds a yellow paper butterfly on a wooden stick. They laugh and preen into their smartphone cameras, adjusting their hair, pouting for selfies. It has the feeling of a sports day or class outing. One girl carries a tote bag with TOKYO STREET GIRL on it. Several have items bearing Hello Kitty logos.

A priest in heavy ivory-white robes with a who-are-you-kidding comb-over (an arrangement known in this part of the world as a barcode) stands with his back to the teenagers behind a small lectern placed in the gutter. From the priest's lectern hangs a scroll upon which is written 'Japanese Military Sexual Slavery The Girls Memorial Church', plus phone, Facebook and web contact details. He is facing some grey hoardings across the street which shield a building site. Four busloads of riot police regard the scene from across the way.

Every Wednesday since 1992 protesters have been gathering here, just across the street from the Japanese embassy (currently being rebuilt, hence the building site), to campaign on behalf of the women who were forced into sexual slavery by the Japanese during World War II. The women are euphemistically called comfort women (the term the movement most often uses); the yellow butterfly is their symbol.

The priest is speaking through a public address system. The children aren't paying a great deal of attention but a few older Korean men and women listen intently. One, in wraparound shades and baseball cap, stares in the direction of the building site, gripping a small Korean flag. Around his neck hangs a banner with an aerial photograph of two rocky islets which I recognise as the disputed Dokdo/Takeshima Islands. The photo has been doctored so that a gigantic flagpole bearing the Korean flag erupts from one of the islets.

Beside the priest is a bronze statue of a young barefoot woman seated beside an empty chair. Her hands are in her lap. I look closer and notice that her fists are clenched. She is garlanded with yellow flowers and offerings have been placed at her feet. This is perhaps the most controversial public statue in the free world, a mute emblem of the seething enmity which continues to undermine what should be a firm alliance between prosperous, democratic, free-trading, peaceable neighbours.

Erected in 2011, it was the first of the comfort women memorials, but many more are now popping up around the world. A few days earlier I had seen a replica outside the Japanese consulate in the southern city of Busan. There is one in Sydney too, another outside the Japanese embassy in Taipei, and recently here in Seoul replica statues have been placed on buses. There are several comfort women statues in the USA; one was unveiled in New Jersey in May 2018.

The comfort women system was set up by the Japanese army in the early 1930s, partly to combat the spread of venereal disease among its soldiers but also to lessen the number of rapes perpetrated on the civilians of conquered countries. Estimates of the total number of comfort women enslaved by the Japanese during the war range from 20,000 to 200,000; some Korean and Chinese sources even put the figure as high as 400,000; a few years ago a BBC documentary settled on 80,000–100,000 women.

Up to 80 per cent of the comfort women are believed to have died, either through injuries incurred during their imprisonment, from diseases contracted from the soldiers or when, at the end of the war, some were forced to commit suicide or were killed by their captors. Of those that survived, many were unable to have children and shunned by their communities. Today, fewer than forty comfort women survive in Korea, the youngest of whom is now well into her eighties.

Women were taken from other countries Japan invaded. Tomasa Dioso Salinog, the most prominent Filipino comfort woman, was thirteen when her father was killed by a Japanese soldier and she was abducted and taken to a 'comfort station' – as Japanese military brothels were called. One Dutch woman, Jan Ruff-O'Herne, who passed away in September 2019, was captured by the Japanese in Indonesia, then the Dutch East Indies. In 2008 Ruff-O'Herne testified at a hearing of the US Congress alongside several Asian comfort women.

A Japanese writer, Kako Senda, was the first to investigate Japan's military brothel system. In 1962 he was editing a collection of photographs taken during the war for a Japanese national newspaper, *Mainichi Shimbun*; the pictures had previously been banned from publication. Among the 25,000 photographs, Senda found one of two women crossing a river, taken in 1938 during the Battle of Xuzhou. It struck him as odd that they had been there, but he then discovered that they were comfort women. Senda published a book about his findings in Japan in 1973, but the issue was not really discussed in the South Korean media or by its politicians until after democratisation in the late 1980s, when press freedom improved greatly. Part of the reason for this was that the 1965 Treaty on Basic Relations had restored official contacts between the two countries, and Japan had paid South Korea £600 million in reparations, equivalent to three times Korea's national budget at the time. Most of the money was used for infrastructure projects by the Park Chung-hee government and it was in both governments' interests to leave the matter alone. But in the 1990s South Korean women's organisations began to campaign on the issue.

A Korean comfort woman, Kim Hak-sun, filed the first lawsuit against the Japanese government, testifying that in 1941, aged seventeen, she had been taken by Japanese soldiers and raped between thirty and forty times every day for a year. In 1992, Japanese historian Yoshimi Yoshiaki of Chuo University unearthed further documents in the state archives, prompting an inquiry by the government, and as a result the chief cabinet secretary, Koichi Kato, made a statement which admitted the Japanese government's guilt and expressed its 'sincere apology and remorse'. While on a visit to Seoul the same year, the Japanese prime minister, Kiichi Miyazawa, made another official statement, which included the following: 'We should never forget our feelings of remorse over this ... As prime minister of Japan, I would like to declare anew my remorse at these deeds and tender my apology to the people of the Republic of Korea.'

In 1993 the Japanese government undertook another, more detailed inquiry, following the discovery of 127 new documents relating to the comfort women, and issued another formal apology, written in close cooperation with the Korean government. It was offered by the chief cabinet secretary, Yohei Kono. The Kono Statement, as it became known, is recognised as the high point in relations between the two countries on this matter. It stated: 'The Japanese military was directly or indirectly involved in the establishment and management of the comfort stations and the transfer of "Comfort Women" ... in many cases recruited against their will, through coaxing, coercion, etc., and that, at times, administrative/military personnel directly took part in the recruitments.' It also included a promise to 'face squarely' the historical facts and teach them in schools. Surviving comfort women were each sent a signed letter from the prime minister of Japan, Ryutaro Hashimoto, which read: 'As Prime Minister of Japan, I thus extend anew my most sincere apologies and remorse to all the women who underwent immeasurable and painful experiences and suffered incurable physical and psychological wounds as comfort women.'

In 1995 the Japanese government set up the Asia Women's Fund to compensate the comfort women, but there was a catch, a legal technicality which has provoked at least some of the resentment of the campaigners to this day. The compensation offered by the Japanese came from donations from private people, not the Japanese state. Had the money been official, it might have negated the various post-war treaties between Japan and the countries it had invaded and risked opening the floodgates to claims from anyone adversely affected by the actions of the Japanese military up until 1945. To move the issue forward quickly, the Japanese government accepted full moral responsibility but insisted that the right to claim material compensation had been dealt with in the treaties. In fact, government money *was* used for the administration of the fund, but most of the cash came from voluntary donations by Japanese people – a quite extraordinary gesture of civic atonement in itself. Within a couple of months, 400 million yen (£2.84 million) had been raised, but many of the comfort women refused to accept payments from the fund, arguing the Japanese government needed to compensate them further under international law.

Over the years many comfort women have taken their cases to Japanese courts, usually represented by Japanese legal teams working for free. In all of these cases the courts have acknowledged the veracity of the women's claims but again concluded (often regretfully) either that the issue of state compensation had been settled by the treaties with China and Korea in 1952, 1965 and 1972, in which these countries renounced their claims for war reparations from Japan, or that a statute of limitations applied. The comfort women campaigners argued in return that those treaties only renounced the right of the Chinese and Korean *states* to sue Japan, not the right of individuals. The United Nations weighed in, pointing out that statutes of limitations do not apply to 'gross violations of human rights'.

Nevertheless, there have been numerous further statements of remorse and regret from Japanese prime ministers over the years, while Emperor Akihito, son of Hirohito, in whose name and under whose command the war was waged, has also done as much as he can within his limited sphere of expression to offer remorse for Japan's actions, leading one observer, Jeff Kingston, director of Asian studies at Temple University, Japan, to describe him recently as 'Japan's leading emissary of reconciliation'.

Often, though, these official apologies and expressions of remorse have been undermined; not all Japanese politicians have felt inclined to maintain a contrite tone, particularly in recent years. Several figures high up in the ruling Liberal Democratic Party, tired of what they see as the South Koreans' insatiable demands for atonement, have called into question historical evidence about the comfort women. In 2012 Prime Minister Yoshihiko Noda stated in the Diet that there was 'no evidence' that they had been taken by force. The mayor of Osaka, Toru Hashimoto, has also said that 'If Korea has this evidence it would be good to see it.' Shintaro Ishihara, former governor of Tokyo, opined that 'prostitution is a good means of making money in times of difficulty, and the comfort women chose to do that'. The current premier, Shinzo Abe, would seem to agree. In 2007 in a speech to the Diet he said that 'it was not as though military police broke into people's homes and took them away like kidnappers'. Others claim that it would have been unthinkable for the Japanese military to have prioritised the maintenance of 200,000 sex workers during the height of their overseas campaigns when they were fighting the Chinese in China, the Americans in the Pacific and the British in Burma. And, where were the Korean men when their women were being taken away? No, they say, the women *chose* prostitution, and in many cases the men who organised the brothels were Korean. This last point probably has some truth to it: by the 1940s Korea had been Japanese territory for three decades, and the locals were involved in the running of the country at almost every level, including the military.

'Who is responsible? The brothel owners, right?' Andrew Salmon told me. 'And as far as we are aware, they were private organisations run by Japanese and Korean pimps.' This can't be a very popular opinion to hold in South Korea, I said. No, said Salmon. 'If you question these things, you will be accused of being pro-Japanese. Why take on that grief? There is such cowardice, a real instinct for saying and doing nothing. I'm fine because I am a foreigner – I can get away with it – but if you are Korean, you don't.' He claimed he had met Korean academics who dismissed aspects of the comfort women narrative but who told him that they were too afraid to say anything about it.

Occasionally though Korean academics do speak out. In her 2013 book *Comfort Women of the Empire* Sejong University literature professor Park Yu-ha presented evidence that *some* of the Korean comfort women were indeed willing employees of the comfort stations, and that the stations were in some cases run by Korean men. It was a more nuanced picture, not in the category of historical denial by any means, but Park was taken to court for defamation by nine former comfort women.

Salmon's take is that generally the Japanese treated the Koreans 'pretty well compared to the way we [the British] treated the Irish or the Indians', but in recent years the South Koreans have 'cherry-picked all the worst possible details and invented others' from the colonial era. The Japanese were only doing what every other imperial power was attempting to do at the time, and the abuse of sex workers is one of the universal tragedies of war. German soldiers raped Russian women as they advanced on Moscow, for instance. The difference was, in the German army rape was illegal; the Japanese institutionalised it.

Out in the murkier reaches of the Internet you will find people who say the entire comfort women issue is a Chinese conspiracy intended to weaken relations between Korea and Japan and thus destabilise America's position in east Asia. Or is it the work of leftist Americans aiming to nudge South Korea towards communist China? Or North Korean infiltrators stirring up trouble in the South? Or is the whole thing a conspiracy by lawyers and NGOs out to make money from the saga? Naturally, such theories and denials infuriate the comfort women campaigners.

In 2006 a group of sixty-four submitted a complaint to the constitutional court of Korea, claiming that the government had been in dereliction of its duties in not taking further action against Japan. The women won the case, and in 2015 the two countries again met around the negotiating table to try and resolve the problem once and for all. In the end, Shinzo Abe agreed that the Japanese government would pay 1 billion yen (£5.6 million), this time from government funds, to the surviving comfort women on condition that South Korea agreed to let the issue rest and remove the comfort women statue from outside the Japanese embassy in Seoul.

Another apology was issued in Seoul by the Japanese government: 'The issue of comfort women, with an involvement of the Japanese military authorities at that time, was a grave affront to the honour and dignity of large numbers of women, and the government of Japan is painfully aware of responsibilities from this perspective.' But as I had seen, the statue remains outside the Japanese embassy. Not only that, but another one went up in Busan in 2016. In protest at what it considered was South Korea reneging on the agreement, Japan recalled its ambassador to Seoul. The Korean government responded that the statue was a civic matter, had been erected by private individuals and was beyond their control – much like the statements and activities of Japanese ultra-nationalists, you could say.

The Japanese foreign minister, Taro Kono – ironically, son of Yohei – issued a statement: 'The Japan–South Korea agreement was a pledge by the two countries that confirmed a final and irreversible resolution to the comfort women issue … Japan has faithfully honoured its pledges according to the Japan–South Korea agreement, and we continue to strongly demand that South Korea act responsibly and faithfully implement the agreement.'

In 2017 Moon Jae-in campaigned for the presidency on a pledge to review the 2015 agreement. 'The Japanese government, the perpetrator, should not say the matter is closed,' he said. 'The issue of a crime against humanity committed in a time of war cannot be closed with just a word. I do not seek special treatment from Japan. I ask only that [Japan] walk alongside us into the future on the basis of heartfelt remorse and reconciliation, befitting our closest neighbour.' After Moon's election, the review concluded that the deal was flawed because there had not been proper consultation with the victims themselves, and that the apology was not 'heartfelt'. The South Korean government dissolved the foundation which had been set up by the Japanese to support the comfort women, but its foreign ministry said that it would not attempt a renegotiation of the agreement. At least, not for now.

In late 2018 the focus shifted to the issue of forced labour during the Japanese occupation when the South Korean supreme court ordered two Japanese companies – Sumitomo Metal and Nippon Steel – to pay compensation to Koreans who had worked for them in the early 1940s. Prime Minister Abe immediately rejected the demand as 'impossible under international law', but there are many more such cases pending in the South Korean courts.

The comfort women and forced labour issues are frequently employed by Korean politicians in election campaigns or when their approval ratings are waning: they are guaranteed vote-winners, a subject all Koreans from left and right, whether pro-America or sympathetic to North Korea, can agree upon. It certainly seemed to work for Moon, and one imagines he might well employ it again in the future if his popularity wanes and the economy continues to stagnate.

In Seoul I met the prominent novelist and poet Song Sokze (also known as Song Suk-je), author of several books including *In the Shade of the Oleander*, which has been translated into English. I asked him what was wrong with the many apologies already offered by the Japanese to the comfort women. The Koreans seem to characterise them as 'I'm sorry if you were offended' or 'I apologise if you were hurt' – sneaky equivocation.

'We didn't really feel that there was much *truth* in their apologies, and every time they apologised, they didn't phrase it right,' he said. 'They say things like "We think it's our fault" or "We should say sorry." You know that kind of phrasing that doesn't really satisfy us Koreans. If they can't apologise properly, they should keep their mouth shut, but if they do apologise then they should put their heart into it.'

What precisely should the Japanese say?

'Maybe something along the lines of "We are sorry for putting Koreans through so much hardship and for killing Koreans, and then taking over the country by force, and also for not apologising properly" and then promise they will never do anything like that again.'

To non-Koreans all of this is sometimes frustrating. Clearly, the Japanese have apologised, officially, several times, and paid compensation. In a nation of 127 million people, there will always be deluded fringe voices, just as there are still Nazis in Germany, Russians who cherish Stalin's memory and, for all I know, fans of Pol Pot in Cambodia.

But according to a 2018 Genron NPO poll of 1,000 people in each country, only 1.1 per cent of Koreans questioned felt the comfort women issue had been resolved, and nearly half felt 'more discussion' was the way forward. In contrast, a 2016 Pew poll revealed that just over half of Japanese people thought they had apologised enough, and 17 per cent felt that no apology was necessary at all, a figure which has not altered much over the last ten years, suggesting the hard-liners are a stubborn minority. However, the percentage of Japanese who did not feel Japan had apologised sufficiently had almost halved over the previous decade to 23 from 44 per cent. So it does seem even Japanese moderates are running out of patience on this issue.

It is not the place of an outsider to tell the Koreans to move on, but they *could*, just as most Taiwanese, Filipinos, Vietnamese, Burmese and Singaporeans have, or for that matter many of those who have suffered from German or Russian or American aggression during the last century. But when discussing this with South Koreans, whenever I mooted that they might try a more magnanimous approach, I would sense something stir deep within them. A light would go out. Their body language would shift. I would feel the air change.

I didn't really understand what was happening until I visited the House of Sharing.

I am standing in a comfort station, a dark windowless wooden hovel. On the wall hang two rows of small wooden tablets, much like the ones you see in traditional Japanese *izakaya* restaurants. In an *izakaya* they would be individual menu items. In the comfort station they list the services offered by the women workers.

The room is a replica, one of the exhibits at the Museum of Sexual Slavery by Japanese Military, part of the House of Sharing complex in Gwangju City, Gyeonggi Province (a different Gwangju from the scene of the 1980 uprising), an hour south of Seoul. The complex is also home to some of the surviving victims.

'One more thing: you notice the washbasin?' Jeong Ho-cheol, who helps run the museum asks. 'It is very utilitarian. It is not for the women's comfort at all. The basin is where the woman would have to wash the rapist's genitalia after she just got raped. And they would have to wash the same condom out. This is an actual condom from that time ...' He gestures to a glass display case nearby in which lies a desiccated lump of rubber.

Some comfort stations housed ten women, some over a hundred. The women would often have to service more than forty men each day. Soldiers in the morning, NCOs in the afternoon, officers from 7 to 8 p.m., commanding officers at 10 p.m. 'Can you imagine having to have sex with more than forty men in one day?' Jeong asks me. 'According to the testimony of one woman, she had done it with ten men, and so she was very painful in that part, so she refused more, but the owners tied her feet so she would have to continue.' There are many, many such stories, he says, often ending with the woman's suicide.

As an example, he tells me about the thirty-five women taken from Korea to service the Japanese military occupying Papua New Guinea. Half of them died on the journey. Half of those who survived the journey died during their time in the comfort station from disease, botched abortions, trauma or suicide. Only seven made it home at the end of the war.

The thirty comfort women – at the House of Sharing they prefer to call them *Halmoni* ('Grandma') – who live here are all in their eighties and nineties, and in most cases extremely frail. Many still suffer from injuries caused at the time of their incarceration.

The House of Sharing is situated on a quiet hillside amid woodland with tomato and rice farms nearby. At its heart is a small amphitheatre-style open space ringed with bronze busts of some of its current and former residents, including Kim Soon-deok, who drew the 'Unblossomed Flower', which became the symbol of the comfort women movement; Kim Hak-soon, the first woman to testify; and Park Doo-ri, born in 1924, who was among the plaintiffs in the court at Shimonoseki, Japan, who unsuccessfully sought an official apology and reparations from the Japanese legal system in 2000. Inside the museum, which is beneath the amphitheatre, one of the first things you see is a map showing all the comfort stations, stretching from Japan and Korea through China to Thailand, Burma, Malaysia, Indonesia and the Philippines, and as far south as Papua New Guinea. The museum estimates the total number of comfort women to be between 50,000 and 300,000. According to the people who run it, 40 per cent of visitors to the House of Sharing are Japanese.

One current resident is Lee Ok-sun. Born in 1927 in Busan, Lee's family was poor so she didn't attend school. In 1942 she was taken from her job at a local hotel by two Japanese men dressed as civilians to Yanji in north-west China. 'It was an occurrence that doesn't even happen in dreams,' she recalled in a TV documentary. 'We had no idea where we were going during the train ride. Instead of going straight to the comfort station like most girls, we were sent to do labour in a different place after being captured.' The labour was hard, and the girls, some as young as eleven, complained. The Japanese soldiers said they would send them home, but instead the girls were taken to the first of many comfort stations where they would work over the following three years until the end of the war.

Lee has described what she experienced as like being in a 'slaughterhouse for humans'. Many of the young women she knew committed suicide by jumping off cliffs; one slit her own throat. During those three years Lee received several injections of an anti-syphilis drug as well as mercury vapour treatments, which left her unable to have children. After the war she remained in Jilin Province in China, settling there with a Korean man who had been conscripted into the Japanese army. The man was enrolled in the Chinese military when the civil war started, and Lee moved in with her in-laws. She never saw her husband again, though she eventually remarried. Lee returned to South Korea to live in the House of Sharing in 2001.

Would I like to meet Lee Ok-sun? Jeong asks. He shows me into the nursing home a little further up the hill. On the way we pass a large statue depicting an elderly woman, naked from the waist up but sunk into the ground from the waist down, as if in quicksand.

The building looks like any other nursing home with a communal living room containing armchairs ranged around its edge. Two elderly women are sitting on opposite sides of the room in silence. I am introduced to one of them. This is Lee Ok-sun. She is slumped, penned in by her Zimmer frame. Her eyes are closed and her chin rests on her chest. She is clearly extremely frail. I am told she has been only taking liquids for the past couple of days, unable to digest anything more, and is in considerable pain. She is wearing purple trousers and a mauve top. She is barefoot. Her hair is a shock of white. Lee Ok-sun has travelled the world to highlight the plight of the *Halmoni*, meeting Holocaust survivors in Germany, testifying in Tokyo and visiting California to submit an affadavit to a California federal court to block the removal of a comfort women statue in Glendale, Los Angeles.

A female carer squats down beside Lee and explains who I am. I hesitate to disturb her, but the carer nods that I should speak. I thank Lee for finding the time to meet me and sympathise with her current condition. Then I ask if she has a message for the Japanese.

The question is translated, and it is as if a light has been switched on in Lee's eyes. Her face becomes animated as she speaks. The carer translates her response.

'The first thing I want is an apology. I don't want to die without getting an apology from the [Japanese] government. I have nothing I want to say to the people because it is not the people who are bad, it is the government who did this to me. I just want an apology from the government.'

Previously she has said that she will not be satisfied until the emperor of Japan kneels in front of her to deliver the apology. Was this still the case?

Lee nods almost imperceptibly as she closes her eyes.

21

DMZ

The next day I drive east out of Seoul in my intermittently self-driving Kia. At one point a couple of police motorcyclists appear alongside me on the highway. For a brief moment I wonder if my autonomous vehicle has reported me for some or other misdemeanour, but they merely wave me aside to make way for the newly elected president himself. Moon Jae-in, I learn later from the evening TV news, was somewhere within the fleet of armoured Cadillac Escalades swooshing past me through the rain, on his way to start the countdown to the Winter Olympics to be held a few months hence in Pyeongchang.

I spend the night in a hotel in Wonju, a prosperous-seeming city of highways and high towers. The rain has not stopped all day. From my window I watch a man, alone on a golf course, putting through two-inch-deep puddles, the living embodiment of Korean determination.

The next morning I make it to the east coast road. This turns out to be one of those great ocean highways, snaking its way between stratified cliffs on my left and crashing waves on the right, with military lookouts up above and the occasional enticing crescent of sand. While the Japanese accessorise their holiday spots with Ferris wheels and aquariums, the Koreans prefer terrifyingly high-altitude zip wires. There was one at the mud festival over on the west coast, and I pass another here that must be a kilometre long and thirty metres high. South Koreans like a thrill ride, a bit of danger, it seems.

Which brings me to the Demilitarised Zone (DMZ), my destination today. This is the no-man's-land between North and South

Korea, four kilometres wide and stretching 248 kilometres from the Yellow Sea coast in the west to Gangwon Province in the east, on the Japan Sea coast. I had heard that on the east coast you could drive to the border unaccompanied, which sounded more interesting than the stagey day trip by coach from Seoul.

I am getting closer to the DMZ now as I arrive at Unification Park, an outdoor exhibition space by the sea featuring a wooden boat used by eleven North Korean defectors in 2009 as well as a North Korean submarine captured off the coast here in September 1996. 'The incident was a great shock to us and incurred our wrath,' explains an information panel beside a red and green submarine, a rackety, rusting Cold War trophy propped up on stilts. It was captured after North Korean infiltrators signalled the sub to come closer inshore, and it ran aground. Inside it is horribly cramped; bits of metal jut perilously at eye level. I notice that some of the equipment has English-language signage.

Further up the road is a military museum with more North Korean trophies – spying equipment captured from the submarine infiltrators, including Japanese cameras, binoculars and rations – and pointed exhibits about other countries which have managed to reunify, such as Vietnam and Germany. As I leave I have a queasy feeling. The Ealing-comedy aspects of North Korea are endlessly entertaining – the state-approved hairstyles, the Korean Central News Agency reporting in 2012 that they had discovered a unicorn's lair, or Kim Jong-il scoring five holes-in-one playing golf – but more than 25 million people live there and have endured appalling conditions over the past decades. In the early 1990s two million are believed to have died as a result of a famine caused by the government's intransigence. Though North Korea is believed to be experiencing economic growth of about 4 per cent these days, many of its citizens still live in poverty, and few have any freedom. And, should *Juche*, the North's state ideology, be threatened, they would not think twice about slaughtering their neighbours. North Korea has the world's fourth largest army.

As I pass Goseong, the last town before the DMZ, I notice that the military posts are now manned and the beaches lined with razor wire. I see a sign beside the highway. I do a double take. It really does say, 'To Moscow. To Be Continued ...' During the Sunshine Policy era in the late 1990s when relations were more 'transactional' between North and South Korea, there were genuine hopes that Highway 7, as the coast road is known, would continue up through North Korea and on across Russia, creating a properly pan-Asian link from Moscow to Busan. That may still come to pass, as the current Moon administration is building friendly ties with the North faster than anyone has witnessed before, but for now people must make do with the ferry from nearby Sokcho to Vladivostok.

Over the final few miles to the border, life continues. Farmers tend their fields; there are residential towers by the sea, and military bases. The air is thick with dragonflies, which splat on my windscreen. Huge concrete blocks stand sentinel on either side of the highway as I enter the last mountain tunnel before the border – presumably waiting to be toppled over to block advancing tanks.

Finally I come to a military checkpoint. A couple of polite young soldiers lean into my open window. Realising I am not Korean, they pass me a laminated information card on which is written, 'Do you have an application form?' I wasn't aware I needed one. I'm not planning on visiting North Korea, I joke. I must turn back, they say, stony-faced. It seems I have missed something called the Security Education Centre, six miles back down the coast road, which turns out to be a facility for separating tourists from their money. I pay to show my passport, fill in a form, peruse the souvenirs (lots of ginseng) and watch a propaganda film about the Korean War, before driving back to the checkpoint. This time the guards give me an 'admission pass' and further instructions. I must 'turn off my black box' (I've no doubt my car has one but equally no idea how to turn it off); I must not overtake military vehicles or take any photographs of military installations; I must drive without stopping to the DMZ viewpoint.

I enter an eerie zone now with little other traffic and few buildings. There is still the odd farmer though, working in fields hemmed in by great slinky-rings of razor wire. I stop by the vast and lavish DMZ Museum. Cabinets display more of the pitiful possessions of North Koreans who attempted to reach freedom, while old magazine covers offer an insight into a period of communist paranoia which I remember well from my own childhood in the 1970s. The cover of *World Week* has a strapline which reads 'In the Grip of the Red Giant'; below is a graphic showing two armoured gloves reaching down from communist China and grabbing the Korean peninsula. Elsewhere, propaganda leaflets dropped by both North and South over the years feature lots of skimpily clad young women. The message seems to be 'Life is better here' (for men). There is also a powerful letter to American soldiers, airdropped by the communists one Christmas during the war. It begins in a friendly fashion:

We are wishing you a Merry Christmas and a Happy New Year. We also have something to talk to you about.

You are far away from those you love, in Korea, a country you never heard of three years ago ... You've been told you came here to stop 'Communist aggression.' But what do your own eyes and head tell you? The Koreans are fighting in their own country. The Chinese are defending their own nearby borders. Neither of these peoples have ever dreamed of invading the United States. It is the US troops who have come here with bombs, napalm, germs and every other weapon of mass murder.

They had a point.

I wander on through a fascinating section dedicated to the wildlife which has flourished in the empty DMZ over the last sixty-five years (every cloud ...) and one dedicated to the other overseas armed forces who fought for the South Koreans, including almost 6,000 Brits. In the gift shop they are selling the produce of the local farmers; this is a major buckwheat-growing region, so there are grains, flours and noodles, incongruous beside the replica uniforms and medals.

The last few miles after the museum take me up to the DMZ itself. Here there is a viewing platform on a hill overlooking the no-man's-land stretch of coast which, as Donald Trump salivated, really is stunning real estate, ripe for condos and casinos. As I stand high above the shore together with a few South Koreans looking at the view through pay binoculars, we hear quavering propaganda drifting out of distant speakers on the North Korean side. It is an eerie, angry bark. I ask one of the other visitors what they are saying, but she giggles and runs away.

I wonder what the Southerners think when they look at the North from their vantage point of wealth and democracy. Superiority? Wistful longing? Pity? The only sign of civilisation in North Korea is a distant mountaintop lookout, while the South Koreans are currently building a snazzy new observation tower here. On reflection, probably not a good sign for the prospect of reunification.

I have something to confess at this point in my journey: this is the closest I will get to North Korea. On the one hand, it would have been good to go there and tick that box. On the other, as with all foreign visitors, my visit would have been very tightly controlled, I would not have been able to talk to anyone interesting and would not have learned anything new. For the bragging rights of a visit, a couple of thousand pounds would also have had to have been dropped into the pockets of this frightful regime, so there is a moral aspect to visiting North Korea. Whether it is the assassination of opponents overseas, the torture and imprisonment of hundreds of thousands of its own people in labour and re-education camps, the public executions, the exporting of slave labour (to build stadiums for the World Cup in Qatar, for instance) or the systematic oppression and control of virtually every aspect of the lives of the entire population down to their very thoughts, the regime in Pyongyang is at least thorough in its tyranny. But the moral aspect was only part of my decision, and probably an excuse if I'm honest.

I was visiting the region just prior to the detente between the US, South Korea and the North which took place in mid-2018, before

President Moon began his remarkable campaign to woo Kim Jong-un. These days everyone (and Michael Palin) has visited, but back then foremost in my mind was that I didn't want to have my brain turned to vegetable soup, as had happened to poor Otto Warmbier, the American college student arrested in January 2016 for stealing a propaganda poster from his hotel while on an arranged trip to Pyongyang. Otto had just been delivered back to the Americans in a coma and died shortly afterwards. America had banned its citizens from visiting the country as a result, and I unilaterally extended that ban to British citizens.

As I walk back down to the car, I pass a monument with a DEC-LARATION OF UNIFICATION drawn up in August 2010 by a volunteer association on the sixty-fifth anniversary of Korean Liberation Day. It traces the origins of the division of Korea, and asks, 'Is this what those who died for this country and declared independence in the March 1st (1919) movement wanted? ... The truth is that even today, we are still pointing guns at people of our own race.'

There is no smooth way to transition from the bleak inhumanity of the DMZ to a park full of giant penises, but it was at Penis Park, a couple of hours' drive back down south along the coast from the DMZ, that I finally fell in love with the Koreans.

Penis Park lies above the fishing harbour at the small town of Sinnam, roughly two thirds of the way up the east coast of South Korea. Its real name is Haesindang Park, but what else do you call a rambling wooded cliff-top garden which is absolutely rammed with gigantic sculptures of the male member? All the pricks are proudly erect; some are several metres in length; most are alarmingly detailed, although testicles are an optional extra. A few of the statues eschew all anatomical verisimilitude and have faces, others have two or more heads; one of them appears to be ejaculating the Prince of Wales feathers. Some are wooden, some are stone, one is bronze; the really big ones are fibreglass.

What I especially enjoy about the park is the atmosphere. All I can hear as I wander around are peals of laughter. This is mostly from female visitors; the men feign bashfulness but laugh along too. At one point a lone male among a tour group of women threatens jokingly to take his own penis out, as if to say 'Why are you looking at these statues, when I've got a real one here?' I cover my eyes in mock horror; there is a pause, and then everyone laughs again.

This is all a bit of a paradox because I had understood South Korean society to be quite puritanical, at least in terms of public exhibitions of anything overtly sexual. Pornography is banned. I didn't see any sex shops anywhere – not that I was looking, I should add. The sexual content of films is heavily censored. Even cigarettes are pixelated. Adultery was illegal in South Korea until 2015; forty-two people were *jailed* for being unfaithful in 2008; and premarital sex is still the exception. And yet here we are in a park full of penises.

South Korea shares this authoritarian squeamishness about sex with China. In 2016 the Chinese government even banned the 'seductive eating of bananas' online. The Japanese, on the other hand, have a comparatively robust and open attitude towards sex and pornography, as evidenced by everything from the iconic *shunga* (woodblock print erotica), most famously Hokusai's *Dream of the Fisherman's Wife* from 1814, which depicts a woman being ravaged by an octopus, to the open consumption of manga porn on public transport. You will find graphic discussions of sex on mainstream television too, although weirdly they pixelate the hairy bits in their porn (I'm told).

Sexual mores are changing in South Korea though, particularly among the young and city dwellers. 'Love hotels' are as common here as in Japan, partly because so many young Koreans still live at home with their parents, and in his excellent book *Korea, The Impossible Country* Daniel Tudor describes the practice of 'booking', in which groups of men and women visit a nightclub and are introduced to each other by the waiters in return for a tip – a kind of speed dating: 'one-night stands from such meetings are very common ... Booking has an old-fashioned Korean element to it – the introduction from the waiter – but the way in which it is now used suggests that young South Koreans today are sexually rather liberal.'

Many of the statues at Penis Park have a totem-pole vibe, penis stacked on top of penis; there are penis wind chimes, and even the park's seats and benches are penis shaped. But pride of place goes, naturally given our proximity to the DMZ, to a military-themed ensemble featuring a three-metre-long knob mounted like a gigantic cannon between two wheels, with three 'soldier' penises standing behind it as if about to light its fuse.

Things get even weirder the higher you climb the cliffs. At one point there is a semicircle of nine white stone penises ranged around two oddly feminine, reclining members. Each of the standing willies is two metres high and has creatures relating to the Chinese zodiac carved into it. There is a museum up here too, giving an actually quite serious ethnographical overview of penis art from around the world. One display tells the story behind the park.

Once upon a time, a fisherman's girlfriend, a virgin, would sit on the rocks below waiting for her beau to return from the sea, but then, one day, a storm swept her to her death. After this tragic but, really, let's be honest, easily avoided calamity, the villagers were unable to catch any fish no matter how hard they tried. That was until one selfless local man ejaculated into the sea. This caused the fish to return, and so, to appease the fish gods or whatever, they built the park. An authentic South Korean cock and bull story, you might say.

22

Seoul VII

I don't want you thinking that Penis Park has left me with a one-track mind, but as I arrive at the piazza in front of Seoul's War Memorial and Museum a rather piquant heavy rock number begins to blare from speakers ranged around the entrance plaza. It is 'Rock You Like a Hurricane' by the Scorpions – sample lyric: 'The bitch is hungry, she needs to tell, So give her inches and feed her well'. As it plays, Seoul's Military Police Motorcycle Display Team enter the square, gliding past the museum's outdoor collection of military vehicles, tanks, boats and planes on their Harley-Davidsons, engines revving, blue lights flashing, and commence a complex routine, repeatedly criss-crossing the plaza.

Most museums would be a bit of an anti-climax after something like that, but this is on a colossal scale and full of interesting stuff. It's thorough too, covering the Imjin Wars and Admiral Yi, the efforts of the Korean Independence Army during the Japanese occupation and of course the Korean War of 1950–3. There is an on-site cinema, which this week is showing *The Bridge On the River Kwai*. I suspect, though, that the South Koreans have a different relationship to the memorialising of international conflict, as the museum also has a wedding hall.

I spend some hours viewing the events of the past century through Korean eyes. The bad guys are very clearly the Japanese, who again are accused of genocide. Apparently, in 1945 they were kicked out of Korea entirely due to the efforts of the Koreans themselves, which would come as news to the Americans, ('Through the ongoing heroic struggle to restore the nation's sovereignty and independence, the Korean people finally succeeded in driving out the Japanese imperialists'). Blame for the current situation on the peninsula, meanwhile, is laid at the door of the Chinese for preventing the unification of the Korean peninsula by intervening on the side of Kim Il-sung. Ominously, the message of the museum is that the conflict 'should be remembered as an unfinished war'.

Aside from losing the credit for ending the war in Asia, the Americans come out of it all very well, but as I look out through the first floor window at the Harley riders, now enjoying a cup of coffee, I find myself playing the old blame game again. I begin, obviously, with the Japanese, without whose interference Korea's twentieth century would have turned out very differently. Perhaps the peninsula would have modernised as a sovereign nation, or then again maybe Russia would have taken it, or China even. In 1910, when Japan annexed Korea, thousands of Koreans fled to China, among them the parents of the young Kim Il-sung. In 1932 Kim joined the fight for Korean independence, by all accounts a determined campaign, during which the Japanese captured and killed his wife, Kim Hye-sun. Veteran Korea commentator Bruce Cumings believes that the fact that the Japanese used other Koreans to fight Kim and his fellow members of the resistance is the prime reason for the poisoned blood on the peninsula today. The Japanese set Korean against Korean in defence of their occupation, and that toxic legacy lingers.

In the 1930s and 40s the man in charge of the munitions factories supplying the Japanese counter-insurgency forces fighting Kim, and also responsible for the Korean forced labour programme, was Nobusuke Kishi. After the war Kishi was initially categorised as a Class A war criminal, but he later founded the Liberal Democratic Party (LDP) and twice served as prime minister of Japan. Not uncoincidentally, he is the grandfather of the current prime minister, Shinzo Abe, who is hoping to succeed where Kishi failed and revise the Japanese constitution to allow its Self Defence Forces to take offensive action. As Cumings noted in a recent article in the *London Review of Books*, the very evening in April 2017 that President Trump dined with Abe at Mar-a-Lago in Florida, Kim Jong-un tested one of his missiles in the direction of Hokkaido – a 'pointed message'. With the kind of symmetry which would be dismissed as fanciful were it to be found in fiction, wrote Cumings 'Kim Il-sung and Kishi are meeting again through their grandsons.'

The Americans must shoulder some of the responsibility for what happened to the Korean peninsula after 1945 – for the division in 1953 and for their support of the military dictators who then ruled South Korea for more than three decades. After World War II, rather than attempt a transparent truth and reconciliation process, the Americans used the Japanese-trained ruling class, including Park Chung-hee, to help administer South Korea. As Michael Breen put it to me, 'The Americans ... they didn't give a shit about the Japanese occupation. It was done. And all the competent people who had worked with the Japanese, the Americans thought, *Well you've been a whore to the Japanese, you can be a whore to us now*, so they actually found these people useful.' Many also point to American decisions in post-war Tokyo as a factor in Japan's failure to atone for its war guilt and crimes, particularly their protection of Emperor Hirohito.

And it was an American army colonel, Dean Rusk, who the day after the bomb was dropped on Nagasaki famously drew the line roughly equating to the 38th Parallel across the peninsula which divides North and South Korea to this day. The Americans feared that the tens of thousands of Korean resistance fighters, Kim Il-sung among them, would side with the Russians, and so moved 25,000 troops into Korea, proposing that the two World War Two allies oversee a five-year transitional period leading to democratic elections run by the United Nations. The Russians opposed this, and in 1948 Rusk's line, originally drawn to demarcate the Russian and American occupation zones, took on a permanence no one had foreseen.

The accepted historical view is that, encouraged by the withdrawal of the American troops, at 4 a.m. on the morning of 25 June 1950 the North attacked the South, supported by Russian tanks. In response the United Nations authorised military intervention, with the USA contributing the overwhelming majority of the UN forces. After initial setbacks the Americans stabilised the situation and pushed north. It was only when General MacArthur's troops reached the Yalu river on China's border that Mao Zedong felt compelled to join the fight on the side of the North Koreans, abandoning his pursuit of Chiang Kai-shek's Chinese nationalists, who had fled to Taiwan. Kim had sent a message by plane to Chairman Mao asking for help, playing the Chinese off against the Russians, as he would for many years. Within two weeks Chinese forces entered North Korea and would thereafter bear the brunt of the fight: 900,000 Chinese soldiers died or were injured, compared to 520,000 North Koreans.

The destructive stalemate raged for two and a half years. Over three million people died, and in the famous words of Rusk the Americans bombed 'everything that moved in North Korea, every brick standing on top of another'. The war ended with an armistice in 1953, but hostilities continued in various forms. The North attempted to kill the South's presidents on four occasions, and in 1974 succeeded in assassinating Yuk Young-soo, President Park's wife and the mother of Park Geun-hye, in the lobby of Seoul's National Theatre. Extreme anti-communist paranoia lasted in the South until the late 1980s; imprisonment and torture awaited anyone even remotely suspected of being sympathetic to communism or the North.

And in 1976 World Word III very nearly broke out at the Demilitarised Zone as a result of some light gardening. A group of US soldiers was sent to trim a poplar tree obstructing the view of UN observers. The North Koreans, who claimed that the tree had been planted by Kim Il-sung himself and as such was sacred, took umbrage at this arboreal aggression and murdered two of the soldiers with their own axes. This resulted in a massive military operation involving twenty-seven helicopters, nuclear-capable bombers, F-4s, F-111s, an aircraft carrier and a crack team of tree specialists (including future South Korean President Moon Jae-in, doing his national service at the time), who managed to coppice the tree at the second attempt, leaving a stump to remind the North Koreans of their resolve.

But the most famous North Korean attack was the Blue House Raid of January 1968, an audacious attempt by thirty-one soldiers from the North to cut off the head of Park Chung-hee. They got within 800 metres of the presidential palace, and though most were killed or captured, one soldier is believed to have made it back to North Korea. Perhaps the lowest point in relations came in 1987 when Korean Air Flight 858 exploded in mid-air – the work of a North Korean agent, Kim Hyon-hui. She was captured and was the first to confirm the long-held belief that the North had been abducting Japanese citizens from their beaches and fishing boats.

I was curious to know what younger Koreans thought about the North and the events of seventy years ago. According to one student I got chatting to in a café one day in Seoul, the answer was, not a lot. 'Nowadays, the younger people have almost no idea about the war,' he told me. I raised my eyebrows. 'Really. It's so far away from their real lives. There is almost no idea that we share an ethnicity [with North Koreans].'

One writer on Korea, Boyé Lafayette De Mente, claims in his book *The Korean Mind* that the schism between North and South Korea existed long before the Japanese arrived: 'The fact of the matter was that historically North and South Korea had been divided by ideological and social gaps often so wide that they behaved very much like separate countries.' A Southern elite had held sway over the North for centuries, and there had always been bad blood between the two areas.

All the South Koreans I spoke to, not just the young, seemed reconciled to the existence of their nuclear-armed neighbour, rather like people who live on seismic fault lines come to accept the risk of an earthquake. 'People are immune to it as a coping mechanism,' as one local put it to me.

How has that numbness affected attitudes towards reunification? The 2018 detente, when Kim Jong-un stepped across the threshold at the DMZ and shook hands with Moon Jae-in, had reunification – in one form or another – as its unspoken subtext: the idea that one day the North and the South would live under one government. But what would that actually look like? Michael Breen had this frank assessment should the North and South ever come together again: 'Day one will be all fireworks and live coverage on CNN. Day two, the poor North Koreans go to the bottom of the hierarchical ladder.' In his book he quotes an assistant South Korean foreign minister of his acquaintance who, strictly off the record, made this unequivocal statement: 'He leaned forward over our coffee cups and spoke in slow, clear syllables. "We ... do ... not ... want ... to ... unify ... with ... North ... Korea."' On the record, the same official offered this: 'We Koreans are a divided people and our goal is to become one again.'

People do *care* about reunification of course, but they are just not that motivated about making it happen. The feeling I had was that most South Koreans see the North more as a problem to be postponed indefinitely rather than the lost half of the family with whom they hope one day to reunite. They don't really see reunification as an opportunity, even though there are obvious advantages for them in belonging to a country with a population of eighty million, including economies of scale and cheap labour. A unified Korea would also be a key overland link between China, Russia and Japan. 'A lot of people say that they want reunification, but they don't have a clear blueprint,' said the journalist Stephanie Sehoi Park. 'Plus, they don't want it to happen in their lifetime. I mean, reunification sounds harmonious and beautiful, but it is going to be so much turmoil and my generation doesn't want to pay the price for it.' How about you let China have it? I asked. 'Nooo! I want the land. They have a lot of natural resources. We need the space.'

The mechanisms and a timescale for reunification are unclear too. 'If it happens rapidly, that is disastrous for South Korea,' said Park Sangin, the economics professor from Seoul University. 'We have to narrow that gap to reach unification. It is much, much worse than the gap between East and West Germany. North Korea is much more isolated than East Germany was, so it is not just the economic gap, it is also the exchange between people.'

Perhaps the main reason reunification is unlikely is that many powerful groups would have much to lose. The military-industrial complex would suffer enormously, particularly in America, something evident from the dramatic drop in the share price of Lockheed Martin when President Moon meet Kim Jong-un in April 2018. Japan doesn't want a single Korea either because it would be more of an economic and potentially military threat. China would probably prefer the peninsula to remain divided too – to threaten Seoul, hold Pyongyang close and keep America and Japan at bay. And America/the West values South Korea as an ally in the region.

Perhaps the most telling statistic I saw regarding the ambivalence of the South Koreans towards reunification was the live Internet search ranking when the two countries' leaders commenced those face-to-face talks. The talks ranked tenth, after various actors and actresses, boy bands, the next day's weather and college acceptance rates. Those were the things South Koreans really wanted to know about.

THE PEOPLE'S REPUBLIC OF CHINA

23

Incheon

My time in South Korea ends in Incheon, an hour or so west of central Seoul. I have elected to continue my 'slow travel' approach and take the ferry which leaves Incheon every evening and arrives in Qingdao on China's east coast eighteen hours later.

First though I have a day spare in Incheon and have heard that, like Yokohama, it has a large Chinese population, having been the main port of entry for Chinese migrants from Shandong Province for over a century. A small Chinatown has somehow survived here, despite Incheon also being the landing place of the United Nations forces in 1950; it is close to the harbour and has a cluster of museums and restaurants. On a dreary, dark Monday evening, with the air cloaked in smog and smelling vaguely of drains, Incheon's Chinatown is a rather desolate place, for all the gaiety of the four-storey Chinese restaurants lit up like fairground rides.

In one I order a bowl of *jjajangmeyon*. These are the classic noodles of Incheon's Chinatown, commemorated with their own museum, where I learn that they were brought here by Chinese labourers in the 1880s. Back then this was cheap, quick, filling workers' food sold from handcarts down on the harbourside. Over time it has acquired a Korean touch of fermented soybean paste and in the 1950s, for some reason, caramel, and is served with the usual generous array of Korean side dishes – pickles, fermented dipping sauces and *kimchi*.

In the 1880s, when Korea opened up to foreign trade, the Japanese concession was located right next to the Qing Chinese area down here by the port. The two were divided by a stairway, which is still here, these days crowned by a more recent statue of Confucius, donated by the city of Qingdao. Incheon has managed to hold on to the largest collection of pre-colonial era Japanese buildings in the country too. I take a wander around a motley congregation of mostly former banks. A stout granite building dating from 1883 with a neoclassical dome was once the Incheon branch of the First Bank of Japan, the first modern financial institution in Korea. Japanese Street has a few more Japanese-style buildings, including some wooden shops reminiscent of the *machiya* you find in Kyoto. The old British consulate is still here too, now repurposed as the Paradise Hotel.

The next day, heavily dosed with my usual cocktail of seasickness medications, I arrive at the port. There is a long queue ahead of me in the crowded departure lounge, but the mood is festive and friendly. My fellow passengers – middle-aged salesmen and lorry drivers – seem a jolly bunch. As we are instructed to climb the gangplank, there is that nervous excitement in the air common to all embarking ferry passengers.

Onboard, the purser shows me to my windowless cabin. There are two beds, one either side of the narrow room. By the door is a tiny toilet and shower room, and at the end of the room a table and bench. The cabin is half filled with cardboard boxes and a tatty black suitcase bulging at the seams and tied with rope, presumably belonging to my cabin mate.

This ferry, like all ferries, as far as I can make out, was cobbled together from vinyl, polyester and Dralon some time around 1974. Every surface is coated with a layer of grime. There is the smell of something fermented about the place; you would not want to walk on the carpet in bare feet – a hazmat suit would be preferable.

I leave my bags and go exploring. The Carpenters are playing over the intercom, and I begin to wonder whether I have bought a ticket to some kind of 70s-themed cruise by mistake. There is a convenience store stocked with instant noodles and cans of Chupa Chups strawberry soda. On one deck I stumble upon a vast open dormitory with rows of mattresses laid out on the floor – an option if my roomie turns out to be a snorer. I inspect the restaurant buffet, which offers rice with a range of catering pans filled with semi-liquid red matter. Later I will try some of the red stuff, and it is so spicy it removes an entire layer from the lining of my mouth.

The ferry departs from a drizzly Incheon on time, inching beneath the mammoth Samsung-built suspension bridge to the airport. I go up top, stand beside a funnel belching thick black smoke like an old minicab and tilt my head back to look up at the bridge's underside. It is properly awesome, and I can't help wondering if I should be up there instead, in a taxi on the way to the airport.

The sea though is calm, for which I am grateful. As I lie on my bed I am jiggled gently back and forth, but during the night I am intermittently disturbed by my cabin mate's operatic teeth-grinding and intermittent weird straining noises. He was there when I returned. His name is Dong, and he is from Beijing. Via a complicated mime routine he explained that he tiles bathrooms, or raises camels, or runs a mime workshop. It could have been any of those. I was left none the wiser about what was in the boxes but assumed he had been conducting business in South Korea. What about THAAD? I asked. I mimed rockets being shot down. His eyes followed my fingers then darted anxiously towards the door. By this point he either believed I worked in the aerospace industry or was a terrorist. I tried something else but, seeing it through his eyes, realised my 'writing' mime could also be misinterpreted. I do 'typing' instead. He probably by now thought I was a pianist.

We then performed an awkward dance around who went to the bathroom first to prepare for bed but eventually turned off the lights. I cannot sleep though. How can I? I am in a box on the sea in my underwear with a strange man who thinks I am a piano-playing terrorist. At around 3 a.m. it dawns on me: *I am on a slow boat to China*. I don't know if it's the medication, but the phrase seems fascinating, and I roll it around my head for hours. Then, at around 5 a.m. we hit a rough patch and the cabin begins to swirl. I feel as if I am in a barrel going over Niagara Falls. I fight the urge to reflect upon my earlier meal of gristly beef in spicy ketchup but some masochistic imperative keeps bringing it to mind. I hasten to the toilet, where we shall draw a veil over the rest of the night's events. But yes, there are times when I want to die.

As I wait to disembark in Qingdao the next morning, the purser corrals me into a special priority departure zone. The rest of the passengers, including Dong, to whom I have bidden an appropriately awkward good bye, queue up in the cabin corridor. While waiting, I witness my first example of blatant queue jumping syndrome (BQJS). Two shabbily dressed Chinese men, one in mirrored sunglasses, the other with an heroic comb-over, arrive late carrying cardboard boxes tied with string, but instead of going to the back of the line simply station themselves at the head of the queue in front of a woman who has been standing there for about ten minutes. The men gaze up innocently at the ceiling. The woman frowns but takes no further action.

As the weeks pass, I will witness this kind of shameless line-cutting quite often in China. It is a cliché for foreigners, particularly English people, to complain about this, so instead I merely offer you my empirical survey of the different strategies employed. Two demographics are particularly prone to BQJS, and each has its specific method. Middle-aged men exude an air of relaxed entitlement, as if sidling to the front of queues is their birthright. Younger women pretend to be engrossed in a Very Important Conversation on their smartphones, looking up at the departures board in a don't-talk-to-me-I'm-multi-tasking kind of a way and using the arm holding the device to shield them from their victims. Both of these techniques were impressive in their brazenness. I could never pull them off. But not once did I see anyone make any kind of protest, much less take action; everyone seemed to just accept that there was always someone who, while you were in the middle of a transaction, would edge up to the kiosk window and thrust a piece of paper or some money beneath the glass to distract the clerk. And the clerk would always turn away to deal with the intruder as if it was the correct thing to do.

During my travels in China I spent many hours quietly brooding to myself about BQJers. I also developed extraordinary peripheral vision, much broader than humans are normally capable of, so that I could block attempts to usurp my place by taking a swift step left or right, or sometimes dummying both ways. Queuing for a ticket to a museum in Shanghai, I engaged in a particularly satisfying bout of this with a diminutive yet determined elderly woman intent on muscling in on my teller time. I shimmied left, I shimmied right, blocking her access to the clerk like Beyoncé's bouncer shielding his charge from the paparazzi. In the end she twigged, and we both laughed about it, but much later, fatigued from weeks of battle, I finally broke down one afternoon while waiting to check into a flight at Shanghai airport. A middle-aged man outflanked the roped-off line, swooshing in at an acute angle like a bird of prey on an unsuspecting vole to the next available check-in counter as soon as the previous customer vacated it.

I was fifth in the queue but decided to mount a protest and shouted to the pathetic individual at the head of the queue who had allowed this to happen, 'What? Why have you let him do that? He just walked in from over there! We are all waiting here!' I gesticulated wildly.

The man at the head of the queue looked round at me, offered the very slightest of shrugs and returned his gaze to the counter. I was powerless; I could do nothing but fantasise about violent acts. When it finally came to my turn, the check-in clerk informed me that my luggage was overweight; I would have to go to another desk to pay some money. She pointed over to the left, from where the queue-jumper had materialised.

'Wait, but then I will have to queue all over again,' I bleated, pointing at the line behind me, which had now grown even longer.

'No, it's OK. You can just come up to the counter,' said the woman mildly.

I realised then that this is what the queue-jumper had been doing. He hadn't been queue-jumping at all. After that I never got het up about Chinese queues again.

★

As I am waiting to disembark from the ferry in Qingdao, a man sits beside me in the VIP area. He is dressed like a Sunday-afternoon explorer in khaki trousers with zips around the knees and a fly-fishing jacket. He has a large rucksack from which dangle a water bottle and binoculars.

'Look at them,' the man says to me in disgust. 'Chinese.'

'Oh, you're not Chinese. Korean?'

The man looks affronted. 'Nooo, Japanese!'

He introduces himself as Mr Norisuke. He is a travel writer. Did I know this ferry was built in Japan? he asks. His body language implies that it is clearly beyond the Koreans to build a ferry of this quality. 'You know –' he leans in conspiratorially '– Korean ferries sink all the time.' Mr Norisuke has views about the Chinese too. The Chinese are unpredictable, he says, and not to be trusted. Being Japanese, he has to be careful, particularly when travelling in rural areas. There are parts of China where the Japanese are still disliked, and though he has never experienced physical violence, he sometimes pretends to be Taiwanese to be safe.

After we disembark, I leave Mr Norisuke to his opinions and get a cab to the station. Qingdao looks to be an attractive leafy city with some appealingly shabby colonial-era buildings. Back at the beginning of China's so-called Century of Shame, when Western colonial powers were having their wicked way with the Middle Kingdom, Qingdao was the German concession city. As well as some nice *Mitteleuropa* architecture, the German legacy lingers in the local fast-food joints, which offer sausage burgers and Tsingtao, which is still one of the biggest beer brands in China.

Qingdao station is an impressive affair – huge, well-ordered, clean. As my journey continues, the stations will grow in grandeur until Shanghai, the main concourse of which is perhaps the largest building I have ever been inside. There is something Swiftian about travelling in modern China. This is one of those lands where everything is out of scale, or out of kilter, and never more so than in the railway stations.

The train I take to Beijing is punctual to the minute, spacious, modern and, according to the display over the carriage entrance, at times hits 306 kilometres per hour. We travel through scenery smothered in a smudgy brown gauze of pollution. Rural China is a compelling mix of heavy industry, smoking chimneys, high-rise apartments, smaller lower-rise settlements of boxy terraces and industrial-scale farmland. Evidently, this is where some of the food comes from to feed 1.37 billion people. At one point in my journey for at least forty minutes I look out upon an endless vista of polytunnels. Considering the speed at which we are travelling, we have probably just passed through a region the size of Belgium.

24

Harbin I

Shiro Ishii was born at the end of the nineteenth century in Shibayama, east of Tokyo close to modern-day Narita airport. Photographs of Ishii in his late twenties show a bespectacled figure with a jutting jaw and an oversized overcoat who looks barely in his teens. In 1920 he graduated from the department of medicine at Kyoto Imperial University. A dedicated, serious and clearly ambitious young man, Ishii would go on to marry the daughter of the university president.

Ishii had a special interest in bacteria, and in 1928 he visited Europe to research historical plagues. Four years later he patented a revolutionary device to purify water which would become known as the Ishii Purifier; he also helped to establish a bacterial research laboratory at the Army Medical School in Tokyo.

This was a turbulent time in the Japanese capital. Against a backdrop of severe economic depression, a militarist elite was working, sometimes violently with mutiny and assassinations, to undermine the cabinet, suppress democracy and enhance the power of the emperor. The militarists were much encouraged by the success of the Japanese Kwantung Army, which in 1931 had taken it upon itself to invade Manchuria in north-eastern China using the pretext of a staged sabotage of one of its own railway lines known as the Mukden or Manchurian Incident. In February 1932, having gone fully rogue, the Kwantung Army then attacked Harbin, one of the largest cities in the region, and installed the last emperor of Qing China, Pu-yi, as puppet ruler of Manchukuo, the name it gave to the areas of northern China and Inner Mongolia it had conquered. The invasion was condemned by the Western world; America, which had major economic interests in China, imposed trade sanctions. In response, Japan quit the League of Nations and became gripped by a kind of war fever, its sense of invincibility fuelled by snowballing military successes and the approval of all this by its 'divine' emperor. Popular support propelled the imperial army to the walls of Beijing, after which, in 1936, Japan entered a pact with Germany and Italy and expanded further into China.

In the midst of all this, Ishii's bacterial lab was transferred to Harbin in 1933, where it was renamed the Kwantung Army Epidemic Prevention Squad. That was merely a cover for an institution which is now better known by its code name, Unit 731, where the young microbiologist oversaw the world's largest research centre dedicated to creating bacterial weapons. This work involved fifty different bacteria and germs, including plague, cholera, anthrax and tuberculosis, with systemised human experimentation and live vivisection.

Unit 731 began in a small basement in the centre of Harbin with experiments on two groups of so-called bandits – the first subjected to a five-minute phosgene poisonous gas experiment, the second injected with 15 millilitres of potassium cyanate, then given 20,000-volt shocks, which burned them alive. In 1939, after some prisoners escaped, the centre was moved to a more secure base in the suburb of Pingfang. The new complex was purpose-built, with a high-voltage fence and three-metre protective ditch. Within its grounds, Ishii would go on to oversee the development of aggressive biological agents, conduct experiments into the effects of bio weapons through testing on humans, animals and plants, and work on epidemic prevention and water purification for the military. Up to 3,500 staff and prisoners were housed on the site, which later gained its own airstrip.

Ishii's prisoners – Chinese, Russian and Korean – were well fed and encouraged to take exercise in order to keep them fit for the experiments, which included exposure to temperatures of $-27°$Celsius to determine the effect of frostbite on Japanese troops fighting in Mongolia. Victims would be laid on their backs, tied to stretchers, some would have bare hands and wear wet socks, others wet gloves and undersized boots, or they would be drunk or have empty stomachs. Others were exposed to airborne infection and poisonous gas, or infected by explosive devices or given deadly injections. Often the prisoners would be subject to vivisection without anaesthetic; medical gauze was stuffed into their mouths to muffle the screams.

The victims were criminals, suspected resistance fighters, spies or often just local Chinese that the Japanese military police didn't like the look of – 'irredeemable recidivists'. Once prisoners had been designated for 'special transfer' to Unit 731, they were dehumanised in the manner of German concentration camp inmates, and referred to as *maruta* – 'logs'. More than 600 prisoners are believed to have died each year.

With Japan's supplies of metals and minerals severely restricted by American embargoes, germ warfare came to be seen as a more sustainable method of killing people than bombs and bullets, and Unit 731 took on a vital role in the war effort. According to some calculations, the facility propagated quantities of deadly bacteria sufficient to wipe out the entire population of the earth.

Germ warfare was used on the battlefield for the first time by the Japanese in July 1939, when a suicide squad from Unit 731 dropped 22.5 kilograms of liquid cholera, typhoid and other bacteria into the Khalkha river in the border regions of China and Mongolia, where the Japanese were fighting the Russians. As the war continued, several more bacteria warfare research centres were set up by Ishii in China: in Nanjing, Changchun, Guangzhou and Beijing, as well as in Singapore and elsewhere in the rapidly expanding Japanese empire.

In 1940, in Quzhou, Japanese aircraft dropped plague-infected wheat germ and other crop seeds over the land. The following year, Unit 731 conducted attacks on Zhejiang, Jiangxi and Nanjing, and in 1941 initiated germ warfare in Changde, Hunan Province. In all, Chinese historians claim that the Japanese used biological weapons 1,919 times in twenty provinces in China.

A few days after arriving in Beijing, I take a train up to Harbin, eight hours north. A couple more hours and I would reach the Siberian and North Korean borders. I am going to visit the Japanese Germ Warfare Experimental Base Museum, built ten years ago on the site of Unit 731. I take a taxi to the museum, an hour from the city centre out in a semi-industrial zone, just across the road from a massive Ford factory. The main building is housed in a sleek black granite monolith. It could be a Scandinavian art museum but for a plaque which reads that it stands as 'a memorial against Fascism alongside the concentration camps of Europe and the zero ground of Hiroshima, reminding the whole world of the need to unite in keeping peace and opposing war'.

Some Japanese still deny the true purpose of Unit 731, but the museum is pretty convincing, not because of the wealth of material evidence it presents, but because of its scarcity. There are some microscopes, fumigators, scalpels, gas masks, the unthinkable 'viscera racks' and 'tooth hooks' – most of which have been handed in by locals over the years – but not much more in terms of physical evidence. The museum could easily have been curated as an exercise in emotive anti-Japanese propaganda but instead it presents its grisly facts in a relatively straightforward manner using eye-witness testimony, much of it from Japanese veterans, academics and journalists.

I take a walk through the grounds, mostly excavated foundations sheltered by open-sided sheds, like Roman ruins often are in Europe. Signs mark the former purpose of each building in the complex, which was built according to German plans. In the so-called Square Building, large-scale experiments were conducted on healthy living captives into bubonic plague, anthrax, cholera, tuberculosis and typhoid. Near the site of the Freezing Lab, a two-storey building which was hermetically sealed to enable experiments to be carried out year round, I see a small sign: GROUND SQUIRREL BREEDING ROOM. The Japanese also bred mice, rabbits, donkeys, monkeys and horses for experimentation.

One newly arrived junior member of Unit 731, a keen rider, later recalled his first encounter with the horses: 'I didn't see the supervisors, therefore I mounted the nearest tethered horse. I said, "Go, go." "What are you doing!" an angry voice came suddenly. Two researchers wearing protective clothing were greatly frightened and ran towards me.' The young man was stripped and sterilised from head to foot. The horse, he later discovered, had been deliberately infected with glanders bacteria, an infectious disease of horses and cattle which was considered for use against humans. Unit 731 also explored various delivery methods for their weapons, including bombs and spraying from aircraft, although their most outlandish idea was to float balloon bombs across the Pacific to the US mainland.

Ishii was one of four brothers. An elder brother died in the Russo-Japanese War of 1904–5, and Ishii would later arrange for the two others to work with him in Harbin – one as a body burner, the other as a veterinary technician, looking after the experimental animals. Many others who worked at Unit 731 were also blood relations or from his home town, classmates or former students, all the better to maintain secrecy.

On 9 August 1945, Unit 731 learned that the Red Army was heading its way. Ishii ordered his staff to destroy all evidence of their work in the furnace. His brother Tadaotoko was given responsibility for killing the remaining prisoners with poison gas or by shooting, and cremating the corpses. The Japanese bombed the complex on 10 August, but infected mice and fleas survived, and plague broke out in Pingfang. In all, 143 people would die of plague in Harbin over the next nine years.

By the time Japan surrendered, most of those who had worked at Unit 731 had fled to Japan via Busan. They had strict orders never to contact each other, identify one another or continue in any way the work of the unit. Some were captured by the Russians, including Kiyoshi Kawashima, head of its Division 1, who at his trial in 1945 testified that there had been over 3,000 deaths at Unit 731 between 1940 and 1945 alone. Several other Unit 731 veterans who made it back to Japan ignored their orders and formed veterans' associations. None was ever punished. Indeed, as the museum in Harbin puts it, many 'reaped exorbitant profits by opening private hospitals and pharmaceutical companies ... [and] occupied important positions in Japanese medical circles'. One, Masaji Kitano, worked in a private medical clinic in Japan and lived until 1986. The man in charge of frostbite research, Hisato Yoshimura, went to work in a medical college. The former head of the anthrax section, Uemura Hazime, joined the Japanese ministry of education. One veteran became vice governor of Hokkaido, another the president of the health school of Japan's Self Defence Forces.

In the 1980s and 90s many Unit 731 veterans offered detailed witness statements describing the atrocities they committed. Some defended their actions as a necessity of war. Others, like Yoshio Shinozuka, who went to work in Unit 731 aged just fifteen, confessed as a form of atonement and appeared as witnesses in Japanese courts to the army's crimes on behalf of Chinese survivors and their families. Japanese journalists and academics have also thoroughly researched the history of Unit 731, perhaps to a greater extent than their Chinese and Korean peers, and as with the Korean comfort women, Japanese lawyers have assisted the relatives of victims in bringing civil suits against the Japanese authorities. Yet there are still Japanese academics responsible for school history textbooks who deny that human experimentation took place in Harbin. In a 2002 BBC *Correspondent* documentary, 'Unit 731', journalist Anita McNaught brought along a suitcase full of evidence – she could barely carry it up the steps to his office – to present to one textbook author, Nobukatsu Fujioka, a professor of education at Tokyo University. Initially he said there was no evidence. Presented with the contents of the suitcase, he claimed it was falsified.

There is plenty of criticism of Japanese deniers of Unit 731 at the museum in Harbin, which talks of 'the right-wing forces' distortion of Japan's history of aggression, gilding its invasion against, and occupation of, other countries with a veneer of respectability, and the revival of the unhealthy tradition of militarism'. It also displays a photograph taken in 2013 of Shinzo Abe at the Japanese base in Higashimatsushima, Miyagi Prefecture. Abe is sitting inside the cockpit of a T-4 trainer jet, smiling and giving a thumbs up. On the side of the plane is the number 731. The caption reads: 'It is inconceivable that Shinzo Abe could not be fully aware of the history of Unit 731. His action reflects the fact that mainstream Japanese society refuses to admit to, reflect on, or apologise for its war responsibilities.'

Ishii fled to Japan on 12 August 1945. He faked his own death, and a funeral was held for him in his home town on 10 November 1945. American investigators eventually tracked him down to Kanazawa, where he was hiding in a shrine functioning as a kind of ad hoc base for Unit 731. The Americans had their own biological warfare centre in Fort Detrick, Maryland, where they were of course prohibited from experimenting on people, and so they were keen to learn what Ishii knew. 'Such information could not be obtained in our own laboratories because scruples attached to human experimentation,' read a report by the US investigators.

Ishii was interrogated at length, initially downplaying the potential of germ warfare: 'In a winning war there is no necessity for using BW [biological weapons] and in a losing war there is not the opportunity to use BW effectively. You need a lot of men, money and materials to conduct research into BW.' He admitted to tests on 'small animals' but denied planning and carrying out biological warfare. But as he came to understand his testimony would not be used or even referred to at the Tokyo Trials, Ishii began to open up and eventually offered all of his research to the United States in return for all charges against him and his team being dropped.[16] He always denied the work of Unit 731 was officially sanctioned by Tokyo, and claimed until his death that the emperor had no knowledge of their research, telling one interrogator, 'The emperor is a lover of humanity and never would have consented to such a thing.' In fact, Hirohito gave the order to deploy biological weapons in a directive bearing his seal in July 1937. He was fully aware, and fully approved, of Unit 731. Ishii died of laryngeal cancer on 9 October 1959, at home in Tokyo, aged sixty-seven.

How is all of this viewed in China today? At the museum I read the results of a survey carried out by UNESCO as part of the museum's application for World Heritage Site status. Surprisingly, the majority

[16] Recent revelations suggest the Americans later deployed plague-infected fleas in the war with North Korea, using Japanese techniques.

of locals in Harbin did not even know about Unit 731 or the museum. Some 76 per cent believed that not all the people of Japan should be lumped together with its right-wingers, while 55 per cent felt that the world should not condemn present-day Japanese.

As I am leaving, I chat briefly with the clerk at the information counter. She says the museum receives 300,000 visitors a year. I ask if many are Japanese. Not so many, she says. Perhaps a couple a week, mostly students. However, it does seem that the facts surrounding Unit 731 are finally achieving mainstream acceptability in Japan. In August 2017 the Japanese national broadcaster, NHK, screened a documentary about Unit 731 featuring the testimony of former staff members, and in April 2018 a list of 3,607 of the unit's personnel dating from January 1945 was published by a Japanese academic at Shiga University.

As I rode in the taxi back to my hotel in the centre of Harbin, I thought about the right-wingers in Japan who claim those who have gone on the record about their time working in Unit 731 have been brainwashed by the Chinese. Do the deniers genuinely believe the unit never existed? Or are they convinced that Japan's Asian war was just and that any action, no matter how morally repugnant today, was justified by the conflict? I suspect that at least some of their resistance comes from wanting to deny ammunition to 'Japan bashers', particularly those Chinese and Korean politicians who use attacks on Japan to boost their popularity. But if the Japanese think such issues are going to fade away quietly, they are very much mistaken. Both the Chinese and the Koreans are determined to memorialise Japanese crimes, and, as I would find out, their efforts show no signs of diminishing.

25

Harbin II

On the morning of 26 October 1909, just before Japan annexed Korea, Hirobumi Ito, the former prime minister of Japan and close friend of the Meiji emperor, arrived at Harbin station, at that time a Russian enclave within Chinese territory. Hirobumi had been negotiating with the Russian finance minister, Kokovtsov, in the wake of the defeat of Russia in the 1905 war and Japan's growing presence in Korea, now effectively its protectorate.

Waiting for Hirobumi at the station with a gun hidden in his lunchbox was a Korean resistance fighter called Ahn Jung-geun. As Hirobumi descended the steps from the train and began to walk along the platform, Ahn emerged from the shadows and fired several shots, killing him. The Russians arrested Ahn but quickly handed him over to the Japanese, who tried and executed him. As with the assassination of Franz Ferdinand a few years later, the killing of Hirobumi had major repercussions throughout east Asia, although it is viewed very differently today by the Koreans and Japanese: the former revere Ahn as a hero, the latter consider him a terrorist.

In Seoul a week earlier I had visited a beautiful museum dedicated to Ahn. Understandably, South Korea today takes the veneration of those who fought for independence against the Japanese very seriously, to the extent, some say, of exaggerating the scale and achievements of the resistance. In the annual presidential Liberation Day speech in 2018, Moon Jae-in claimed, for instance, 'The struggles of the Korean people for independence were more relentless than those in any country around the world. National liberation was not given simply from the outside.' I wonder whether the French, whose resistance to the Germans was pretty significant, or the Americans, who liberated Korea, would agree?

The four glass cubes which house the Ahn Museum could not be more prestigiously located, in Namsan Park, on the hill which dominates central Seoul. Inside, the museum explained the context of Japan's annexation of Korea following what it called the thirty years of 'national crisis' which had started with the Ganghwa Treaty of 1876 through to the full annexation of Korea in 1910. Ahn Jung-geun was born in the midst of all this in 1879. As a young man, he converted to Catholicism and later travelled to Shanghai in an attempt to meet the provisional government of the Republic of Korea in exile there. Ahn returned to Korea when his father died in 1906 and, according to the museum, vowed not to touch a drop of alcohol until Korea achieved independence. Not content with teetotalism, Ahn and his comrades also cut off the first joint of their ring fingers while swearing an oath to restore the independence of Korea. One exhibit in the museum recreated the aftermath of this voluntary maiming with a bloody severed fingertip resting, spotlit, upon a folded handkerchief.

In 1908 Ahn left for Siberia, aiming to raise an army to attack the Japanese. He hatched his plan to assassinate Hirobumi while visiting Harbin. The museum has a full-size tableau recreating the moment he fired the fatal shot. Photographs show him after his arrest with chains around his waist, a handsome young man with a broad open face, high forehead and wispy moustache. He claimed to be a lieutenant general in the Korean Righteous Army and therefore a prisoner of war. 'I did not kill for vengeance,' Ahn wrote in his statement to the Japanese. 'I killed for the peace of east Asia.' Despite massive international interest in the case – *The Times* reported, 'Japan's modern civilisation was as much on trial as any of the prisoners' – the death sentence was passed and Ahn was executed on 26 March 1910.

Four years after the Ahn Museum opened in Seoul, the South Korean president, Park Geun-hye, persuaded the Chinese to open a memorial museum to Ahn within Harbin station itself. Park knew that any kind of antagonism towards Japan played well with the South Korean electorate, and the Chinese authorities perhaps also realised that they could make political capital out of the friction Ahn still generates between Japan and South Korea. At the museum's opening a Chinese foreign ministry spokesperson, Qin Gang, said, 'If Ahn Jung-geun were a terrorist [as some Japanese claim], what about the fourteen Class A war criminals of World War II honoured in the Yasukuni shrine?'

I thought I would try to see this new museum in Harbin station while I was in the city, and head off there the next morning from my hotel.

Harbin is home to about ten million people, and everything about it, from the apartment blocks to the public squares, department stores and government buildings, is constructed on a gigantic scale. The city has developed so quickly there seems to have been no time for the niceties of suburbs or commuter belts or planning, just forests of beige tower blocks, their facades already crumbling, then arable land, then industrial zones, each placed seemingly at random. The exception is Zhongyang Dajie, the rather lovely tree-lined main shopping street, where you can still sense some of the city's Russian-Jewish past as you walk beneath the Chinese flags which fly from flagpoles by the kerbside.

In the late nineteenth century the Russians had persuaded the Chinese to allow them to use Harbin as the administrative centre for the Trans-Siberian Railway, connecting Russia to the year-round warm waters of Port Arthur – near present-day Dalian on the western side of the Korean peninsula. Moscow encouraged thousands of Jews to move to what was little more than a village on the banks of a river, promising them relief from the periodic pogroms which erupted in European Russia. After the 1917 revolution, the Jewish community in Harbin became the driving force of the city's economy and business, as well as its flourishing cultural life, but conditions for the Jews deteriorated with the arrival of the Japanese in 1931, and most of Harbin's Jewish community eventually left for Australia and Palestine.

A reputation as a centre for classical music is one legacy of Harbin's Jewish heritage; a ragbag of baroque, Renaissance and art nouveau buildings also survives. Some have been restored and bear plaques explaining their history, written in a rather Borat-esque style (one referred to it having been owned by 'a Jew named P.A. Birkwiky', for instance; another had a plaque explaining it once housed 'the National Bank of Jews'). Other Russian remnants include onion-domed Orthodox churches and wedding-cakey early-twentieth-century banks and department stores, one of which houses the tourist information office. I go in to find out more about the city's history and current attractions, but the staff seem genuinely alarmed that an actual tourist is asking them questions, so I leave before causing them any further distress.

Back on the cobbled Zhongyang Dajie, all the familiar European luxury brands are present, and many shops also sell Russian blueberries, vodka, furs and dolls. That piece of music, the one that always seems to accompany cossack dancing, blares from many of the buildings. In a square halfway down the street, couples are ballroom dancing, and further down a Russian orchestra is playing to a small audience. There is also an unexpectedly prominent Japanese presence on the streets – sushi and tako-yaki restaurants, a clothing brand called Harajuku and Japanese fast-food chains like Yoshinoya, but on only one of Harbin's historic buildings do I find any reference to the Japanese era. Perhaps tellingly, the building is a semi-derelict stumpy little tower. Its plaque is badly cracked and covered with paint drips and merely notes that the tower had been 'built and used by Japanese in the 1930s'.

Finally I arrive at the south side of Harbin station but I am separated from it by many, many lanes of fast-moving traffic. I try for several minutes to cross but the risk of death is significant. A man with two squirrels on leads walks by and I am momentarily distracted. I resort to trying to hail a taxi just to cross the road, but none will stop.[17] Eventually, an old man on a moped pulls up alongside me and beckons me to climb on the back. The man has a broad and friendly smile revealing Gothic teeth. He is wearing an open-faced pink helmet and tatty leather jacket. He has no spare helmet and his bike is as decrepit as his dentistry, but this is my only chance to reach the station, so I hop on the back.

The man takes off at buttock-clenching pace and weaves us through the cars and lorries to the other side, where I disembark a little shakily, give him a few notes and thank him with the enthusiasm of the condemned man reprieved.

It turns out not have been worth either of our efforts. After wandering around the station for a while I am told by a railway functionary that the Ahn exhibition hall has been removed. Apparently, this happened soon after the Americans installed their THAAD anti-missile system in South Korea. Ahn's memory really was then nothing more than a pawn in a political game.

---

[17] Taxis were an interesting experience in Harbin. Most of them smelled as if the previous passengers had shat themselves and then died. Worse, one of them played Kenny G for my entire, hour-long ride. Also, in Harbin it is apparently perfectly normal for your taxi to stop during the journey to take on other passengers. The first time this happened I wondered if I was being abducted. The taxi driver pulled over to pick up a man with a suitcase who climbed in the front without even acknowledging me. We proceeded as normal to my destination, where I was (over-) charged for the trip. The second time, I was in the front passenger seat and a father and son climbed in the back. We had a brief friendly sign-language exchange and actually it was rather cosy.

26

Beijing

I always understood that World War II began on 1 September 1939 when Britain and France declared war on Germany, but there is a strong argument that it started by accident more than two years earlier, right here at the Marco Polo Bridge on 7 July 1937.

The exact chain of events has always been disputed. What we do know is that there was a skirmish between Japanese and Chinese nationalist troops stationed beside a bridge in Wanping, ten miles south-west of Beijing. Some say the Japanese accused the Chinese of kidnapping one of their soldiers, demanded to be allowed access to the nationalists' camp to retrieve him, but were denied. Another version has the Chinese troops opening fire on a group of Japanese soldiers who refused to answer a 'Friend or foe?' challenge. Whatever the truth, the Marco Polo Bridge Incident pushed the strained relations between China and Japan into a full-on war lasting eight years and resulting in 14 million deaths and 80 million refugees.

Beijing was still under Chinese nationalist rule at the time, but Japanese troops had been stationed outside Wanping since 1901 as part of an agreement following the Boxer Rebellion, an anti-colonial uprising which had been crushed by an alliance of Western and Japanese forces. In 1937 the demoralised Chinese 29th army was stationed within spitting distance of Japanese troops exultant about their military successes in northern China and hungry for more action. A militarist faction in Tokyo had been urging further expansion in China, but other players, including the emperor, were concerned this would weaken the Japanese front with Russia. The shots fired at the Marco Polo Bridge that night would take the decision out of their hands.

*

I have taken the train to Wanping after returning to Beijing from my Harbin trip and walk across the elegant white granite bridge decorated with hundreds of carved lions. Foreigners have always referred to the bridge by the name of the Italian traveller who first brought it to the attention of the West, describing it as being 'so beautiful that there is hardly another that can rival it', but it isn't actually called the Marco Polo Bridge; in China it is known as the Lugou Bridge and is the oldest in the country, dating from 1192. Remarkably, it was still carrying motorised traffic as recently as the 1980s.

I walk on through Wanping's impressive double gate and city walls, which still bear bullet holes from the fighting of 1937. There is a touristy high street on which I find the Museum of the War of China's Resistance Against Japanese Aggression. As with the vast National Museum in central Beijing, which I had visited the previous day, this also claims that Mao's communists resisted and defeated Japan almost single-handedly after Chiang Kai-shek's nationalists 'gave away' north-east China to the Japanese.

To the Communist Party of China (CPC) history is a malleable thing, to be altered according to its needs. Previously, Chinese children have been taught that the war started here in 1937, but it is now being described in Chinese school history textbooks as the 'Fourteen-Year War of Resistance against Japanese Aggression', back-dated to the original invasion of Manchuria in 1931. One thing does remain constant: the crimes of the Kwantung Army. This is how the museum presents them:

> They brutally slaughtered, persecuted and destroyed Chinese people ... cruelly killed war captives, enslaved laborers, forced 'comfort women' into service, launched bacterial and chemical warfares, conducted colonialism in occupied regions, promoted enslaving education, poisoned the Chinese people with opium, controlled China's economic lifelines in areas such as mining, transportation, culture, finance and trade and plundered

China's economic and cultural resources, committing numerous criminal offences, bringing forth great sufferings to the Chinese people and leaving the darkest page in the history of modern civilisation.

In the final rooms of the museum is the evidence, including numerous gruesome photographs of slaughtered Chinese people. One shows five severed heads dangling from a post; others feature villagers being buried alive by Japanese troops, the corpses of toddlers poisoned in the May 1942 Beituan massacre in Hebei Province, corpses covering the riverbank in Nanjing, and one picture of live prisoners being used for bayonet practice. Beside the photos is a Japanese torture device, supposedly used in China in the 1930s: a cylindrical metal cage, its interior lined with spikes, into which victims were placed and rolled around.

Though just about everything has changed in the fabric and psyche of this country since 1945, the war lives on in the collective memory of the Chinese people, and not just thanks to museums such as this; they are also reminded of Japanese crimes daily via their televisions.

Virtually every day in my various hotel rooms as I travelled through eastern China, flicking through the TV channels I would come across a drama about the war. These series tend to conform to a basic template: the Japanese officers are pantomime sadists, moustache-twirling baddies, pitiless in their slaughter of innocents, while the Chinese troops are light-hearted, uncomplicatedly heroic, ready to sacrifice their lives for their comrades. And good-looking. Among their number there was always an improbably young and attractive woman, whose beau was usually captured by the Japanese and tortured, sometimes to death, accompanied by maniacal cackling. In the end, however, the cowardly Japanese would always be undone by some brilliantly clever plan concocted by the Chinese – who were always communists, never nationalists.

Similar anti-Japanese wartime dramas are hugely popular in South Korea. In Seoul a week or so earlier I had been to see a new movie,

The Battleship Island, directed by Ryoo Seung-wan, set in the final weeks of World War II and following a group of desperate unemployed Koreans tricked by the Japanese into working as forced labourers in the notorious coal mines of Hashima Island. It focused on a bandleader – a widower – and his eight-year-old daughter. The film was easy enough to follow even in Korean. Again, all of the Japanese characters were sadists: the camp commander actually did have a twirly moustache, another officer had a Hitler moustache. Spoiler alert: at the last end of the film the bandleader dies in his daughter's arms.

It was the very last seconds of the film which stayed with me: the daughter is in tears at her father's death but then she suddenly stops crying and looks defiantly straight into the camera. That look – expressing determination, hatred, revenge and, I guess, *han* – electrified those around me in the huge Imax cinema in Seoul. As the house lights went up, the young woman in the seat next to me was sobbing loudly. I turned to see an elderly Korean couple behind me. The wife was struggling down the stairs, so I gave her my hand. 'Did you understand it?' the woman asked me. I did, I said. What did she think of it? I asked. 'The Japanese,' she replied with a stern look. 'We must never forget what they did to us.' *The Battleship Island* went on to break South Korean box office records.

'Chinese people don't really take those entertainments seriously,' Dr Sun Cheng, a former foreign policy adviser to the Chinese government, tells me when I meet him later in the day at my hotel in central Beijing. On his visits to Tokyo, Japanese politicians often used to complain to Dr Cheng that China should restrict these kinds of dramas, but he didn't take any notice. 'You know, the viewers see the Japanese soldiers are so weak, and they ask, "Well, why did the war continue for eight years then?"'

A Chinese student I talk to in Shanghai later in my trip tells me, 'The younger generation are tired of those grand nationalistic dramas. They are all *so* melodramatic.' He admits that his peers could still be quite nationalistic, 'but they aren't xenophobic', and he says anti-Japanese comments online often provoke disagreement.

'They'll write, "Why are you talking about this? We're trying to watch a food video!"' Another Chinese student I correspond with via email confirms that his peers don't really buy the CPC's nationalism: 'If someone sings the national anthem loudly in school, all their classmates will think they are really funny.'

But forces within the Communist Party of China – not to mention the South Korean entertainment industry – clearly believe it is worth keeping anti-Japanese sentiment simmering until, as happens from time to time, they need it to boil over. One example of this came in 2012 following the nationalisation of the disputed Diaoyu/Senkaku Islands by the Japanese government. They have been the source of ongoing tension between Japan and China and Taiwan for years. In 1996 some silly buggers from a right-wing Japanese group stunt-landed on the islands (forbidden by the Japanese because they know it upsets the Chinese) and built a lighthouse. Cue protests in China and Taiwan, and more silly buggers, this time from Hong Kong, carried out their own landing. There was another bust-up in 2010 when a Chinese fishing trawler hit a Japanese patrol boat near the islands, but in 2012 it all really kicked off when another band of silly buggers from Hong Kong landed again, setting off further tit-for-tat landings.

In Beijing the Japanese ambassador's limousine was attacked, a man ripping the flag from its bonnet. Ambassador Uichiro Niwa, inside the car at the time, was shaken but unhurt. 'They were only students,' Niwa, now seventy-nine, told me when I met him in Tokyo. 'I was a student demonstrator in the 60s – I had the same experience. He was a young, crazy boy. I am not afraid of that.' Meanwhile, Shintaro Ishihara, governor of Tokyo and an outspoken nationalist, was campaigning to raise funds to buy three of the islands from their Japanese owners. Ironically, Niwa was, and remains, a moderate and warned against privatisation. Still, the attack on his ambassadorial car shocked Japan, and Niwa was recalled to Tokyo. The Japanese government proceeded to purchase three of the islands for around £16 million in an attempt to damp down the issue, but the Chinese reacted again with violent protests in several cities over three days, forcing Japanese factories in China to close temporarily. Some believe the protests were staged or encouraged by the Chinese government – or at the very least, they could have prevented them; it's not like they don't have expertise in controlling public protests, after all.

These days Japan does seem to have the most substantial claim to the islands, but they would be of great value to China militarily because they lie in a crucial sea lane between Taiwan and Japan. Ownership would also bring an expansion of China's 'exclusive economic zone', allowing it to tap the oil, gas and other mineral reserves which are believed to lie beneath the seabed around the islands. These are not to be sniffed at; one estimate put the reserves as enough to fuel China for eighty years or more. But, as with the Dokdo / Takeshima Islands dispute with South Korea, from the point of view of the Japanese, it is as much a demonstration of resolve on their part. The issue remains on standby, one feels, should it need to be reactivated by the Chinese.

'Personally, I am very worried, very pessimistic about the future of these two countries,' Dr Sun Cheng tells me when I ask him for his more general predictions for Sino-Japanese relations. He points to the collapse of the Soviet Union in the early 1990s as the moment when relations began to deteriorate. The USSR was a kind of common enemy for Japan, the US and even China, but these days China sees Japan and the US as rivals, particular in maritime terms. 'Japan thinks China is a threat, but China doesn't think Japan is a significant threat. China really wants to get a good relationship with Japan, but it seems that Japan doesn't want to establish a good relationship with China.' Dr Sun places a good deal of the blame for poor post-war China–Japan relations on the Americans, drawing a comparison with post-war Europe. 'They supported the uniting of Europe to fight back against the Soviet Union, so Germany gave very strong and firm apologies, but the United States has not supported Asian unity in the same way because China had a different political ideology.'

Things are escalating militarily. China now has the world's second largest armed forces while Japan's military spending is at its highest level ever. In 2018 the countries spent £133 billion and £38 billion on their respective militaries. Writing in the *Guardian* recently, former Beijing correspondent for the *Financial Times* Richard McGregor warned that the two countries could go to war 'within the coming decades'. The oft-quoted Thucydides Trap posits that, as with Sparta and Athens, a rising power and an existing great power are destined to go to war. It has almost become a cliché to predict this outcome for China and the US, but it is not unthinkable that Japan could be China's opponent in a future conflict. Dr Cheng believes that the two countries have lost all mutual trust, partly because 'The Japanese government doesn't teach their citizens enough about the war.'

I point out that NHK, the Japanese state broadcaster, had recently screened a thorough investigation of Unit 731. The Chinese were 'really happy about that', Dr Cheng said, but he thinks that Japan's growing militarism is creating instability. Japan has always had this idea of itself as the saviour of Asia in the face of Western imperialism, something which Dr Sun feels is rather ironic given that after the war Japan became a de facto colony of America. 'Japan needs to learn to respect contemporary China and what it has achieved and get rid of this superiority complex. Unless it does this, there are only going to be problems in the future,' he tells me. He believes China is seeking better relations with Korea as a bulwark against Japan, and that should the North and South reunify and the Americans leave, Korea will become an ally of China. That will be bad news for Japan and America. 'It is one of the most complicated issues in the world,' he sighs.

Not everyone agrees with predictions of war between China and Japan. Ren Xiao, of the Institute of International Studies at Fudan University in Shanghai and previously first secretary at the Chinese embassy in Tokyo, told me the idea was a 'ridiculous' prospect. Everyone was militarising, he said, but things had stabilised between the two countries and, besides, Japan was only a middle-ranking power and had been for years. 'China's GDP is now more than double Japan's.' As a result, the Chinese didn't really worry that much about the Japanese, although that was a difficult thing for the Japanese to adjust to, more in terms of their state of mind than anything.

'As a nation, as a people, they are ambiguous, vague,' Xiao added. He felt the Japanese had not 'sincerely condemned' their past, pointing to history textbooks which describe the imperial army as 'entering' China, rather than 'invading' it. He firmly believed there was such a thing as national character, and that the Japanese had been shaped by being an island nation. 'They always reserve something. I know Americans who have interacted with Chinese, Koreans and Japanese, and they always find that Chinese are easier to make friends with. If you compare the Japanese to Germans [in terms of war apologies], there must be something very deeply different in their psyches.'

Now we were getting to the nub of the matter. Dr Sun Cheng had said something similar: 'The Japanese mind is different from other people's.' He and Xiao were suggesting that, deep down, in their very souls, there was something *not quite right* about the Japanese – an indifference, a lack of empathy, a superiority complex – which makes them capable of committing the grossest atrocities upon their fellow men. I had heard – and would hear – this again and again from Koreans and Chinese during my travels.

The Chinese television journalist Wenming Dai said it to me when I met her in Shanghai: 'There is something wrong with the Japanese national character: it can go to extremes. When they make things, they make them perfect, they go to extremes. When they are cruel, they go to extremes as well. I do think there is a red line which goes from that to fascism. Historians say don't generalise, but I think there is something particular about the Japanese.'

Others took an even stronger view: 'Barbarians. Savages. Devils – Japanese devils – that's the common take [from students],' Chih-yun Chang, a Taiwanese historian Dai introduced me to in Shanghai told me when I asked him about Chinese perceptions of the Japanese. Chang teaches in Shanghai and was regularly surprised by his students' views of the Japanese. '[My students think] there is something wrong with them. They are evil – as if it is a definite truth. They love Japanese culture, they like each other in many ways, but they also weigh history. The Chinese are very aware that the Japanese can be extremely savage, particularly when you are weak. There is always that awareness in the back of the mind.' One Chinese student I asked about this believed that it was bushido which set the Japanese apart. The samurai moral code – 'bushido' means 'way of the warrior' – was revived by the militarists during the later years of Japanese imperialism and focused on a kind of devotional self-sacrifice, epitomised by the act of seppuku (ritual suicide) and the kamikaze.

Certainly, trust between the two nations remains low: in a 2016 poll more than 80 per cent of Japanese people did not trust China. A 2017 joint survey of 2,500 people by Japanese think tank Genron NPO and the China International Publishing Group revealed that 90 per cent of Japanese people had an 'unfavourable' or 'relatively unfavourable' impression of China, while 67 per cent of Chinese felt that way about the Japanese. Encouragingly, 44 per cent of Chinese people wanted to visit Japan, and the percentage of Japanese people who thought that relations between China and Japan were 'bad' or 'relatively bad' had fallen to 45 per cent from 72 per cent the previous year – the first time it had gone below 50 per cent in the seven years of the survey. And both Japanese and Chinese people were more positive about the future relations between the countries.

So from some angles relations between China and Japan seem shaky, from others quite healthy. One hopeful development is the extraordinary growth in tourism from China to Japan in recent years. In 2017 a record number of tourists visited Japan – 28.7 million, up almost 20 per cent on the previous year – in large part due to increased cruise-ship traffic. Chinese made up the largest number of visitors – over 7 million – slightly ahead of South Koreans in second place, but they accounted for almost 40 per cent of tourist spending in Japan, three times the second biggest spenders, the

Taiwanese. So many Chinese tourists are flying to Nagoya that they are having to build a second runway at the airport.

'The Chinese are fans of Japanese culture, and it is a top tourist destination because, I tell you what, Japan has things China doesn't have at the moment: tranquillity, attention to details, perfectionism – that's what we don't have,' journalist Wenming Dai told me. 'And Japan is admired for being able to protect its heritage very well, while here we are losing our past.'

Despite his criticisms, former diplomat Ren Xiao was also a fan of Japan. 'There are many things China can and should learn from Japan; we will always see it as an important neighbour. It's clean, orderly, people are polite, so when they return from Japan, they only say nice things.' Dr Sun Cheng too had great respect for contemporary Japan. 'It is a highly developed country – economically, its education, science, civilisation. Their products are really high quality. We Chinese love to travel there, and, though we know our GDP has developed fast, when we go to Japan we can see that we will have a way to go to match them. We need Japanese technology, and Japan needs the Chinese market. It's a good balance.'

'My generation, we are fascinated by Japanese culture – manga, anime. I really want to visit Japan,' a Beijing-based student, Yao Guiling, told me one day when I met him for a coffee in one of the city's Hutong alleyways. Yao – English name Frank – had contacted me via email a couple of years earlier to ask some questions about a book I had written about Scandinavia, and we had kept in touch. I asked him for one word to sum up Japan. 'Harmony,' he said. 'All that Chinese people want is a harmonious relationship with Japan. We see more of a threat from America, but even America we look at as both a friend and an enemy.' The Chinese should never forget what the Japanese did to them, the 'shame' he called it, and it didn't help that he felt the Japanese still hadn't apologised properly. 'Maybe the people are sincere, and some scholars, but the government is not good. They have not said, "We did it and we are sorry from the bottom of our heart." They cannot just put history aside. Facts are facts.'

Sometimes fascination with Japanese culture expresses itself in unexpected ways. The Chinese can't get enough of Japanese porn, for instance. Former Japanese porn star Sora Aoi has over 18 million followers on Weibo, China's version of Twitter, making her more popular than most American pop and movie stars. When she announced her engagement in early 2018, the post got several million likes. And then you have *jingri*. This roughly translates as 'Japanese in spirit' and is a category of cosplay in which Chinese people, exclusively men from what I've seen, identify as Japanese. *Jingri's* particular fetish is for the pre-1945 Japanese imperial army. In 2017 two *jingri* made headlines in the Chinese media when they were arrested, dressed as Japanese imperial soldiers, posing in front of a massacre site just outside Nanjing. Others have been caught posing in costume in front of the Nanjing Massacre Memorial Hall. As a result there were calls to make wearing the old imperial Japanese military uniform illegal. China's foreign minister, Wang Yi, called them 'scum among the Chinese people'.

Back at the war museum near the Marco Polo Bridge, the final rooms bring me up to date with Sino-Japanese relations. There is a warning that the world must be on 'high alert for wrongdoings' on the part of the Japanese, such as historical revisionism, comfort women denial and Yasukuni shrine visits, but also an insistence that those relations are now characterised by 'peace and friendship'. There is a photograph from May 1995 of the Japanese prime minister Murayama Tomichi visiting the museum.

In the visitors' book he wrote, 'Face history, and pray for permanent peace between China and Japan.'

27

Qufu

I have come to see a limestone cave in the side of a mountain half an hour's drive outside the city of Qufu in Shandong Province. It's not much of a cave. I have to crouch to see inside. There are no prehistoric drawings or majestic stalactites within, but it is a very important cave because two and a half thousand years ago a baby called Kong Fuzi laid his legendarily ugly head right here and suckled from a tiger as an eagle fanned him with its wings to keep him cool in the summer heat.

Kong Fuzi is better known as Confucius, the great sage of Asia. His father, Shuliang He, was the governor of the district, so presumably the family was relatively well-to-do and of high standing. So why was his wife giving birth in such discomfort? One story has it that she was caught short on her way home, but another legend tells that Confucius was such an unsightly baby his parents abandoned him here on the side of the mountain. He was then adopted by the tiger, who brought him to this cave to feed him while the eagle kept the unprepossessing child cool.

He was worth the effort. Confucius is considered one of the greatest moral teachers in history, whose seminal writings, *The Analects*, emphasise among other things the importance of education and obedience within hierarchies. In 500 BC China was an agricultural society, so Confucius has plenty of analogies featuring yokes and ploughs. The country was also a patchwork of warring regions, not yet unified, so he has lots to say about living in harmony with others. He describes five key relationships in which one figure is duty bound to obey a superior. These are:

Ruler to subject

Master to servant

Parent to child

Husband to wife

Friend to friend (the only equal relationship, assuming it is
    between two men)

Over the centuries his teachings have come to mean all sorts of
things to all sorts of people, which makes it almost impossible to
define what Confucianism or neo-Confucianism really mean today,
let alone tease out any direct influence on how people actually live.
But I'm going to give it a go anyhow.[18]

To reach the Qufu cave I have taken a high-speed train through
the sepia scenery of eastern China. From Qufu station there was
then a notably hair-raising taxi ride to Mount Nishan in the countryside twenty miles south-east of the city. My taxi driver doesn't
so much drive as careen, the car emitting ominous death rattles as
all the dashboard warning lights flash like some mad slot machine.
At one point an alarm sounds. He pays it no heed. Outside, traffic
lights of various hues blur by. Red, green, orange – they don't
matter. They are just lights. Finally we come to a halt in some kind
of fly-tipping wasteland, the car park at the entrance to the site of
Confucius' birthplace.

There is not another soul here apart from the napping ticket clerk
in his kiosk, and I see no one else during my entire visit to the
rambling temple complex up among the pines. Where is everyone?
I had visited Bethlehem a few weeks earlier with my family and
queued for an hour as part of an unexpectedly rowdy crowd
attempting to force its way down into the subterranean cave where
Confucius' European counterpart was born. So Jesus 1, Confucius 0.

---

[18] Neo-Confucianism was an eleventh-century attempt to rid his teachings of
creeping metaphysical aspects. It retained Buddhist and Taoist elements, but was
much stricter and placed a greater emphasis on poor people knowing their place
and staying there. So, yes, quite contradictory.

Later that day, back in Qufu, I wander through the massive Confucian temple in the centre of the city and end up at the great man's grave. Again I have the place virtually to myself. On this evidence, the appeal of Confucius to modern Chinese tourists seems limited, but Qufu still milks its cash cow for all he is worth, branding itself the 'Oriental Holy City', though Confucius was neither holy, nor his philosophy a religion.

What is the truth about Confucius' influence on contemporary China and beyond? I want to find out more about the great sage in the hope that it will help me understand better why east Asian societies function as they do, but also perhaps to gain some insight into the interaction *between* the nations. I had formed a theory that Confucius' ideas had brought a uniquely toxic edge to the twentieth-century conflicts between Japan, China and Korea, and their aftermath. For centuries China had been the Middle Kingdom, the centre of the civilised world – the elder brother, in Confucian terms. From China had flowed, downwards, all the blessings of agriculture, writing, bureaucracy, porcelain, philosophy, religion and so on. These technologies and knowledge had passed through the Korean peninsula before filtering down to Japan, a process which created its own hierarchy of civilisation, prestige and power between China, Korea and Japan – a tributary system in which Korea and Japan from time to time offered symbolic gifts or paid respect to China in return for favourable status, with Korea as the middle brother and Japan as the youngest and, in the Confucian order of things, the lowest of the siblings. So, imagine the upset when for fifty years or so the little brother attacked and invaded his elder siblings, raping, pillaging and killing hundreds of thousands of Koreans and Chinese and bequeathing them a legacy of half a century more – admittedly often self-inflicted – suffering upon his departure in 1945. Japan of course also suffered the devastation of mass – and atomic – bombing the same year, but within twenty years had righted itself and, economically at least, inverted the hierarchy all over again: dominating the region as the wealthiest nation for another half-century. So the little brother had trounced his elder siblings not once but twice, a heinous Confucian transgression.

This notion of an ancient geopolitical family hierarchy in east Asia is hardly an original observation, and many take issue with it. For a start, perspectives differ depending on which state you identify with. Bruce Cumings, author of numerous books and articles on Korea, advises us not to fall into the trap of thinking of it as the middle brother. 'Korea was never "Sinicized",' he writes, adding that it would be improbable if Chinese culture simply passed down through the peninsula, unaltered, to Japan; the Koreans adapted Chinese teaching as the Romans did with Greek civilisation. 'The real story is ... the unstinting Koreanisation of foreign influence, and not vice versa.' Korea may have been a tributary state of China, or even a vassal, but this was often on Korea's terms because it suited the Koreans at the time; they required Chinese military support against Japan, for instance.

One historian I spoke to in Hong Kong – who also said some stuff which might get her into trouble, so asked not to be identified – agreed, assuring me that the Confucian order was a mirage created by the Chinese, and that from the fifteenth and sixteenth centuries onward in particular the relationships between the countries grew much more complex as maritime trade and communications expanded. 'The Chinese were simply lying to themselves, and others used that to their advantage when it suited them,' she said. The countries China viewed as vassals didn't necessarily see themselves that way. Within Korea, for example, there were always people who were pro-China, more independent-minded or even pro-Japan. Even when the Japanese and Koreans adopted Chinese ways – of writing, eating or whatever – they would do their best to make them their own as quickly as possible, 'because they felt it would make them feel and look inferior if they simply copied from the Chinese'.

Nor were the Japanese the type to accept cultural crumbs from China's lazy Susan. They were quite capable of modernising themselves, thanks in part to European influence in the sixteenth century, and, as we saw with the Imjin invasions, Japan imposed its power and technology on its neighbours too at times.

Tai Tai-kin, the *Zainichi* academic and specialist in relations between Japan and Korea I had met in Tokyo, agreed there *was* something to my Confucian hierarchy theory, but felt that it was largely a Korean fantasy. 'The Koreans believe that Japanese culture started with accepting and learning Korean culture. They think they were a huge contributor to the formation of the state of Japan during ancient times, but that Japan returned this only with aggression in the twentieth century – that is the story in South Korean textbooks.' Tai-kin told me such claims were 'nonsense' but that 'because of their closeness to China, the Koreans despised and looked down upon Japan'. He also thought that the process of Westernisation following the Meiji restoration, which saw Japan ascendant 'does bring a special sense of humiliation for Korea, that they had to be ruled by a country that they thought was lower than themselves'.

What about Confucianism as a more general influence *within* each of these societies? This too is tricky to assess. A common view of the Koreans, for instance, is that they are Confucian socially, Buddhist spiritually and shamanistic when it comes to everyday superstition. As for modern-day Japan, it is even harder to unpick Confucianism from all the other ingredients in the cultural cooking pot: Buddhism, Taoism, the cultural developments during the Tokugawa *sakoku* era, the American influence after the war and of course Shinto. But there is a great deal of Confucianism in Japan's paternalistic, highly bureaucratic, elitist style of government.

Journalist Martin Jacques identifies a key difference with the Japanese though: while Chinese Confucianism 'included benevolence among its core values, the Japanese instead laid much greater emphasis on loyalty'. This emphasis grew more pronounced over time, leading to the unquestioning emperor worship on which much of the militarism of the early twentieth century was founded. In Chinese Confucianism leaders have a responsibility to act wisely and justly, whereas in Japanese Confucianism, Jacques claims, the emphasis is on the obedience of inferiors. Incidentally, in *When China Rules the World* Jacques also suggests that China's current economic colonisation of resource-rich countries like Laos and Cambodia is evidence of a new Confucian order being imposed by Beijing.

At a fourteenth-century Confucian temple in the Chinese capital – where I spotted a photograph on display showing Japanese soldiers offering sacrifices there in 1938 – I asked a couple of visitors, two men in their early thirties, whether they felt Confucius had anything to say about contemporary China. They looked at me as if I were asking them whether foot-binding was still going on. Yet, in a recent BBC Radio 4 documentary, Rana Mitter, director of the University of Oxford China Centre, whose knowledge of China is beyond reproach, described Confucius as 'the man who gave China its cultural DNA'. Mitter believes his legacy continues into the present day.

One Chinese student I got talking to at a coffee shop just after I visited the massive temple agreed that Confucianism had had a very deep influence on his education and on contemporary Chinese society. You could see it in the way older people were respected in China today – on public transport for instance, he said. The young man believed there were important lessons to be learned from his writings – 'We very truly value them' – but conceded that they had also been misused by unscrupulous rulers to control, exploit and oppress the people.

Superficially at least, Mao Zedong and Park Chung-hee both did their best to eradicate Confucianism from their respective societies, the former because he judged it oppressively anti-egalitarian, the latter because it conflicted with his capitalistic ambitions. But you could argue that communism and Confucianism have some synergies: both address the challenge of how individuals function within collective societies, and neither have any time for mysticism or gods. Confucius was certainly an egalitarian when it came to education. And Chairman Mao's 'Little Red Book' owed at least a formal debt to the *Analects*. The CPC is keenly aware that social order in China is very much dependent on it continuing to deliver economic development and stability, which chimes with Confucian notions of the responsibility of rulers and is perhaps why the Chinese people tolerate restrictions on their liberty; even the younger Chinese I speak to never seem especially het up about democratic reform. It is a classic Confucian trade. And it is telling that the Chinese cultural centres which the state is opening around the world – its answer to the British Council – are called Confucius Institutes. Meanwhile, in terms of President Park's economic miracle in South Korea, his *chaebol* did – and still do – seem to function on Confucian principles, with the I-know-my-place deference of workers within their corporate hierarchies and the blind obedience to superiors. And the Koreans' mania for education is straight out of the Confucian playbook too.

Later on in my trip, I asked people in Taiwan whether theirs was a Confucian society. 'Not in *any* sense,' French sociologist Frank Huyard assured me, although he also denied that China was Confucian too. American lecturer and Taiwan expert Michael Turton agreed: 'The word Confucian is just tossed around by journalists, but no one ever unpacks it to see what it means. It could mean so many things. It is a Western term, used by Westerners to tell Westerners what's going on. If I tell you this is Confucian, I mean it is authoritarian and hierarchical. But when you look at the legislature in Taiwan, 40 per cent is female. There are female business owners, female academics. Women wield a lot of power here.' It does seem that Taiwan has broken free from the Confucian loop.

Accusations of generalisation, Orientalism or cultural essentialism can also be levelled at anyone suggesting that some or other behaviour has its roots here in this cave outside Qufu. For instance, the American writer Malcolm Gladwell was criticised by some in Korea when he suggested in his book *Outliers* that repeated fatal errors by Korean Air pilots were due to what he termed Korea's 'cultural legacy', by which he basically meant a Confucian deference to superiors. Gladwell implied that co-pilots were afraid to draw pilots' attention to, say, the mountain looming ahead or the flaming starboard engine – that kind of thing. His theory does seem a bit ridiculous, but then you go to Korea, you read anything about Korea or you meet actual Koreans, and, well, you can't help but see *everything* through a Confucianist filter. Korea is often held to be the most Confucian society on earth; some Koreans even claim him as one of their own, based on rather sketchy claims that Confucius' grandfather was born in Korea. The first Confucian school was founded there in AD 372 and Korea used China's bureaucratic entrance exam system for centuries. Confucian thinkers still feature on banknotes.

Confucius does get blamed for many of Korea's ills, not least by the Koreans themselves. A few years ago a book called *Confucius Must Die for the Country to Live*, laying just about every lamentable aspect of Korean society at the feet of the bearded one, was a bestseller in South Korea. The *Washington Post* ran a piece recently in which two academics similarly blamed Confucianism for the country's horrendous culture of sexual abuse and gender inequality, and the great sage is usually cited when people talk about the high-pressure approach to education in South Korea. Bruce Cumings believes Confucianism also reigns in North Korea: 'the assumption that North Korean communism broke completely with the past would blind one to continuing Confucian legacies there: its family-based politics, the succession to rule of the leader's son, and the extraordinary veneration of the state's founder, Kim Il-sung'.

Public manifestations of Korean–Confucian male entitlement occasionally go viral these days, to highly entertaining effect. When politician Kim Moo-sung, once considered a presidential hopeful, arrived at Gimpo international airport back in 2016, film footage showed him swaggering through the automatic doors of the arrivals hall, thrusting his canary-yellow suitcase off to be caught by a bowing aide who had been waiting obediently to receive it. Kim didn't acknowledge the man or even break stride but, staring straight ahead, kept on walking, presumably to his chauffeured limo, as he sent his suitcase spearing off at a tangent like a booster rocket from a space-shuttle launch. The viral video provoked amused horror worldwide, leading to discussion of the treatment of subordinates by powerful Koreans. Kim responded to the ridicule with confused indignation.

So much of how Koreans conduct themselves and interact with each other seems to be determined by Confucian hierarchies, even in the supposedly relaxed environments of bars and restaurants. When you raise your glass, you should be careful not to raise it higher than your elders or superiors, for instance. And Koreans simply cannot bear to see a solo diner refill his own glass or cup.

One night in Kwangjang market in Seoul I sat at a counter around one of the open kitchens, eating *bindaetteok* (mung bean pancakes). Beside me were two men in their early twenties, enjoying some sashimi. We exchanged pleasantries, and then they left me to my meal, but each time I went to refill my cup of *makgeolli* – a yeasty-milky fermented rice drink – they would literally flinch. The younger one, seated further from me, would instinctively reach out to take the bottle to refill my cup, just as Confucian protocol dictated, before pulling himself back. Eventually I felt compelled to ask them about this. It was an instinct, the younger man told me, laughing. Something he had done all his life. I was curious how Koreans managed this kind of social ranking on a day-to-day basis. How was one person's superiority ascertained by the parties in a conversation and then expressed?

'There is the polite way of speaking and the impolite way,' explained the elder of the two men. 'It's not so much about social status or money, although if it is obvious that someone is rich then you might be more polite to them. Age is the first, most important thing and then gender. But unfortunately older people often too easily choose the impolite way of speaking to younger people.' If in doubt, one Korean will literally ask how old the other is and adjust their mode of talking accordingly, using one of seven different forms of address. 'When you meet someone for the first time, if you think that you are going to have more to do with them in the future, you will just ask, so that you know whether to use the polite form or not.' The younger of the two will thereafter treat the elder with deference, agreeing with his opinions, laughing at his jokes, pouring his drinks and so on.

I attempted a little impromptu role play.

'So, you'd say, like, "Hi Alan, my name's John. We're going to be working on this project together ..."'

My fellow diners nodded.

'And then you'd ask, "So, how old are you?"'

'Yes, that's how it would be, right at the beginning of the conversation, just like that. Among students we might just use the impolite form, no matter what the age; there is a kind of anti-ageism culture now.'

We continued for a while with me offering various scenarios – what if you were richer than your teacher, or she was female and you were male? 'Of course, you would respect her because she is a teacher and so of higher rank than any student' – but in most circumstances women ranked lower than men.

I had assumed it was a question of using the imperative form when one was being less polite – 'Tell me the way to the station' instead of 'Would you mind telling me ...' That kind of thing. But apparently it is all in the conjugation of the verb. 'If you put something like *yo* at the end of the verb, like *ka-yo*, then that is the polite way, if you just use *ka*, then that's the impolite way,' the elder of the two told me.

Yet, even in Korea, the most Confucian society on earth, there are things which are decidedly *un*-Confucian. The way the *chaebol* are structured conforms to Confucian protocol; their bosses turning up at court in wheelchairs on intravenous drips, feigning illness and denying responsibility for their crimes, does not. An essential element of Confucianism is that leaders have a responsibility to act honourably – to 'exercise government by means of virtue', as Confucius put it – but that is rarely how the *chaebol* families operate. And where is the Confucian veneration for elders in the Korean obsession with employing plastic surgery to look younger?

*

Back in Qufu, after another taxi death race, I check in to my hotel. It is a strange place, a complex of ersatz traditional houses ranged around a concrete garden in the shadow of the old city walls. With the city empty of tourists, they have given me an entire house to myself. Designed to cater to the special requirements of Confucian scholars, it has an office with an ornately carved desk equipped with brush-pen and ink, and behind it a large bookcase lined with – I'm guessing – the works of Confucius.

On my last afternoon in Qufu I look around the temple complex. It is over a thousand years old with stone pillars carved with dragon reliefs, ancient cedar trees leaning on wooden supports and beautiful pavilions with yellow and green tiled roofs and triple upturned eaves, including the Xingtan Pavilion, where Confucius is said to have lectured. In one of the buildings are some inlaid panels depicting scenes from Confucius' life, rendered using semi-precious stones. They show the sage in the traditional manner, with flowing blue robes and triple-peaked hat. His heavyset face and thick black beard puts me in mind of a Chinese Barry White.

In the oldest existing illustrations of Confucius' life (of any Chinese life), thirty-six woodblock prints from 1444, I learn of his birth, when a unicorn came by with a heavenly book in its mouth. Unicorns were recurring visitors to Confucius, apparently. He once got very upset over the killing of a unicorn and decried the lack of morality and justice in China it implied. Then, according to the English translation, there was the time he 'lived on vegetarian [sic] and prayed to the Big Dipper'. Often dragons also descended for reasons I couldn't really follow, and on one occasion, as Confucius was praying, a rainbow appeared and then turned into a piece of yellow jade, which must have been nice.

I walk out of the temple grounds and continue past the city walls to the cemetery where Confucius was buried when he died, aged seventy-three, in 479 BC. As I stand looking at his surprisingly simple, grass-covered burial mound amid the gloomy pines, I try to sum up my conclusions about the great sage and his legacy in these countries.

All those supposedly Confucian characteristics – the emphasis on education, respect for elders, valuing the family, the desire to avoid losing face, the sexism, the entitled old men – you find them everywhere in the world, don't you? Patriarchal hierarchies and class systems are, unfortunately, universal. I think about that old *Frost Report* 'Class System' sketch with John Cleese looking down on Ronnie Barker, who looks down on Ronnie Corbett, who knows his place. Old Kong Fuzi would have nodded along contentedly to that. And plenty of countries hate each other without having 2,500 years of indoctrination by a strange-looking man raised by a tiger and an eagle upon which to place the blame.

In the late 1990s a Danish sociologist, Geir Helgesen, conducted a survey of Asians and Scandinavians which among other things asked whether or not they agreed with the proposition: 'The ideal society is like a family.' Some 80 per cent of Chinese and South Koreans agreed but so did over 70 per cent of Scandinavians, for whom Confucius is about as relevant as the preachings of cable TV evangelists. In other words, perhaps Confucius resonates for Asians simply because his teachings are universal – they speak to us all.

28

Nanjing

I arrive in Nanjing by high-speed train. Straightaway it seems like a city in which one might actually want to live, unlike sombre, neurotic Beijing or ossified Qufu.

Nanjing has been the capital of China at various points through the country's history, and it still has plenty of that grandeur with broad tree-lined avenues and lively public spaces which are transformed with futuristic light shows at night. It feels as if I have finally arrived in the twenty-first century. There is even a public bike rental scheme, although the locals tend to leave the bicycles piled as if for a bonfire on the pavement when they are finished with them.

Above all, Nanjing has really great food, a lot of it Japanese. In fact, I will see more Japanese restaurants here than in any other Chinese city: *izakaya*, sushi, ramen, *donburi* and *yakitori* places galore, and there are even Japanese convenience stores. The Hello Kitty Café is doing a roaring trade too, and in an underground mall I see Japanese patisseries, retail brands like Muji, Uniqlo and one shop just called Japanese Designer Brand. There is even a vending machine dispensing live crabs. And it doesn't get much more Japanese than that.

I resist drawing any trite conclusions about the relationship between the people of Nanjing and their former Japanese occupiers from all this but do decide to take it as an encouraging sign. At least the Japanese are not considered the mortal enemies they might be here because, for many still today, the name of this city is synonymous with one of the most depraved, large-scale war crimes ever to have been committed: the Nanjing massacre of December 1937 to January 1938.

By the autumn of 1937, the Japanese had taken Shanghai and were moving north towards Nanjing. Following months of bombing by planes flying from Nagasaki, in December 100,000 troops of the imperial army, under the command of Emperor Hirohito's uncle-by-marriage, Prince Asaka Yasuhiko, entered what was the capital of China, routing 150,000 Chinese nationalists. They were under orders to take no prisoners. The Chinese retreat turned to chaos. As the *New York Times* reported on 11 December 1937, the disarray was partly the fault of the Chinese commanders: 'In many cases the individual [Chinese] generals have been more concerned with the safety of their personal wealth and their vast landholdings in the path of the Japanese invaders than with the defence of the city.' On 13 December, many Chinese soldiers were still trapped within the city walls as the Japanese embarked on a murderous spree which lasted several weeks. The scale and nature of the killing shocked the world then as it still does today. According to one estimate, 57,000 Chinese prisoners were killed at one location alone – near Mufu Mountain, north of the city.

By this stage of their campaign, the Japanese soldiers seemed utterly desensitised. There were live burials, killing competitions, disembowellings, decapitations and death by fire. Victims were ordered into freezing ponds; others were attacked by dogs. One soldier, Nagatomi Hakudo, speaking almost sixty years later, recalled what he saw: 'Soldiers impaled babies on bayonets and tossed them still alive into pots of boiling water. They gang-raped women from the ages of twelve to eighty and then killed them when they could no longer satisfy sexual requirements. I beheaded people, starved them to death, burned them, and buried them alive, over two hundred in all. It is terrible that I could turn into an animal and do these things. There are really no words to explain what I was doing. I was truly a devil.'

One of the most notorious incidents was the killing contest between two Japanese sub-lieutenants, Mukai Toshiaki and Noda Takeshi of the Katagiri Unit, at Kuyung in the days just before Nanjing fell. The two men had a wager to see who would be first to behead one hundred Chinese. The competition was reported with great enthusiasm by the *Japan Advertiser* on 7 December 1937. In the chaos the two men lost count and so increased the target to 150 beheadings, which was also reported in the paper. Toshiaki and Takeshi were later captured by the Chinese and brought to trial in 1947. Both denied the contest, saying it was made-up propaganda. They were executed by firing squad in 1948.[19]

Estimates of the death toll between December 1937 and January 1938 range from 50,000 to 300,000 and in some cases more. The latter is the official figure quoted by the Chinese state based on evidence presented at the post-war trials held in Nanjing, but the sheer chaos of war and the massive numbers of refugees in China at the time make it impossible to arrive at a true figure. One historian told me off the record that none of the Chinese historians he had spoken to believed 300,000 died. They put the death toll at 50,000–80,000, he said, but there does seem to be a general consensus internationally, including by the Tokyo War Crimes Tribunal, of around 200,000. To put even the lower estimates into context, 61,000

---

[19] One of the swords supposedly used in the competition somehow ended up in the Taiwanese Armoury Museum in Taipei, its blade inscribed in Japanese '107 people killed in the Nanking battle'. Recently, a violent and bizarre postscript was added to the sword's story. In August 2017 a fifty-one-year-old man, Lu Chun-yi, smashed the glass case, stole the sword from the museum and walked a few hundred metres around the corner to the Presidential Office Building, where he attacked a military police officer in an attempt, it is believed, to gain entry in order to behead the president, who was in her office at the time. Lu, subsequently revealed to be suffering from mental issues, was also carrying a Chinese flag. The policeman was struck on the neck, but he survived. Members of Lu's family told investigators that he had become obsessed with television programmes from Chinese state networks, like the wartime series I had been seeing. One of his family was quoted in a Taiwanese newspaper as saying, 'These Chinese TV programmes had strong effects on him, as he became a fervent political enthusiast, with extremist pro-China views and actively supporting Taiwan returning to the "Chinese Motherland".'

British civilians and 108,000 French civilians died during the *entirety* of World War II.

The taking of Nanjing made headlines around the world even at the time. In his *Sonnets from China*, published in 1939, W. H. Auden drew a clear line from the Chinese capital to the Nazi death camps in his poem 'Here War Is Simple'.

And maps can really point to places
Where life is evil now:
Nanking; Dachau

Today there are Japanese people who deny the Nanjing massacre ever took place. One Japanese historian has written that precisely forty-seven Chinese civilians died. Others quibble about the definition of 'massacre' or the timeframe (Was it the first week after the Japanese arrived or six weeks thereafter, as prescribed by the 1946 Tokyo Trials?) or how to define 'Nanjing' – the entire district or just within the city walls. The deniers include the Society for the Dissemination of Historical Fact, a Japanese right-wing group which has a conspiracy for just about every accusation levelled against the imperial army. In terms of Nanjing, they say the Chinese were the barbarians: it was *they* who burned the city and committed atrocities, and anyone who disagrees is a communist.

Among other critics of the accepted Nanjing narrative are prominent Japanese politicians like the former mayor of Nagoya, Takashi Kawamura. In 2012 he made a speech claiming the acts of the Japanese military were 'conventional acts of combat'. In 1990 a former governor of Tokyo, Shintaro Ishihara, told *Playboy* magazine, 'People say that the Japanese made a holocaust there [in Nanjing], but that is not true. It is a story made up by the Chinese … it is a lie.' A former minister of education, Fujio Masayui, dismissed it as 'just a part of war'.

A more realistic defence might be that terrible things happen in wars, in all wars; that few nations are innocent when it comes to war crimes; that many armies have operated a 'take-no-prisoners' policy; and many victorious soldiers have rampaged, raped and looted. The My Lai and Amritsar massacres are two of the better known occasions on which American and British troops killed unarmed civilians in Vietnam and India respectively. During the battle for Okinawa Americans executed Japanese prisoners, as did British soldiers in the Burma campaign.

Others try to explain or excuse the brutality of the Japanese in Nanjing by pointing to the fact that the soldiers had been systematically brutalised during the army's bushido-infused training. The 'imperial way', a kind of emperor-led spiritual nationalism, had also programmed them to believe in their own racial superiority, rendering them indifferent to the suffering of their enemies, whom they considered less than human. They were on a mission to 'purify' Asia. In his book *Horror in the East* Laurence Rees quotes Yoshio Tshuchiya, a veteran of the Japanese military police who served in China, as saying that they thought of the Chinese as 'like bugs or animals ... The Chinese didn't belong to the human race.' 'I felt like I was just killing animals, like pigs,' Rees quotes another veteran of the army in Northern China as saying. 'I thought that this was the way for the Japanese imperial army to do things. I was just totally convinced.'

Legitimising his army's conduct with his divinity was Emperor Hirohito. One Japanese soldier taken prisoner by the Chinese and tried after the war was Masayo Enomoto. In his testimony he said, 'I was fighting for the emperor. He was a god. In the name of the emperor we could do whatever we wanted against the Chinese.' Who knows how many ordinary Japanese soldiers truly believed their actions were sanctioned by the emperor's mystical authority, but this is certainly what they were taught.

For decades after the end of the war, the crimes of the Japanese did not rank highly among the priorities of the Chinese government, which benefited in various ways from good relations with Tokyo. In a speech in 1964 on the occasion of the visit of the chairman of the Japanese Socialist Party, Mao Zedong said, 'Japanese militarism was tremendously advantageous for China in that it allowed the Chinese people to take back power.' Mao's gratitude was perhaps double-edged, but it is undeniable that the CPC did benefit from Japan's colonial war against its rivals, Chiang Kai-shek's nationalists.

So for many years conserving and memorialising the story of what had happened in the 1930s and early 1940s in China was mostly left to those who had directly experienced the horror or individuals otherwise motivated to ensure the events were never forgotten. One of the more remarkable examples of these civic-minded historians is Wu Xianbing, who has single-handedly created a private museum dedicated to the Nanjing massacre.

'It started off out of pure anger,' Mr Wu tells me when I visit him at his museum on my second day in the city. 'But I realised anger was not enough. I wanted to teach people about what had happened and translate my anger into action.'

Wu is a stocky man in his mid-fifties. Today he is dressed in jeans, a white baseball cap with a red star and sensible thick-soled brown shoes. He looks like a factory boss, which it turns out is precisely what he is. When my taxi deposited me at the address I had been given for his museum, outside a rather tacky gold and red building in a light-industrial zone of the city, it looked to me more like a down-at-heel office, which again is precisely what it was. In 2004 Mr Wu repurposed the administration building of his furniture business into the Museum of the War of China's Resistance Against Japanese Aggression.

I had been expecting a fanatic, but Mr Wu is an eminently reasonable man. His approach to the war, to the Japanese and to current relations between the two countries is balanced and lucid. 'The point for me is not to evoke hatred or bring out bad memories, it is to show people that this is what has happened, to remember it and to learn from it,' he says as he shows me into his large office, its walls lined with books and bulging files. There are boxes around us on the floor overflowing with yet more papers. He has over 40,000 books on the history of the war, he says.

On my way to meet him I visited the official Nanjing Massacre Memorial Museum close to the Jiangdong Gate, where the remains of many victims have been found. As with the Unit 731 museum in Harbin, the official Nanjing institution is housed in a dramatic example of modern architecture – a grey granite triangular monolith surrounded by a gravel park filled with monuments and statues. But, says Mr Wu, the official museum is 'from the point of view of the leaders, the generals, the big players'. At his he wants to explore the Nanjing massacre through the perspective of ordinary people. 'To show that everyone has their own lives, but war breaks them all. This shows the humanity.'

I follow him into a large rectangular room with exhibits ranging from swords to chamber pots, helmets and Japanese flags, newspaper cuttings and the now familiar photographs of the slaughter. Though clearly curated on a tight budget, it is all well presented.

Wu's family came to Nanjing after the war, so he has no personal connection to the massacre other than being born here. He felt compelled to start his own museum – funded entirely out of his own pocket – when he read about Japanese prime ministers visiting Yasukuni. I point out that they haven't done that for some years now. 'Yes, but they still send gifts. Deep down I don't believe they have acknowledged what they did. Lots of Japanese ask me, "Why don't you let it go, forget about the past?"' He tells them that China was the victim, and victims and perpetrators have different perspectives and different rights. What about all the Japanese restaurants and companies and brands I had seen in Nanjing? Don't they show that the Chinese people had forgiven and forgotten? 'Society is complicated,' replies Mr Wu levelly. 'That is economics; it doesn't mean that Chinese people forget history or what they went through during the Japanese occupation.' He still believes that the Japanese are withholding evidence about the events of 1937.

Mr Wu invested a large amount of money to start the museum – he doesn't feel comfortable telling me how much, he says, but I later read it ran to over £200,000 – and has now devoted twelve years of his life to it. He is married with a grown-up daughter, but his family and friends didn't really understand what he was doing, he says with a shrug. Even with around 40,000 visitors a year, he doesn't make any money from the museum, but in recent years the government has started supporting him financially.

I venture that perhaps most Chinese people have moved on and maybe he should consider doing so too. 'I agree with you – we should look to the future – but the people who can't let go of the past are the Japanese. From the 1950s to the 1980s none of this was mentioned in Chinese society. It was only when it became acceptable in the Japanese mainstream to deny history, when the right wing took over, then it became a problem.' The first Japanese history textbook denying the massacre (and terming the invasion an 'advance') was published in the early 1980s. The Chinese authorities began building the official Nanjing Memorial Hall in 1984.

'I like Japan. I think modern Japanese society is among the most civilised in the world,' continues Mr Wu. 'But most ordinary Japanese, especially the young, they don't know anything of the Japanese history in China; they never mention the massacre because the politicians try to suppress this information. School textbooks – how can they use so few words to describe something as big as the Nanjing massacre? I think a lot of younger Japanese would be shocked if they knew the truth.'

Every time he visits Japan, which he does often, Mr Wu is disturbed to see there are fewer and fewer books about the massacre. In 2014, with the help of some Japanese NGOs, he took an exhibition of some of his material to Hiroshima and Nagoya. He has had help from 'hundreds' of Japanese people over the years with fundraising, and Japanese people are the most numerous overseas visitors to the museum. He hoped to take his exhibition to Tokyo in 2019 but hadn't yet found the right Japanese partner.

'Of course there are trolls, people online. Sometimes they write to me and are threatening or get aggressive, but I have never experienced any physical attack. Sometimes they come here.' Japanese right-wingers have visited his museum? I ask, astonished. 'Yes, I would even say I would call some of them friends. There are different types of right-wingers – centre right, moderate right, extreme right. Listen.' He stops walking and turns to me. 'I believe in communication. Without that, you never get further. There is no point in being angry or getting emotional about one person's version of history. It is better to know what they are thinking and use truth to fight them. Why are they saying this? Where do they get their information from?'

What did he say to those who allege that some or all of the evidence about the massacre was fabricated by the Chinese authorities? 'There are eight hundred photographs taken of the events, and none of them were taken by Chinese; they were all taken by foreigners, mostly Japanese, but also by the Westerners who were here.' New photographic evidence continues to come to light. In September 2008 photographs were found in the home of a Kobe resident showing Japanese troops burying Chinese people alive, for instance. The photographs were first published by the Japanese newspaper *Asahi Shimbun*. 'If these photographs were faked, then they weren't faked by the Chinese, but the truth is, evidence has come from multiple sources: mostly Japanese, but Americans, Chinese and Europeans.'

Appalled by the slaughter, in the first days after the Japanese arrived a group of European residents in the city rushed to set up a safety zone for refugees. A similar zone had been set up during the taking of Shanghai in mid-1937. In Nanjing the group included John Rabe, a German businessman and member of the Nazi Party, who personally harboured 600 Chinese refugees at his home, earning the sobriquet the 'living Buddha'. Today those Europeans are remembered with gratitude by the Chinese for providing a haven for an estimated 250,000 people, and the official museum has a large display dedicated to them. There were also several foreign reporters in the city, including Tillman Durdin of the *New York Times* and Charles McDaniel of Associated Press. In February 1938 an American priest, George Fitch, did much to bring the

Nanjing massacre to the attention of the world by smuggling a Super 8 film made by a missionary called John Magee out of the city and to the US.

The foreign reporter who has done more than anyone else to bring the Nanjing massacre to the attention of people in the West in more recent years is Chinese-American journalist Iris Chang. In 1997 she published *The Rape of Nanking: The Forgotten Holocaust of World War II*, which became an international bestseller.

From Mr Wu I learn that there is an entire museum dedicated to Chang about three hours' drive north of Nanjing in Huai-an. I visit it the next day, curious to see how the Chinese have memorialised an author who did so much to bring one of the darkest moments of their recent history to global prominence.

The museum, a purpose-built cross between a Chinese mausoleum and a park café, stands alone in the middle of a park overlooked by dozens of thirty-storey buildings. There is nobody guarding the entrance, so I just walk in. It is freezing cold and completely empty of people. Chang gazes down beatifically from portraits, photographs and plaster busts. There are relics – a sweatshirt, her childhood piano – a mock-up of her bedroom, childhood poems and drawings, and an IQ test from Mensa to illustrate her precocity. A text on display early on reads:

Iris Chang
Pure and innocent
Poetic and rainbow-like

I learn that Chang was the daughter of Chinese-American Harvard graduates and attended the University of Illinois. Her early career was spent rewriting computer software instruction manuals before she got a job at the *Chicago Tribune*. Finally we get to the book, which she began researching in 1993. Chang was outraged by what she saw as the continuing denial of the Nanjing massacre by certain sections of the Japanese establishment, calling it the 'second Japanese rape'.

A PBS *Newshour* television segment from the mid-1990s featuring Chang and the Japanese ambassador to the US runs on a loop on a screen in the museum. It is captioned: 'Iris turned a Japanese ambassador into jelly in less than thirty seconds.' I watch the film a couple of times. I think it is worth word-for-word transcription because it goes right to the heart of the Japan apology issue. Chang is in the studio, the ambassador is on a live feed.

CHANG: Can the ambassador himself say today, on national TV, live, that he personally is profoundly sorry for the rape of Nanking and other war crimes against China?

AMBASSADOR: We do recognise that acts of cruelty and violence were committed by members of the Japanese military and we are very sorry for that and we understand that the memory of those who suffered lasts long and I personally think that this is a burden which Japanese people will have to carry for a long time.

The ambassador goes on to say that he has examined twenty textbooks and they all mention Nanjing, and that the Japanese make conscious efforts to teach what happened.

INTERVIEWER (TO CHANG): Did you hear an apology?

CHANG: I don't know, did you hear an apology? I didn't really hear the word 'apology'. And I think that if he had said genuinely 'I personally am sorry for what the Japanese military did during World War II' I would have considered that an apology, I think that would have been a great step in the right direction. But again there are these words such as 'regret', 'remorse' and 'unfortunate things happen'; it is because of these types of wording and the vagueness of the expression that the Chinese people are infuriated.

Admittedly the ambassador is not the most charismatic of characters and he struggles in a second language, but he does *literally* say 'we are very sorry', live and on national TV, as Chang demands. He at no point uses the words 'regret', 'remorse' or 'unfortunate things happen', as she suggests. It is as if she is not really listening, as if she does not want to hear anything but equivocation from the ambassador.

Following what appears to have been a nervous breakdown, perhaps brought on by the stress of her work on a follow-up book about American prisoners of war in the Philippines, Chang committed suicide in 2004, leaving behind a three-year-old son. She had been diagnosed as bipolar and for some weeks prior to her death believed she was a target of the CIA and/or Japanese right-wing extremists and the Bush administration.

Chang's book has been criticised by many academics – both Western and Japanese – for its exaggeration (she claims the death toll was 'well over' 350,000, for instance), her 'emotionalism' and, in likening Nanjing to the Holocaust, of a skewed 'comparative victimology'. She also skims over the many Japanese who carried out pioneering research into the massacre before her. For three decades beginning in 1965 Japanese historian Ienaga Saburo waged a famous legal battle against the Japanese government regarding what he regarded as their suppression of the truth in school history textbooks, for instance. Expressing these kinds of views can be life-threatening in Japan. In 1990 the mayor of Nagasaki, Motoshima Hitoshi, was shot in the chest for suggesting that Emperor Hirohito bore some responsibility for the war. Yet from Chang's book one would conclude that all Japanese were equally in denial.

Mr Wu is characteristically reasonable when I put the criticisms of Chang to him. 'Without her book, a lot of people in the West would not have known about the massacre. I realise people say she exaggerated and was very subjective, but I think she made a great contribution, and the more research is done, the more people realise that her book was accurate.'

Chang's conclusion to *The Rape of Nanking* is more conciliatory, rightly pointing out that there is nothing different or 'other' about the Japanese. 'No race or culture has a monopoly on wartime cruelty,' she wrote. All societies are capable of the brutality of Nanjing. 'Japan's behaviour during Word War II was less a product of dangerous people than of a dangerous government, in a vulnerable culture, in dangerous times ...'

29

Shanghai I

If Nanjing had felt like arriving in the twenty-first century, Shanghai was like an Epcot Center vision of the future, albeit seen from circa 1988. The evening I arrive by high-speed train, I join the tourist crowds down on the Bund, the iconic Hunangpu river embankment lined with turn-of-the-last-century Beaux Arts buildings. These sturdy granite blocks and clock towers once housed the institutions of Western imperialism and always remind me of Liverpool's old waterfront. These days they house European luxury brand flagships, five-star hotels and high-roller restaurants: Western imperialism by consumer stealth.

Over on the other side of the river, the towers of Pudong are shrouded in cloud this evening. Their red aircraft warning lights glow through the mist. It is said that when Pudong was being constructed in the 1990s they built the equivalent of ten Manhattans within a decade. Today the glassy skyscrapers jostle for attention in the jagged skyline, each a wilder shape than the next. My gaze is drawn to the Shanghai World Financial Center, nicknamed the bottle opener on account of the square opening at the top. The story goes that the Mori Company, the Japanese developers, originally designed the opening as a circle, but the authorities felt this was uncomfortably reminiscent of the sun on the Japanese flag and made them change it.

I cross the river using a weird tourist tunnel ride affair which, with its BBC Radiophonic Workshop-style soundtrack and kaleidoscopic light show, makes me feel like I am in the opening credits to *Dr Who*. Once in Pudong, I visit a similarly kitschy history museum at the base of the Oriental Pearl Tower – one of those cherry-on-a-cocktail-stick buildings – which walks me through the official Chinese version of Shanghai's recent past. Much of this focuses on the locals' 'heroic' resistance to the 'nimble-footed' Western imperialists who commandeered and corrupted the city in the late 1800s with their 'flowery smoking houses' (combined opium dens/brothels). Back then Shanghai had a reputation as a good-time city, the New York of the East, but the pleasures of the few were founded on the miseries of the many. It is no coincidence that the city gave birth to the CPC in the early 1920s.

I end that first evening's walk at the former British consulate building, a large vaguely Mediterranean-looking villa at the far end of the Bund, built in the 1870s with a veranda overlooking a mani-cured lawn shaded by magnolias. These days it is a smart hotel and bar. It is almost empty as I enter. A pianist plays 'Memories'. I order a drink and imagine games of croquet, G & Ts and Victorian ladies fanning themselves in the heat as coolies labour in the distant docks bearing tea chests on their backs.

When I first visited Shanghai a few years ago, I braced myself for a bland megacity of identikit high-rises and gargantuan shopping malls, but I was instantly captivated. It has what I believe proper travel writers call texture, by which I think they mean that you can still see old people sitting in doorways smoking. Away from the luxury brand megastores, Shanghai is still enjoyably chaotic, a great city for flâneurs. This visit I flân around for a couple of days, mostly in the former French Concession with its shady avenues lined with plane trees and art deco villas, and the brick tenements in Xintiandi, where the CPC was founded by Mao, among others, in 1921. In the side streets around Nanjing Road, colonial Shanghai's main drag, grocers, ironmongers and dumpling sellers jostle for your custom. Scarlet slabs of fresh-ish meat hang over the pavement outside open-fronted butchers' shops. I brush shoulders with a shoulder of pork as I dummy my way out of the grasp of a seedy individual trying to entice me into one of the many massage parlours dotted among the tourist hotels.

One evening I meet up with two young locals, Søren, the friend of a friend from Denmark, and his schoolfriend Ben, at a noodle place on the edge of the French Concession. Most young Chinese take a Western name at some point, they tell me above the noise of the packed restaurant as we wait for the waitress to take our order. 'Søren' became a fan of Kierkegaard during his time studying philosophy at university, which had taken him to Denmark, where he had met our mutual acquaintance, while Ben got his name in kindergarten (it means 'stupid' in Chinese, so is considered cute). He has friends called Hulk, Apple and even Titty, he says. I'd been spending a lot of time in the company of older academics so wanted to hear about things in China from a younger perspective, particularly how they reconcile living under CPC restrictions in the social media age.

'Nowadays in China you have young people doing things that nobody in China has ever done before – the Internet culture is wild,' says Ben. 'And that means the basic conflict is about the obedience of children to parents. We are all trying to negotiate with the older generation to figure out strategies for dealing with them.' There had been a breakdown in communication between parents and children, which, though par for the course in the West, was something new for China. Both Søren and Ben, who work in finance and the tech sector respectively, had had conflicts with their parents, at times even cutting off contact with them. Søren knew a girl from his small home town in Shandong who had moved away on the day of her graduation. She had a place at a good university, which was where everyone expected her to go. Shandong is a very conservative province where the conventional path is to become a teacher or an administrator in local government – low-paid drudgery but a job for life. Instead, she had arranged an internship at a company in Shanghai, and left without telling anyone. 'She just took her bags, got on a bus to Jinan and transferred to the train to Shanghai. Cut herself off from her family,' Søren marvels.

'Young Chinese people are looking more and more outward. We all want to study abroad,' says Ben, who has studied in the US. That is the dream: to get to an American university. The traffic goes both ways. 'At my college in Shanghai we were basically half Chinese students and half international.'

I had assumed both young men were from middle- or upper-middle-class backgrounds, but Ben's father works in a factory and his mother is a primary school teacher. He had a traditional childhood in a provincial town and it hadn't been easy moving to cosmopolitan Shanghai. 'I graduated from this really Chinese, really communist kind of school, with a strong nationalist identity. When I first came to university here, it was kind of awkward for a while to know how to talk to the other students.'

We talk about the Chinese online message sites, an often bizarre parallel universe where, to circumvent censorship, Xi Jinping is depicted as Winnie the Pooh and Peppa Pig is banned for 'promoting gangster culture'. Younger people spend a lot of time mocking the older generation online, Ben says. In the run-up to the national holiday for Chinese new year, when everybody is expected to return home, the sites fill up with people offering advice on how to deal with parental interrogations of the 'Why aren't you married yet?' 'How is your promotion coming along?' sort. '[One piece of] advice was to change the focus – so before Auntie starts asking why you aren't married yet, you say, "Happy new year, Auntie. How is your daughter? Has she found a boyfriend yet?"' says Søren.

Both young men tell me that they circumvent the Great Firewall of China by using VPN (virtual private network) servers, as I am doing while travelling here. VPNs work pretty well: I can use Twitter without any problem even though it is officially banned in China. Whenever I speak to Chinese people about Internet censorship in China, they all say exactly the same thing: that it is terrible, that the government is treating them like children, that it is an infringement of their human rights and ridiculous that a reputed 30,000 government employees work full-time monitoring discussion sites, and so on. But each and every one of them then happily admits that they have a VPN, which means they labour under no such restrictions.

'Fewer and fewer people get their information from CCTV [state TV] now,' another Chinese student told me. 'Many of my friends don't even have a TV in their home.' She explained that the control of information wasn't so much about the things the authorities broadcast but more what they muted. The names of previous presidents are not searchable on Weibo (China's answer to Google), for instance, 'but most people don't care about that; they do care a lot when ordinary people are harmed though, and that kind of scandal can't be suppressed. If my Weibo account got sealed one day, I'd register another the next day and tweet about why censorship is unreasonable.'

This last exchange is from an ongoing email correspondence I have with a couple of Chinese students who have contacted me over the years as a result of a book of mine being published in China. I always ask them about their lives in China, and they patiently explain that, no, they do not have democracy in the Western sense, but that the system they have functions as well as that in the West. After all, as one student put it to me, 'It is true that a vote can be a symbol of democracy, partly, but when the result of the vote can be easily shaped by outsiders, can we still say that vote means democracy?' Both systems are influenced by propaganda, he said. He read reports about their government's human rights abuses in the Western media but, wrote another student, 'If there is that much imprisoning, beating and restrictions, how can our government still have such a high level of support?' This is true. A poll conducted by the Edelman Trust Barometer, an independent international organisation, rates the Chinese people's trust in their institutions at over 80 per cent, higher than any other country in the world. The UK scores 36 per cent, the US 33 per cent.

Ben and Søren are products of China's one-child policy, only recently discontinued when the country's leadership belatedly realised it was facing a demographic and gender-balance crisis. Sex-selection abortions mean that in some provinces the ratio of boys to girls is 123:100. By 2020 there will be 30 million more men aged 24–40 than women in China. To put it a different way: China is missing more than 60 million females. This is doubly problematic because of China's patrilocal system, in which a bride moves into her husband's family home and then takes care of his parents in their old age. The gender imbalance has also caused an astronomical increase in the cost of a dowry – the bride price, as it is known in China. Even in rural areas a bride price can easily run to £10,000, in some cases several times that.

Everyone knows that the Japanese are getting older too. For the first time since records began, there were fewer than one million births in Japan in 2017. The fertility rate has slumped to 1.43 babies per woman of child-bearing age (the replacement rate is 2.07); Shinzo Abe has pledged to raise that to 1.8 by 2025. He had better get started. The statistics are frightening. The population of Japan fell by a record 403,000 people in 2017 every day 1,000 more Japanese people die than are born. By 2053 the population is set to fall below 100 million from the current 127 million; by 2065 there will be just 88 million Japanese people, and over 65s will make up around 38 per cent of the population. Among them will be around 7 million people with dementia, with a shortfall of around a million care workers to look after them.

South Korea is in an even worse situation. It has one of the lowest birth rates in the world: in 2017 it reached a record low of 1.05 – in Seoul it was 0.84. Its population is ageing faster than any other country, faster even than Japan's. The decline started in the early 1960s, when it was believed that cutting the birth rate was essential to boosting the economy; back then it was 4.5. The government encouraged as many women as possible to go on the pill, and female sterilisation programmes continued into the 1980s. The result is that, according to the UN, by 2026 almost a quarter of the population will be over 65. The Korean government has spent billions incentivising childbirth, including the introduction of universal free childcare.

China's crisis is slightly mitigated by the sheer size of its population, which is projected to peak at 1.5 billion by 2028, but the birth rate is currently 1.57 and declining. By 2050 over a quarter of the population will be over 65. After the CPC changed to a two-child policy in 2015, the birth rate did rise by almost 8 per cent but fell back by 3.5 per cent within a year.[20] And, because China's population is ageing at a much earlier stage in the development of its economy than Japan's and South Korea's have, it is less likely to have accrued the funds necessary to cope with its impending gerontological imbalance.

What is causing the population decline in these countries? First, whenever any country gets richer, fewer babies are born (Taiwan's birth rate has also declined, from 7.04 in 1951 to 1.17 in 2016), but the problem is more visible in east Asia because Japan, South Korea and China are notoriously averse to immigration. Second, young people in all three countries are now living with increasing financial insecurity and fewer career opportunities. The work landscape has changed, becoming far less stable. In Japan, once the spiritual home of jobs-for-life, around 40 per cent of the workforce is in temporary or part-time work, while only about a quarter of graduates can expect to secure one of the increasingly elusive, relatively secure posts at the large corporations. This has a clear knock-on effect on marriage and procreation. For many the idea of one day having a house and a spouse is becoming increasingly remote.

In 2016 Japan's National Institute of Population and Social Security Research published a poll of around 15,000 Japanese men and women aged 18–34 which showed that nearly 70 per cent of unmarried men and 60 per cent of unmarried women were not in a relationship, compared to 48.6 per cent and 39.5 per cent when the first survey was conducted in 1987. Over 40 per cent of the total surveyed were virgins, up from 36.2 per cent of men and 38.7 per cent of women

[21] The end of the one-child policy might be a good thing from the point of view of the ageing population, but it was pointed out to me by one young Chinese woman that it could also have negative effects. 'The last generation of Chinese girls got a better education and more attention growing up. In this way, the one-child policy improved the status of women in China.' Now she said she was worried that they would end up like women in Japan, a situation she found lamentable, citing the recent news story about female applicants to Tokyo Medical University having their grades doctored to give men an advantage.

in 2010. Though 90 per cent of people said they hoped one day to marry, over a quarter said they had effectively given up looking for a partner.

It is a similar story in South Korea. 'The cost of having children is so high – buying a house, education and so on,' Youngruk Cheong, an economist at Seoul National University, told me when I asked him about the reasons for population decline. In the 2012 edition of his book *Korea: The Impossible Country* Daniel Tudor estimates that the cost of raising a child in South Korea is equivalent to almost half the per capita GDP. The Koreans and Japanese also know from bitter experience that their countries' working culture of extreme hours and intolerable conditions is not compatible with being young parents. Many are afraid to take the maternity/paternity leave on offer because they know it will hamper their careers, or even lose them their jobs.

It could also be argued that traditional – some would say outdated – values are to blame for much of this. South Korea has the fewest births out of wedlock among the OECD countries – only 1.9 per cent, compared to the average of 39.9 per cent. Similarly, part of the explanation for Japan's demographic nightmare might be found in news stories like one from 2018 in which a woman working in a private nursery school in Aichi Prefecture was forced to *apologise* to older colleagues when she became pregnant.

There have been some meaningful and progressive initiatives from the governments of the east Asian tigers. South Korea and Japan now lead the OECD in paid parental leave for fathers – offering fifty-three and fifty-two weeks respectively, compared to two weeks in the UK and zero in the US. Even in Sweden, home of 'latte papas', paid leave for fathers is a mere fourteen weeks. Meanwhile, the Chinese state has launched campaigns encouraging single women over twenty-seven to get on with it and find a mate, or risk becoming a 'leftover woman'. And, erm, 8 November is Bra Day in South Korea, when men buy bras for women.

There is perhaps one bright side to these frightening demographic projections: they might just prevent these old enemies from going to war in the future. There are half a million fewer eighteen-year-olds in Japan now than there were twenty years ago. Some 37 per cent of Japanese military personnel are now over the age of forty (compared to 9 per cent in the US), and Japan is already experiencing a severe shortage of recruits, particularly ones willing to fight. American political scientist Mark Haas has termed this phenomenon 'geriatric peace', the idea being not so much that there won't be enough young people to fight (technology will probably alleviate that problem), but that governments' priorities will lie elsewhere, on care for the elderly for instance.

30

Shanghai II

The South Korean comfort women campaigners have been hugely successful in promoting their cause worldwide – to the extent that, I think in many people's minds, the issue is exclusively a Korean one. They even made it to Broadway recently with *Comfort Women: A New Musical*, which was revived in 2018 and supported by the Korean Council for the Women Drafted for Military Sexual Slavery by Japan.

I was interested to find out why the Chinese government had not campaigned for their victims with the same vigour as the South Koreans, or memorialised them in the same way it has the victims of Unit 731 and the Nanjing massacre. Was there some aspect of the issue which made it tricky to address for the Chinese leadership, or might they be keeping it up their sleeves for the future?

It turns out that there is a small museum dedicated to the Chinese comfort women in Shanghai Normal University. I arrange to meet its curator, Su Zhiliang, a leading researcher into China's wartime sex slaves.

Outside on the lawn in front of the building in the pleasantly leafy grounds of the university campus is a bronze statue of two women, each with a yellow woollen scarf around her neck, just like the statues I had seen in Korea. The statues represent a Korean comfort woman and a Chinese comfort woman, Zhiliang explains when I meet him upstairs in the university building overlooking the garden. The empty seat represents other victims of sexual abuse in the world.

'Every single war in world history involved sexual violence towards women,' he tells me. 'But it is usually carried out by individual soldiers, so [it is] personal behaviour. The difference is, in this case, it is the Japanese government that discovered that using women, Chinese women, as sexual slaves, could cheer up their military, so they decided to use women as a tool. This is a war crime.'

Su is in his early sixties. He has an open unlined face framed by a parabola of thinning plastered-down hair. During our interview he keeps his coat and scarf on, which adds to his general air of a man on a mission. He has just returned from Seoul, where he participated in an International Women's Day parade, and he is due to leave any minute for the airport on another campaigning trip.

Su has been researching the Chinese comfort women since the early 1990s. He was studying in Tokyo when a Japanese professor drew his attention to the fact that the first imperial army brothel was established in Shanghai, his home town. He was appalled that he hadn't known this and in his own time set about collecting testimonies, artefacts and documents relating to the Chinese comfort women. 'I thought it would be quite a small thing, that there were maybe four or so brothels in Shanghai, but I discovered there had been 170. The scale was beyond imagining.'

As well as academic research, Su and over a hundred of his students have been involved in welfare projects to help the surviving comfort women, raising and distributing funds, visiting them regularly in hospital and their homes. He believes there were an estimated 400,000 comfort women during Japan's imperial period, perhaps half of them Chinese. He admits a definitive figure is difficult because of the destruction of records by the retreating Japanese and the chaos in China after the war, but says, 'there are some researchers who believe the figure could have been one million'.

Here, as at the House of Sharing in South Korea, the artefacts on display are shocking in their mundanity. There are condoms provided to the Japanese soldiers and sourced from veterans in Japan, a jar of potassium permanganate used as disinfectant and even architectural salvage from a long-demolished Shanghai comfort station. The museum is small, just one room, and includes confessions from Japanese soldiers involved with the setting up and running of the brothels, as well as testimonies from many of the women with whom Su and his researchers have made contact. There are relics from their later lives – the unbearably poignant belongings of elderly women, like combs, mirrors, and porcelain teacups. Su currently has just twenty women on his list of surviving victims, most of whom are in their late eighties or nineties and in precarious health. They have spent much of their lives ostracised by their communities and live in poverty.

Su agrees that, compared to South Korea, the issue has had a relatively low profile in China. 'That's the nature of Chinese people, to be more soft and to go gently,' he says. '[The comfort women] are kind of neglected here because we have such a massive population and it is just impossible for the government to take care of everyone.'

There are several other reasons why the plight of the Chinese comfort women is less well known. After the war, with millions starving, migrating, imprisoned or killed, caring for abused women was not a priority. The subsequent convulsions of the Cultural Revolution and the Great Leap Forward further sidelined the history of China's occupation. Also, many of the women chose to hide their pasts, committed suicide or died as a consequence of their ordeals. And when in 1972 China restored diplomatic relations with Japan in return for massive investment from Tokyo, it formally waived its claims to any further compensation for the war. At that time it was in everyone's interests to let the past rest.

In her book co-written with Su Zhiliang and Chen Lidei, *Chinese Comfort Women: Testimonies from Imperial Japan's Sex Slaves*, Peipei Qiu ventures that Confucian attitudes might also be to blame because they 'demand that, at all costs, a female remain a virgin until marriage, even if that means risking her life; hence, a survivor of rape was deemed impure and was regarded as a disgrace to her family'. A piece about the Chinese comfort women in the *Financial Times* in 2015 similarly claimed that 'their wartime rape [is] shrouded in Confucian delicacy'. But no society is as Confucian as South Korea's, so this explanation seems unconvincing to me.

A historian I spoke to in Hong Kong speculated that the Chinese felt shame over not having been able to protect their women, but again why would they be different from the Koreans? Others speculate that the Chinese government is wary of encouraging legal action by civic groups or individuals against the Japanese state because it might lead to Chinese people suing their own government for its many crimes – which range from land seizures to human organ harvesting, imprisonment for political reasons, anything remotely connected to Tibet, the imprisonment for 'reprogramming' of as many as half a million Muslim Uighurs in Xinjiang, and so on, and on. Unfortunately, this has echoes of the 'whataboutism' employed by Japanese apologists to attack Chinese researchers into Japanese crimes – as in, 'What about all the terrible things the Chinese did to themselves?' Su Zhiliang acknowledges this. 'We do need to reflect on what we did to ourselves. I'm not only looking at what outsiders did to us. Of course, it is difficult for huge political reasons. It is also difficult for people to discuss on a personal level.' Su continues: 'For example, the victims who are still alive now [in China], one of them doesn't want to be mentioned at all, not her name, not her picture, nothing related to her personally, so it is very difficult for us to look at this, and for the media to investigate.'

It shouldn't be forgotten that the Chinese situation was different from the Koreans': the Koreans were colonised, while China was at war with Japan – perhaps this is a factor. One Chinese person I spoke to about his country's reticence on the issue said the problem was that you could never present the comfort women as a positive narrative. Other aspects of the war could be manipulated in one way or another, but the comfort women story was just all bad. Not a productive narrative for those Chinese state television wartime dramas, for instance.

Some are openly hostile to the subject being researched at all. In the early days of his research Su Zhiliang received threatening phone calls from locals asking why he needed to dig around in all these sexual matters. Why not just let it all be? He also believes that

Korean people are more patriotic, and more single-minded: 'Once they set their mind on something, they go for it until the end.'

At the end of our time together, just as I am leaving the museum, I ask Su if any of the buildings which housed the military brothels remain. I am assuming not – the question is really an afterthought – but it turns out that there are several, including what he claims is the *first ever* Japanese military comfort station, dating from 1932. It is at No. 1, Lane 125, East Baoxing Road, a little way north of the old British consulate. It was once the Daiichi Saloon, a dance hall, and is currently home to about seventy migrant workers. He shows me recent photographs of the building including, inside, a wooden frieze featuring Mount Fuji which still decorates the lintel above a doorway. There are hopes one day to turn it into a museum and memorial, he says.

Accompanying me on my visit today to help with translation is Liyan, a friend and documentary maker who lives in Shanghai. She and I look at each other. We are both thinking the same thing: *We need to go and see this place.* We clarify again its exact location, say our good byes to Su Zhiliang and his students, and jump in a cab for the ride across the city. After an hour the taxi drops us off outside a Japanese restaurant.

It takes a few minutes to get our bearings, but there it is right across the street, the former comfort station, a robust-looking grey-brick two-storey building with arched windows, part of a walled compound. We approach it warily, peering into the front courtyard to see – yes – the entrance shown in Su's old black and white photographs; there beneath a scattering of pot plants are the same art deco-style curved tiled steps. Two elderly women are tending to hundreds of pieces of ginger which they have laid out to dry in the alley beside the building. The women know of the building's former purpose, they say. 'I would never live here alone,' one of them tells Liyan. 'But it's OK to be here surrounded by people.' Another woman in slippers and a pink overcoat says she has lived in the building for forty years but doesn't want to talk any more about its history.

After Liyan has asked permission, we enter the building's unlit hall, which is cluttered with boxes, old enamel adverts, buckets and bicycles. Washing hangs from exposed water pipes as, in one corner, does a hunk of drying pork. The building has been subdivided into rooms with plasterboard walls and plywood doors. There is a shared kitchen in which a couple of women are tending to some pots on a stove.

Before Su left to catch his flight, he had told me that when he started his research the government wanted him to stop. 'It was too sensitive, but I thought it was so important, not only to China, but for the whole world to learn about this. If we don't reflect on this, if we don't look at it seriously, will it happen again? I ask you,' he said, stopping and turning to me. 'If this happened to your grandmother or a woman you know, what would you do?'

31

Hong Kong I

If you recall, I started this journey on the beach at Kurihama mulling over my grand historical hypothesis that the Americans were the cause of all east Asia's woes. If Commodore Perry had not insisted that Japan open up, the Japanese would not have modernised, militarised, marched and massacred their way across the continent. If the Americans hadn't given the Japanese that traumatic lesson in gunboat diplomacy, they might never have forced their own unequal treaties upon Korea, before annexing it and then invading Manchuria. The Kwantung Army would not have gone rogue and rampaged as far as Burma and the Philippines. There would have been no American bombing of Japan. Perhaps the nationalists would have prevailed and China would not have gone communist (that's 20 million lives saved), the Korean peninsula would not have been split in two by a terrible war and the Kim dynasty would not have commenced its seven-decade totalitarian reign culminating in the current nuclear threats. Taiwan would not be mired in its present geopolitical pickle, and America would not have spent the post-war decades supporting brutal dictators there and in South Korea – 'deforming post-war Asian affairs', as the biographer of Emperor Hirohito Herbert Bix described their meddling.

I could go on. The Vietnam War wouldn't have occurred, and what would have happened in Russia? But of course this kind of post-historic blame game is for fools; my hypothesis is absurdly simplistic, hopelessly misguided, downright misleading and quite, quite wrong on a number of key matters.

No. It is the British who are to blame.

At least this is now my conclusion having spent my first day in Hong Kong visiting its history museums, all of which make very clear that, right here in south-eastern China, around two hundred years ago, the British concocted a wicked plan to enslave millions of Chinese through opium addiction, and it was *this*, not the Americans' aggression, which paved the way for the country's Century of Shame.

Actually, I'd been hearing this historical narrative since I'd visited the National Museum of China in Beijing a couple of weeks earlier. That had an entire section dedicated to the Opium Wars of the 1840s and 50s, a dark stain indeed on British history which, I am newly convinced, is the root cause of all the problems which beset contemporary east Asia today.

The Beijing museum likened the British to 'a swarm of bees, looting our treasures and killing our people. They forced China's ruling Qing dynasty to sign a series of unequal treaties that granted them economic, political and cultural privileges and sank China gradually into a semi-colonial, semi-feudal society.' This is the version of history that the Chinese learn in their schools, museums, cinemas, newspapers and via their televisions: that the British government conspired deliberately to destabilise China through the illegal sale of opium. It is not untrue.

Since the mid-eighteenth century the British had been buying tea and porcelain from China despite the fact that the Qing had restricted the trade to a few go-betweens in Canton and to just a few months of the year. These restrictions were a frustration for the East India Company and the motley crew of chancers, thieves and adventurers who muscled in on the trade when its monopoly was abolished in 1833. Britain's tea addiction was on such a scale that the country had a serious trade deficit with China, which at that time was the largest economy in the world, larger than all of Europe combined. The deficit was exacerbated by the Qing's refusal to accept anything but silver in exchange for their goods and their almost total lack of interest in everything else the British had to sell them. There was, however, one product of the British empire on which the Chinese were rather keen: opium, produced in Bengal. The fact that this wonderful multi-purpose drug, which could treat malaria, diarrhoea and insomnia, and make you feel *really* good, had been illegal in China since 1729 did not deter British traders. By the late 1830s they were selling the Chinese 40,000 chests a year, each containing about 63 kilos of opium, through the Hong traders in Canton. It was said to be the most valuable trade in any single commodity in the world, and contributed significantly to the coffers of the British government in India. And with the opium came another pernicious invasion, Christian missionaries, who arrived on the same boats, acted as interpreters for the smugglers and distributed their literature alongside the drugs.

In 1838, with public disorder growing because of the illegal opium trade, the Qing emperor in Beijing dispatched the famously conscientious bureaucrat Lin Zexu to Canton to give the British a slap on the wrist. That spring, in an echo of the Boston Tea Party, Lin blockaded the British warehouses, confiscated 20,000 chests of opium and destroyed it in lime pits at the fortress at Humen, on the Pearl river delta. The British withdrew and dropped anchor a little to the south beside some disease-ridden rocks overlooking a harbour long bedevilled by pirates. The Chinese were feeling pretty triumphant at this point.[21]

In London some called for a military response, but there was also a great deal of opposition to attacking China, including from the opposition leader, William Gladstone, then a Conservative, who said that he did not know of a conflict 'more calculated in its progress to cover this country with permanent disgrace'. In response, the government claimed that the heads of executed British traders had been displayed at the gates of Canton. This was a lie, the nineteenth-century equivalent of a sexed-up dossier, but the foreign secretary, Viscount Palmerston, was successful in pitching the sending of

---

[21] Canton, now Guangzhou, is still China's biggest drug smuggling port; these days it's ketamine and methamphetamine. The region is home to a sixth of the country's registered addicts. They still sometimes destroy seized drugs at the Humen fortress.

warships to China as a moral crusade, and is hated to this day by the Chinese.

The British saw the fight as being on behalf of the entire civilised Western world against the arrogant, obstreperous, so-called Celestial Empire, and with memories still fresh of the humiliation of the king's envoy Lord Macartney by Qianlong back in 1793, Palmerston knew this would play well with his electorate. Forty-five years earlier, the emperor's response to Macartney's gifts of barometers and airguns, in an attempt to open China to trade, had been gloriously supercilious: 'We have never valued ingenious articles, nor do we have the slightest need of your manufactures.' Chinese arrogance had not been forgotten. The British went to war.

The Chinese brought matchlocks to the fight, the British brought flintlocks and the world's first iron warship, the *Nemesis*. The British were aided too by the Qing's almost comically incompetent and corrupt provincial officials. Some Cantonese troops misconstrued an instruction from their Beijing masters to fire their guns as little as possible, and turned up for a battle with no guns whatsoever – a double shame, as the soldiers in question were notably good shots. On another occasion, troops from a landlocked province became seasick on a mission to reclaim an island. So desperate did things become that, as the British sailed up the Yangtze in 1841, the Chinese toyed with the idea of hurling live monkeys onto their ships with firecrackers strapped to their backs. This from a nation which had been the greatest power in Asia with a population of 328 million, more than the entire British empire. For several months after hostilities commenced, the emperor didn't even realise he was at war with Britain or for that matter know where Britain was located. Lin sent a report claiming that the British would easily be defeated because 'Their legs and feet are closely bound by their tight trousers, which makes bending and stretching inconvenient.' When the British navy arrived and swiftly destroyed the Chinese defences, Lin simply invented victories and reported them to Beijing. Thousands of Qing troops were effectively massacred for the loss of mere tens of British. The British compounded their crimes by stealing 20,000 tea seedlings, which were eventually used to create the Indian tea industry in Darjeeling, thus ending China's tea monopoly for ever.

The 1842 Treaty of Nanjing awarded the British those disease-ridden, pirate-plagued islands, known as Hong Kong, but the British wanted more. In 1856, on the flimsiest of pretexts, they had another go at the Chinese, sailing, together with some French warships, as far as Beijing, where they razed the emperor's summer palace, the 'Versailles of China', to the ground, leaving it 'a dreary waste of ruined nothings' as one British witness described the aftermath. With the eighth Earl of Elgin, son of the Parthenon marbles felon, overseeing proceedings, they looted countless treasures, including the empress's dog. This was later given to Queen Victoria and renamed Looty, which sounds like a storyline from *Blackadder* but did actually happen. Items from the summer palace still occasionally crop up in auctions, such as one of the fabled twelve zodiacal heads from a palace fountain, which was owned by Yves Saint Laurent and put up for sale after his death.[22]

The Second Opium War was ended by the Treaty of Beijing, which forced the Chinese to legalise opium and open up the interior of their country to foreigners for the first time. This is still presented to the Chinese people by their government as the greatest humiliation ever visited upon the country, and that includes the Japanese invasion.

So, my new domino theory of historical blame goes like this. If the British East India Company had not been such a bunch of brigands, they would never have attempted to flood China with opium; the Chinese would not have had to enforce their sovereign right to ban the trade; the Opium Wars would not have taken place and

---

[22] The twelve heads are considered by many to be the ultimate lost treasures of Qing art, and the Chinese government blocked the sale of YSL's piece. What's more, in recent years, there has also been a spate of intriguing thefts from European museums in which the thieves have exclusively swiped items looted from the summer palace, leading some to suggest that either the Chinese government or patriotic billionaires are taking back what is rightfully theirs.

contributed to the fundamental weakening of the Qing dynasty, leaving them vulnerable to internal conflicts such as the catastrophic Taiping and Boxer Rebellions and the end-of-empire machinations of Empress Cixi. China would not then have been vulnerable to the external threat of the Japanese in the 1890s, when it was defeated after coming to the defence of Korea, or forced to relinquish Taiwan and other territories to Japan.

I want to put my new theory to the test so arrange to meet a local history professor in Hong Kong. I hope you don't mind, but I'm going to take the liberty of changing her name. She only asked that some of her comments be off the record – mostly regarding the current regime in Beijing – but to avoid any risk of her being identified at all, I am going to call her Professor Yang.

She and I meet in a trendy coffee bar in Kowloon, a short ride across the harbour from Hong Kong island on the Star Ferry. I put to her my theory that the British were to blame for everything.

'No, no, no. Blame the Chinese!' replies Professor Yang, replacing her cup on the table and waving her hands dismissively. 'Qing China was already in a state of decline. The Opium War was only a symptom of that, and everybody took advantage of it. Even the Chinese, they took the chance to kick out their alien rulers and adopted nationalism.'

Professor Yang invited me to consider a few questions. Were the Chinese really so passive? Did they have no free will? Were they really anaesthetised by the poppy so easily? Doubtless many Chinese enjoyed a functioning relationship with the drug on a recreational basis and experienced no serious side-effects, just like thousands in Britain at the time, where you could buy opium in chemists. It would have been a very weak country indeed to let a few junkies drag it down. The truth is that the Opium Wars and the ensuing Hundred Years of Shame were a mess of the Qing's own making, a result of corruption, incompetence and distractions elsewhere in what had become an unmanageably vast empire. Yes, the British traders in Asia were unprincipled racists who cloaked their illegal actions in the rhetoric of a 'civilising' power, and the British navy's campaigns were indeed so one-sided they can be described as mas-sacres – the Japanese have cited them when defending their own mass killings in China – but there was no grand conspiracy to enslave the Chinese through addiction; the British just spotted and exploited a commercial opportunity.

Professor Yang was keen to emphasise that the Qing themselves were invaders. The emperor at the time of the Opium Wars, Daoguang, was the eighth-generation descendant of Manchu khans. The Manchu were a non-Chinese people who had invaded from the north, ousting the Ming in 1644. Just like the British and later the Japanese, the Qing had been expansionists, pushing the country's borders as far as Tibet and the Uighur empire, doubling its total area. By the late seventeenth century, attempting to move into Burma and Vietnam, the Qing over-extended themselves and were subse-quently unable to rule effectively what had become – and remains – less a country, more a continent.

The Qing were deeply resented in many parts of their empire, particularly in the south of China, where the British were considered by the Cantonese no more alien than their rulers from the north. In fact, soon after the Second Opium War, the British were able to form military units of local Hakka Chinese. As Julia Lovell puts it in her excellent history of the first Sino-British conflict, *The Opium War*: 'The situation begs the question of what kind of political and social community Qing China was, that a bloody struggle against foreign invaders should for so many become an unmissable oppor-tunity to fleece the government ...'

As we wrap up our coffee meeting, Professor Yang assures me that there is little point in me beating myself up over what my forebears did in her homeland: 'Imperialism was a global phenom-enon; no one could stop it. Japan had already tried to expand onto the Korean peninsula in the sixteenth century. You can't blame air for allowing fire!'

Why am I so preoccupied with events of the nineteenth century? Because history is repeating itself in twenty-first-century China, and the Communist Party of China is using nineteenth-century British aggression to justify its domestic and overseas agenda to its people and the outside world. That is why the CPC is so invested in the historical blame game, why every Chinese child is taught that China is on a mission to avenge the Opium Wars. That's why the section of the National Museum in Beijing dealing with the Opium Wars is said to be Xi Jinping's favourite; one of his very first official acts on becoming president was to visit it. That's why new members of the party are sworn in before the ruins of the summer palace in Beijing. The Opium Wars are a crucial element of CPC propaganda. As a 2017 article in *The Economist* put it, 'The Opium Wars still shape China's view of the West.'

Look at it another way. Why did the Qing crumble? Because hubristic expansionism had created a vast and diverse empire which it found impossible to maintain; because the empire lacked natural resources; and because their maritime strength was no match for a rival power. Beijing is facing precisely the same challenges today but is determined to have the right answers this time.

China has twenty-two provinces and is home to fifty-six different minorities, who by some estimates speak three hundred languages or dialects. As Ben Chu puts it in his book *Chinese Whispers*, the country is still 'a multi-ethnic empire masquerading as a nation'. It still lacks natural resources and feels threatened by maritime powers – primarily the US but also Japan. Its leaders' solutions to these age-old problems are, respectively, to control communications with censorship, surveillance and if need be repression; the economic colonisation of parts of Africa, South East Asia and South America, offering infrastructure in exchange for raw materials vital for the Chinese economy; and the creation of the greatest navy in the world. I have no idea whether the men who work the bulldozers and dredgers which are rapidly turning the Spratly chain of islets into a naval base in the South China Sea sleep beneath stirring 'Hundred Years of Shame' posters, but it's not unthinkable.

The CPC's use of the Opium Wars as anti-Western propaganda is a relatively recent development. Back in the 1960s, when Chairman Mao was attempting to repair relations with Japan, America and

Europe, if they were mentioned at all, blame for the wars was more typically placed on the stupidity and cowardice of the Qing rulers, not on foreign opportunists. After Mao's death, the modernisation of China followed a Western approach, so there was even less of a need to raise the spectre of 1842. It was only after the Tiananmen Square massacre of 1989 that the leadership in Beijing realised there was capital to be gained by stirring up indignation at the Westerners' nineteenth-century destabilisation of China and outrageous looting of treasures – useful distractions for a population increasingly dissatisfied with the pace of democratic and economic reform. Parallels could be drawn between the nineteenth century and alleged Western meddling in late-twentieth-century China, which the CPC improbably claimed had inspired the students to protest in central Beijing.

As Zheng Wang, a professor at Seton Hall University in the US, puts it in his survey of Chinese history textbooks and memorials *Never Forget National Humiliation*, 'the Communist government's ideological reeducation of the public ... relentlessly portrays China as the victim of foreign imperialist bullying during "one hundred years of humiliation"'. In that snappy way of academics, he calls it 'the institutionalisation of manipulated historical consciousness'. But the CPC didn't just use the Opium Wars to distract attention from Tiananmen, it was around this time that anti-Japanese propaganda also began in earnest in China.

'There are some who believe that after Tiananmen Square the Chinese thought very strategically about how they might make that PR problem go away, so they decided to give the Japanese the biggest PR problem of all time, to drive a wedge between Japan and Korea and the US,' Andrew Salmon, the British historian and journalist I had met in Seoul, told me when we had spoken about the comfort women campaign, which also began in South Korea at the same time. 'And you know, the more time goes on, the more I'm thinking that maybe there actually is something to it.' (Along with Western imperialists and the Japanese, Beijing also blamed the Taiwanese for the Tiananmen protests, and halted what had been improving relations with Taipei for a while after 1989.)

And so in the 1990s the CPC began to teach the China-as-victim version of events in schools, to encourage on-message TV dramas and movies about the Opium Wars and to build over four hundred memorials and museums across the country commemorating them. Their propaganda efforts even extended to computer games. Julia Lovell recalls that in 1997, prior to the return of Hong Kong, a Chinese computer game company launched Opium War, a game in which players could 'use wisdom and courage to exterminate the damned invaders'.

Chinese vengeful resentment about the Opium Wars reminded me a little of Korean *han* and how that had been harnessed by the Seoul dictatorship in the 1970s to motivate its workers. But by stoking anti-foreign feeling in this way, there is a risk that public anger might one day turn against the government. In promoting the comfort women issue, by drawing attention to one historical crime on Chinese soil the CPC might well lead people to examine other more recent episodes in which the guilty parties are a little closer to home. As Lovell writes, 'Properly controlled public memory of the Opium War and later acts of imperialism provides a politically correct pressure valve for venting strong feelings in the PRC's tightly controlled public sphere. Carelessly managed, these same feelings spill out into something dangerously subversive.'

32

Hong Kong II

Thanks to Professor Yang, I didn't need to feel quite so guilty about my almost pathological infatuation with Hong Kong, which is good because few places on earth are as magical to me. When I am here I bristle with excitement like a dog who's just seen a squirrel, except the feeling is constant. It had the same effect on me the first time I visited just before the British handed it back to the Chinese in 1997. This time, for two days I just walk and look and feel and smell and clamber about the island's snakes-and-ladders hillsides, occasionally hopping onto one of those decadent outdoor escalators, then hopping off to marvel at a creeping banyan tree, or I sit for a while in a park listening to the ceaseless birdsong, which makes me feel like I am in a giant open-air aviary, or breathing deeply the aroma of durian and diesel fumes. The cityscape is spectacular, especially at night, but it's the everyday things that transfix me – the rattan baskets of black garlic left to dry on traffic islands in the middle of the street, open-fronted shops selling dried fish swim bladders and tree fungi the size of dustbin lids, and the raucous dim-sum halls stuffed with pensioners and grumpy white-coated waiters.

As I wander, I feel a strange, painful nostalgia for the years I spent living here in my twenties. Which is odd, as I have never lived in Hong Kong. *The Germans probably have a word for this feeling*, I think to myself as I gaze out across the bay, conjuring entirely false memories of glamorous parties on the Peak, trysts with heiresses at the Mandarin Oriental and high-rolling trips to play baccarat in Macau.

Though there are still English street names and branches of Marks & Spencer, and though you see the Queen's profile on some coins, and the cars have their steering wheels on the right-hand side, I suspect my wistfulness is less about the passing of the colonial era and more a sense of the sheer miraculousness of Hong Kong, the mere fact of its existence – after the 1842 Treaty of Nanjing, many back in London grouched that all we'd won was 'a barren island with hardly a house on it'. It is miraculous too that Hong Kong remained in British hands right up until the end of the hundred-year lease, although for a few years it was of course under Japanese control.

The Japanese attacked Hong Kong within hours of bombing Pearl Harbor. On my second day I visit the fortress built by the British, high up on the cliffs above the eastern end of the harbour, where the Japanese took control of the island in December 1941. Today the fort houses the rather excellent Hong Kong Museum of Coastal Defence, set up during the British era. Up on the battlements you can still see the bullet holes from the Japanese attack in 1941.

Though the Japanese had been stationed in nearby Guangzhou since 1938, the British never entertained even the possibility that those weedy-looking little Asian men would attack, let alone defeat the might of the British empire. The governor of Hong Kong, Sir Mark Young, twice rejected Japanese demands to surrender before finally capitulating on Christmas Day 1941.

Upon their arrival, the Japanese took around 9,000 prisoners of war, many of whom were sent to labour camps in Japan. They then set about applying the same approach they had adopted in Korea: Hong Kong would now become part of Japan. They replaced the Hong Kong dollar with the military yen, began to revise Hong Kong's educational system to present Japan in a positive way, teaching those locals who remained Japan's language, culture and etiquette – all to promote their Greater East Asia Co-Prosperity Sphere project, a Japanese empire by another name. All symbols of Western imperialism were eradicated.

The reality of Japanese occupation was rampant inflation, severe rationing and outbreaks of cholera and tuberculosis. In 1945, when the Japanese left, Hong Kong was devastated, with 230 shipwrecks cluttering the harbour. It was functioning again within ten months.

Strangely, there was little if any animosity towards Japan in the years after the war, partly because many Chinese left or were removed by the Japanese. The population declined by about 1.8 million to leave only about half a million by 1945. Also, although Hong Kong was crucial to Japanese operations in three large theatres of the war, it was not much more than a military base, and a great deal of the day-to-day administration of the enclave was delegated to a puppet regime. By the 1950s, Japanese companies were already operating out of the territory, which rapidly returned to being a major international commercial port.

At the end of World War II Chiang Kai-shek asked for the territory to be handed over to his Chinese nationalist regime, and until Yalta it looked like he would get his way. It was only courtesy of the Americans that the British were allowed back, out of fear that, with the nationalists vulnerable, it might fall into communist hands. On their return, the British used a more progressive approach, allowing the Hong Kong Chinese some say in the governing of the territory. 'All these reforms were introduced by a rather young group of British officials, many of whom had grown up here,' Professor Yang told me. 'That explains a lot why people in Hong Kong are still rather grateful to the British.' And after their 1949 victory in the civil war the communists didn't press for Hong Kong's return, at least not initially. They realised that the window of trade and communication to the outside world that the territory provided was of vital importance to China.

At the history museum on Kowloon I was stopped in my tracks by a photograph of Margaret Thatcher in her be-coiffed pomp, part of an exhibition about the negotiations prior to the return of the territory to China. It was like coming face to face with a despised school teacher; I literally shivered. The exhibit offered a telling insight into one of Thatcher's many delusions: at the start of negotiations with Deng Xiaoping, she believed the Chinese might actually leave the colony in British hands. That was never going to happen. Instead, like someone hastily flushing their stash down the toilet as the police arrive, the British tried to democratise

Hong Kong in the final years of their occupation, although real power remained in the hands of a small group of conservative businessmen.

Deng reassured the locals that his 'One Country, Two Systems' policy would preserve Hong Kong as it had been, at least until a final merger with the rest of China in 2047. Back then most observers and locals believed that by that distant date China would have moved more in the direction of the Hong Kong model than the other way round, and that China's economic reforms would automatically lead to more openness and freedom, but of course the opposite has happened and democracy is slowly being suffocated in Hong Kong.

Wenming Dai, the Chinese television journalist I had met in Shanghai, had told me that Hong Kong was experiencing a major identity crisis. 'They don't know what their purpose is any more,' she said. 'They've lost their USP. They want to be like Singapore, free and international, but Shenzhen [the neighbouring city, connecting Hong Kong to mainland China] is outperforming them economically.' Many other parts of China were just as international these days, she added, but in Hong Kong the middle class was being squeezed out of the property market.

The 2014 Umbrella Movement saw thousands of Hong Kong residents demonstrate for greater democracy, in particular that Hong Kong's leader be elected democratically instead of being chosen by Beijing. Many activists were arrested, including several publishers and academics. One pro-democracy activist, Howard Lam Tsz-kin, claimed that he had been kidnapped by mainland agents who tortured him using a staple gun. He was charged by Kowloon City court with 'making a false report to a police officer', and in July 2017 the Hong Kong high court disqualified four elected pro-democracy legislators on spurious grounds.

During my visit there are elections for the Legislative Council, a body left over from the fag end of colonial rule, when the British permitted half the seats to be elected democratically; these days the Chinese government selects most of the other, unelected half. Some of the sitting members had been disqualified because they had given speeches critical of China, and replacement pro-democracy candidates had been banned for running in their place on even more spurious grounds. As I wander across the island I pass several polling stations. They look encouragingly like polling stations back home; there are even canvassers for the pro-democracy parties outside. I ask one of them whether the elections are free and fair. Is there interference from Beijing? 'What do you think?' she replies.

The next day, when the votes are counted, the pro-democracy candidates lose two of their possible four seats, resulting in the loss of what little power they had. There was a low turnout, indicating a lack of faith in the process. Voters were also deluged by sophisticated large-scale social media campaigns, and, according to other rumours, bewildered elderly voters were mobilised to vote for mainland candidates.

One local I talk to about this in a café in Central, a pro-democracy Hong Konger, mentions other factors. 'Beijing has done two things: they have given the pro-Beijing candidates much greater financial support, and they have moved in loads of mainlanders, low-income unskilled workers, to live in West Kowloon and redrawn the boundaries to ensure that those votes count as much as possible. These are people who have come from poorer areas, but they've been given decent accommodation, and they are then asked to vote for the party's choices.'

Tomorrow I will catch a plane to the final country on my circumnavigation of east Asia, Taiwan. I knew that the Taiwanese eye the fate of Hong Kong nervously. Mainland China has been alternately threatening and bribing the Taiwanese to accept its authority and re-enter the embrace of the Celestial Kingdom, as Hong Kong has been forced to do. But my Hong Kong local had a message for the Taiwanese: 'Being part of China means you will gradually lose something you treasure – your rights, your ways of life. Just basic things you take for granted in a modern, open society will be lost, starting with Facebook. And those supposed economic benefits of reunification with China? They will never reach the general public, only the elites.'

TAIWAN

33

The Republic of China

My first task after leaving my bags at my hotel in central Taipei is to pay my disrespects at the Chiang Kai-shek Memorial Hall, an open-fronted monument a bit like the Lincoln Memorial, which looms over a large square in the centre of the capital. It is all very imposing, with eighty-nine steps (one for every year Chiang lived, from 1887 to 1975) leading up to a hall. As your eyes adjust to the darkness inside, before you, flanked by two Taiwanese flags, you make out a gigantic bronze statue of the man himself, seated, in robes, on a throne. This is the generalissimo, as he was known in the West, usually with an ever so slightly mocking tone, chairman of the Kuomintang (KMT) government of the Republic of China from 1928 throughout the war with Japan and the subsequent civil war with the communists, and thereafter president here in Taiwan, to where he fled in 1949 and lived until his death. Chiang was also a murderous military dictator who denied the Taiwanese democracy for decades and oversaw a regime in which thousands were imprisoned without trial, executed or simply disappeared.

A statue to such a man in the middle of the capital of what is now a wealthy advanced democratic nation might strike one as strange, but this is Taiwan; things are complicated here.

When the Japanese surrendered in 1945, officially they relinquished all their Chinese territories to Chiang's nationalist government, including Taiwan, which had been a Japanese colony since 1895. There were almost half a million Japanese living here when representatives of the KMT began to arrive in 1946; only 28,000 Japanese were deemed crucial to keeping services going, and the rest had to leave, allowed to take just two bags of belongings with them back to Japan.

The Taiwanese people had been anticipating the arrival of a brave and noble nationalist army which had held the Japanese at bay for many years and was still fighting the communists in mainland China, but the men who began to arrive on boats from the mainland at the docks in Taipei in 1946 were a corrupt and raggedy rabble, among them a large criminal element. They proceeded to commandeer property and food supplies, take over private homes and, in some instances, commit assault, murder and rape.

'The initial PR was that the KMT were going to bring democracy, get rid of the Japanese occupiers, that the island was returning to the motherland,' explains Jerome Keating, an American teacher and historian I met on my first afternoon in Taipei. 'But when Chiang Kai-shek's people actually arrived, they started looting the place of all the rice and the steel to support the war effort [against the Communists] on the mainland, hence you got the Taiwanese phrase "Pigs have replaced dogs."' The Taiwanese had never in their history experienced a shortage of rice, but they did after the KMT arrived.

The Americans supported the KMT in their fight against the Japanese and then against the communists, but by 1947 they had grown weary of Chiang's corruption and withdrew, or 'lost China', as the historians have it. The nationalists' many years of resistance to the Japanese had allowed the communists to regroup, and they finally triumphed in the civil war, Mao declaring the People's Republic of China on 1 October 1949. On 10 December Chiang Kai-shek followed those earlier KMT émigrés to Taiwan, where he proceeded to rule as the leader of the self-declared 'Free Chinese' government in exile until his death.

Mao's forces did attempt to follow Chiang to Taiwan, attacking the Kinmen Islands, which are only a mile or so off the mainland and almost one hundred miles from Taiwan, but the communists were defeated thanks in part to the assistance of Japanese military advisers, among them the last imperial governor of Taiwan, hired by the generalissimo personally. Chiang was nothing if not pragmatic: his hatred of communism trumped his hatred of his former colonial adversaries. And fortunately for Chiang, the communists had to attend to the Korean War, which broke out in 1950 and saw UN troops threaten to cross the Chinese border. Mao gave up on a full invasion of Taiwan, and the KMT dug in for the long haul. Also fortunately for Chiang, by this point it had dawned on the Americans that Taiwan could be an important base in the resistance against the march of communism in east Asia after all, and they sent the 7th Fleet to protect it.

Back at the memorial, Chiang's statue smiles a tight smile, mouth closed, a grimace really, as if he knows he is on borrowed time. As I look up at him, the guards suddenly commence their regular changeover routine. This turns out to be one of those Pythonesque silly-walk affairs, with exaggerated strutting, knee bends and abrupt 180-degree heel-turns. It is a courageous performance in a way, teetering on a tightrope between compelling and ridiculous.

I might find it strange to see a monument to a dictator in a now-democratic country but it is hardly without precedent: Napoleon was guilty of crimes against humanity yet lies in splendour in Les Invalides, and there are still prominent monuments to Franco in Spain, not least his tomb in the Valle de los Caídos. Things might be changing in Taiwan though, as in the couple of years since the opposition Democratic People's Party won both the presidency and the Legislative Yuan, the process of Taiwanisation has slowly pushed back against decades of KMT-led mainland Chinese cultural influence. This process has included calls to repurpose the monument. The statue has been vandalised too, and hundreds of other statues of Chiang have been relocated to a rather surreal park on the outskirts of the city, a kind of dictator's limbo.

A short walk away from the Chiang memorial is a very different monument to his era of rule – the 2/28 Memorial Museum, dedicated to one of his regime's early atrocities, which took place on 28 February 1947. Resentment had been brewing towards the new arrivals, and when KMT agents killed a local woman they had caught in possession of some smuggled cigarettes, there were protests outside the government building. Shots were fired on the crowd with fatal consequences, and the protests spread. The KMT government – still in mainland China at that stage – sent military reinforcements, who embarked on a brutal crackdown. According to some estimates as many as 10,000 protesters were killed.

The incident heralded the period known as the White Terror, after the colour of the helmets worn by the feared military police. Free speech was suppressed, and all opposition effectively banned. Some estimates of the number of Taiwanese people murdered or disappeared during Chiang's reign are as high as 100,000 – certainly it is up in the tens of thousands – but until the pro-democracy movement achieved the island's first free elections in 1996, discussion of the events of February 1947 remained taboo.

Taiwan's journey to democracy has been circuitous and occasionally baffling to outsiders. As with the first properly democratic presidential elections in South Korea in 1987, which saw the Koreans elect as president Roh Tae-woo, a former general who had been involved in suppressing the pro-democracy movement in the early 1980s, the moment the Taiwanese got the chance to choose their president in 1996, they also appear to have been struck by a kind of political Stockholm syndrome and promptly elected a KMT candidate, Lee Teng-hui, who had been hand-picked for the role by Chiang's son, Chiang Ching-kuo, who had succeeded his father as president in 1978. The opposition Democratic Progressive Party (DPP) did eventually win a general election – in 2000 – but the KMT still maintained control of the Legislative Yuan and won the presidency back in 2008. It is only since the DPP's Tsai Ing-wen won the presidential election in 2016 that the opposition party has held the presidency and a majority in parliament, which is why it is only now that Taiwan is seeing steps towards a 'transitional justice movement', the equivalent of South Africa's Truth and Reconciliation process.

Complicating matters is the fact that there are many who still view Chiang as a great man, the saviour of Taiwan. As with Park

Chung-hee in South Korea, Chiang Kai-shek oversaw rapid indus-trialisation and an ensuing economic miracle through a government-led focus on specific manufacturing sectors. In some respects, Taiwan's economic miracle was even more miraculous than that of its fellow Asian tiger, with growth averaging almost 9 per cent for thirty years, and its wealth consistently outstripped China's in per-capita and real terms. Taiwan has been a top-fifteen global economy for over twenty years, all the more remarkable given that, like Korea, it has virtually no natural resources and two thirds of it are mountainous. And, as with South Korea's President Park, Taiwan's economic success persuaded many Taiwanese to turn a blind eye to Chiang's crimes. One young Taiwanese woman I talked to told me she and her mother had often argued about their former ruler. Her mother defended him, called him a hero and claimed that the Taiwanese had much to thank him for. 'But what about the people he murdered?' the daughter would ask. 'They deserved it. They were attacking him. It had to be done. It was necessary,' said her mother.

Mike Liu, a history professor at Academia Sinica, one of the leading educational institutions in Taipei, is involved in a new research project to discover what happened during the White Terror. 'People don't deny that thousands were killed by the regime; even my family knows some of the victims,' he told me. 'But for many people Chiang Kai-shek is some kind of father figure because he saved them from communism.' Even opponents of the KMT give the party credit for the land reforms it imposed early in its reign. Having learned from their mistakes in China, in Taiwan the nation-alists made sure compensation was paid to those who lost land, and the process took place in an orderly fashion. No one lost more than 60 per cent of their holdings, and the compensation was often re-invested in starting new companies, which boosted the post-war economy, or it was paid in the form of shares in the Japanese companies which the KMT nationalised, such as Taiwan Sugar.

'Yes, the KMT were evil in some respects,' Steve Crook, a teacher and journalist who is a British resident of the southern city of

Tainan, told me when I visited the city a few days later. 'But they had some achievements. They were one of the few regimes in history to suffer a catastrophic defeat and get a second chance.'

So, the KMT's legacy is complex. On the negative side, in Taiwan they helped to foster one of the most all-pervading cultures of organised crime in the world. 'One of the things about Taiwan that always blows my mind is that for everything that's formal and legal there's a grey market equivalent,' long-term American resident Michael Turton told me. 'There are banks, and there are underground banks. There are legal factories and illegal factories. There is a legal lottery, and there is a black-market lottery. There is this whole shadow world.'

During the KMT's first couple of decades ruling Taiwan criminal gangs were used to maintain social control and to do some of the dirtier work of the dictatorship – the disappearances and beatings. Goons would also attack pro-democracy protests. Today the gangs influence businesses from construction to logging, private education (not quite as big as in South Korea but still significant) to, Turton tells me, claw machines. What? Those grabbing things in amusement arcades? 'Yes, they are a good way to launder money. You see them all over Taiwan but no one ever uses them. Everyone, somehow, is intertwined with a gangster business. We all do business with them, but most of us don't know when we're doing it.' (I should add, I do not wish to besmirch *all* Taiwanese claw machines: I am sure there are some which are not implicated in money laundering).

It is impossible to avoid coming into contact with organised crime in Taiwan, even when you vote, or rather especially when you vote. According to the book *Taiwan: Nation-State or Province* by John F. Cooper, 15–20 per cent of local councillors are criminals. Michael Turton, who is a prominent blogger on Taiwanese matters, told me of one city which the mayor wanted to turn into the artisan coffee centre of the country, so he offered tax breaks for coffee shops. The result? Gangsters moved in to the posh coffee business to take advantage of the tax breaks. In the 1980s in another city the entire council was populated by underworld figures. A former prominent Kuomintang legislator was a gang boss. 'In Taiwan, they treat [organised crime] as if it is another life option,' says Turton.

Another local, who preferred to remain anonymous for reasons which will become apparent, told me, 'In my wife's family there is a cousin and an uncle, and they are running three illegal gambling places. Everybody knows it. They are loaded with money. The rest of the family is very respectable – doctors, teachers ...' The two groups – legitimate and illegitimate – meet regularly at family gatherings, she said. When I asked my anonymous local if any politicians ever run for election on a clean-up-the-gangs platform, she laughed. No one would dare, she said. They would be killed. Besides, almost all political factions are connected to organised crime in one way or another. In May 2018 some 310 gang members were arrested because they were suspected of attempting to interfere in local elections. One political party, the China Unification Promotion Party, was even founded by a former gang leader, Chang An-lo, the so-called White Wolf, who has served a ten-year prison stretch in the US for drug trafficking but now insists he is a career politician.

At the centre of gang culture in Taiwan are the temples. Taiwan's temples were connected to the education system and the preserve of elite intellectuals and academics. When the Japanese left, the KMT purged a great many from this class, leaving a vacuum in the temples. Into that vacuum stepped the gangs. These days Taiwanese temples are the political, social and illicit business nexus of their communities. If you want to know who the prominent local gangsters and businessmen are, you go down to your temple and read the association names on the noticeboard. The temples are conduits for vast sums of money, donations and favours – Taiwan's equivalent of Masonic lodges. Their big annual get-together is the *Mazu*, the largest religious procession in the world, which lasts for eight days. Over a quarter of a million people take part, and according to my anonymous source a good portion of the money raised ends up in dubious pockets.

The most famous Taiwanese gang is the Bamboo Union, possibly the largest criminal gang in the world, with an estimated membership of 10,000. Based on the Chinese triad organised crime syndicate model, it emerged in Taipei in the 1950s when a KMT-linked group of young teens formed in opposition to local gangs. It thrives to this day on the usual mix of extortion, protection, illegal gambling and prostitution, as well as online fraud, and has trading links with North Korea.

The accepted existence of a semi-legitimate criminal subculture in Taiwan reminded me of the yakuza in Japan, with which the Bamboo Union have fraternal links. Actually, a lot of Taiwan reminded me of Japan, from the electronic toilets to the scrupulously clean and efficient public transport, and as in Japan there are no overweight people, not even a sumo. There are differences though: couples hold hands in public and even kiss, which you almost never see in Japan. The Taiwanese also chew betel nuts, so the pavements are decorated with reddish-brown splats. Taiwan is cheaper than Japan too: dining out is perhaps half as expensive, and you can cross the capital on public transport for less than a pound. It smells different too: often of mothballs, presumably because the insects here are truly epic, but you also occasionally come across an unearthly and repellent odour. On my explorations of Taipei's night markets – wonderfully festive food corridors lined with steaming stalls and flashes of wok fire – I would sometimes pass a stall wreathed in the distinctive highly noxious fumes emitted by fermented tofu.

Stinky tofu is just one facet of a hugely underrated food culture which combines Fujianese, Shanghai and other regional Chinese foods and even some European touches dating from the seventeenth-century arrival of the Portuguese and Dutch on Taiwan's shores, along with Japanese cuisine every bit as good as you get in Japan. One of the most appealing aspects of eating in Taiwan is that the Taiwanese are not so hidebound by tradition as the Japanese, but they still take matters of the table very, very seriously – reverently even, as I discovered when I visited the National Palace Museum.

When Chiang Kai-shek limped across the Taiwan Strait from China he also brought with him the country's gold reserves and a trove of treasures from his homeland. The latter, originally part of the imperial collection, had been packed into 19,000 crates and spirited away from Beijing when the Japanese invaded in 1937. Nearly 3,000 crates were eventually brought to Taiwan by the nationalists for 'safe keeping', and today their contents are on display at the National Palace Museum, in the foothills to the north of Taipei.

The museum skirts over its larcenous origins: the pieces were 'inherited from the Qing imperial court and passed through many places before being moved to Taiwan', I read when I visit on my third day in Taipei. The sheer volume of Song ware and Ming vases on display is astounding, but at the very heart of the museum, displayed in individual, alarmed glass cases, in their own dedicated room to which people queue for *ages* to gain access, are the national collection's two most highly prized pieces, presumably the most prized pieces of art in all of Taiwan and by extension – I decide to believe – in all of China.

They are not vases or silk wall hangings, terracotta soldiers or jewellery. These are pieces quite unlike any I have seen in such a high-profile location in such a prominent museum. One is a lump of naturally occurring stone, banded jasper, not much bigger than a baseball, but mounted on an ornate gold stand. It dates from the Ming dynasty and, thanks to its different-coloured strata, looks precisely like a hunk of pork which has been braised in soy sauce. It is labelled MEAT-SHAPED STONE and is so appetising that you could easily imagine sticking it in a steamed *bao*, sprinkling over some peanuts, coriander and onion, and stuffing it in your face. The other piece, also Qing era and the symbol of the museum, appearing on all the promotional posters, is a beautiful *bok choy* cabbage carved out of jade. Look closely and you can see a locust clinging to its leaves. The two pieces would work pretty well together on a plate.

Given their origins, it is not surprising that the ownership of the museum's treasures is highly disputed. As with the artefacts looted from Beijing's summer palace by the British and French, China has lobbied for years for its cultural heritage to be returned from Taipei. This has led some cheeky Taiwanese independence campaigners to make the Chinese an offer: Taiwan will return the lot, braised pork included. In return, they ask for just one thing: that Beijing acknowledges Taiwan to be an independent state.

34

Chinese Taipei

'People in my father-in-law's generation, in their eighties or nineties, they served in the Japanese army. He cries when he sings the Japanese anthem, even today. In his heart he thinks of himself as Japanese.'

On my first evening in Taipei I have dinner with Michael Turton, who has lived in Taiwan for over twenty years. He is telling me about his Taiwanese father-in-law; he says most Taiwanese think fondly of the Japanese. The only real difference between the generations is the intensity of the fondness for Taiwan's former colonial rulers. Turton teaches English at a university in northern Taiwan. His students 'idolise' Japan, he says. 'To them, Japan is all the things Taiwan could be.'

I had been hearing rumours of this Taiwanese love for Japan from Chinese people and from South Koreans throughout my journey. Japanese people were especially keen that I visit the country. I was curious to find out why the Taiwanese colonial experience was so different from that of the Koreans or, for that matter, any of the other countries Japan invaded in the first half of the twentieth century. Following the Fukushima disaster in Japan, for instance, the Taiwanese sent more money than any other country to help the recovery. So yes, I'll admit it: I've come to Taiwan in search of a positive end to my journey in terms of Japan's relationships with its neighbours.

There is a suggestion that Japan didn't actually want Taiwan, or at least came to regret accepting it as part of the terms of the Treaty of Shimonoseki in 1895, after their unexpected victory over Qing China in the First Sino-Japanese War. For a while it looked like taking Taiwan had been an early learner's mistake by a wannabe colonial power. The Qing secretly congratulated themselves on palming the Japanese off with Formosa, as it was called by the Portuguese. They considered it a land of pirates, headhunters and really very spiteful insects; 'not a place for humans' as Yu Yonghe, the Qing explorer, famously put it; an earlier emperor had described it as 'a mud ball in the sea'. As for the Taiwanese, they were at a loss as to what exactly they had to do with a war that had taken place a thousand miles away, and many resisted the occupation, at least initially.

Slowly the Japanese prevailed, though not without violence. Their tactic was to divide and rule Taiwan's numerous indigenous tribes. In the Wushe Incident of 1930, for instance, hundreds of Seediq tribesmen attacked a Japanese sporting event in protest at their loss of land and the enslavement of members of their tribe. The Japanese retaliated by offering bounties to other tribes, who killed over two hundred Seediq in a two-month campaign. In one museum I see a grisly photograph of the bounty hunters with a Japanese military official, posing in front of a small field of heads.

Taiwan would come to mean many things to the Japanese. It was somewhere to settle their growing population – thousands were encouraged to move there to cultivate the land. It was a source of food, timber and other materials which were increasingly important as their conflicts multiplied. It would become of huge strategic importance during Japan's South East Asia campaigns and the Pacific War. It supplied manpower for the military, mining and other industries back home. And it was a showcase for Japanese colonialism. The Japanese do seem to have genuinely wanted to make Taiwan a model colony. Quite a few Taiwanese I spoke to mentioned the sewage systems they built, for instance – overseen by a Scottish engineer, William Burton. The Japanese also electrified the island and built roads and railways, schools and banks. As in Korea, agricultural output improved exponentially under Japanese rule, and over the fifty years they were there the population grew from 2.6 to 6.6 million. The Taiwanese were encouraged to learn Japanese, worship at Shinto shrines and take Japanese names, but this doesn't seem to have rubbed them up the wrong way as it did the Koreans, probably because Taiwan had no real cohesive identity prior to 1895: it was not a sovereign country with centuries of homogenous culture.

Eventually, over two generations, many Taiwanese would come to think of Japan as the motherland, the font of all knowledge and authority. It would become the goal of the elite to send their sons to Tokyo to study, and over 200,000 Taiwanese served in the Japanese imperial armed forces, 30,000 losing their lives.

In January 1945, aged twenty and just graduated from agricultural school, Kuo Chen-tsun was conscripted into the Japanese army. He joined more than willingly, indeed proudly. 'It was my duty to serve Japan,' Mr Kuo tells me. He was raised during the Japanese occupation, had a Japanese education, and still speaks fluent Japanese. 'It felt very natural to me to serve in the Japanese imperial army,' Mr Kuo says via a translator, 'because at that time, through my education, my background, social contacts, I was already Japanese in my thinking, in my mind.'

Call-up papers in hand, Mr Kuo went by train to Fongshan in southern Taiwan to join around a thousand new recruits for three months of instruction. He was selected for officer training, the first of his family to take this route, something of which he remains proud.

Mr Kuo, ninety-three, walks with a stick but is straight-backed and sturdy-looking, with a thick head of hair. I can imagine he must have been an imposing young man. Today he is wearing large dark glasses, a brown shirt and grey slacks. We have met at the National Human Rights Museum, housed in what from 1968 to 1987 was the Jing-Mei Military Law Detention Centre of the Taiwan Garrison Command. This is where anyone who dared to speak out against Chiang Kai-shek's post-war dictatorship was tried, sentenced and imprisoned without any recourse to justice.

During the war many Taiwanese fought with the Japanese imperial army against the Chinese on the mainland, but it was Mr Kuo's destiny to be posted to East Timor with the 47th Regiment. He never made it there because the Americans dropped the bomb on Hiroshima and ended the war before his ship sailed. He did not hear the famous statement of surrender from Emperor Hirohito, but when he was informed by his superior officer he remembers being 'very disappointed that the Japanese empire had lost, that we the Taiwanese had lost, as we were Japanese subjects'. He realises of course that many of his compatriots did not return from the war but was disappointed not to have had the chance to use his training. He is not a member of any veterans' groups; there are no such organisations for Taiwanese former imperial soldiers, he says, but the Taiwanese still build memorials to Japanese engineers and so on.[23]

'You have to understand that the way in which the Japanese ruled Taiwan was totally different from the European powers colonising Asia,' says Mr Kuo. 'The Japanese built up the country, built up its economy.' All the most beautiful buildings in Taipei today are Japanese, he says. The bridges they built could cope with typhoons; the ones built later under the KMT regime have fallen down. And while Japanese colonial rule grew harsher in Korea, particularly in the 1930s, the Japanese continued to treat the Taiwanese relatively well. The feeling was that they were not so much colonial subjects as partners in a joint modernisation project, on a mission to repel the Western colonial powers. 'The Japanese actually *wanted* the Taiwanese to become their citizens. And in terms of Asia at the time, the Japanese were the most advanced yellow race.'

Journalist Jason Pan, who has put me in touch with Mr Kuo and is kindly helping with translation today, winces at this. 'The yellow

[23] One such memorial takes the form of a shrine and statue to a twenty-year-old Japanese fighter pilot, Sugiura Shigemine, who is fondly remembered for remaining in his crippled Mitsubishi Zero during a dogfight with American aircraft from the 3rd Fleet in October 1944, managing to steer it clear of a village and crashing it instead into a field. Today Sugiura is considered a deity, General Flying Tiger. When I read about him, just before arriving in Taiwan, it struck me that while the Koreans were erecting statues to shame the Japanese, the Taiwanese were doing the opposite.

race – this is an old term,' he interjects apologetically. Clearly though, this was how many felt at the time.

'The Japanese did a lot of savage things and killed innocent people, but they were fighting a war,' says Mr Kuo, who questions the reliability of many of the tales of savagery. Perhaps the Americans used these stories for wartime propaganda purposes, he suggests, and the Chinese have since embellished them. If you read the Japanese accounts, they entered Nanjing without much trouble. And the atomic bombs were worse than anything the Japanese did because they killed civilians indiscriminately. 'There were even unborn babies killed. And that is against military law,' says Mr Kuo.

I ask about his feelings towards the Japanese emperor at the time. 'He was not really a god, but a unifying force, at the centre. Not an absolute authority.' It is a misunderstanding that soldiers in the imperial army were trained to die rather than surrender, he says. 'What we were taught was, don't die needlessly. Of course we were ready to die, but our instructions were to stay alive and try to escape.'

It is clear that Mr Kuo still feels a sense of loyalty and love for Japan. He feels very differently about the mainland Chinese. The KMT looted property, raped Taiwanese women and destroyed the intellectual class, he says. They wanted to impose fear on the island and make a statement: '"We are the new master." They forcibly occupied everywhere, took away peoples' houses.' Mr Kuo blames the Americans. 'If the Americans had supported the Taiwanese people, we would have become an independent country.' The KMT particularly resented the Taiwanese who had collaborated with and fought alongside the Japanese – 'They came over to Taiwan and saw all these people wearing kimonos and singing Japanese songs,' as Steve Crook put it to me. To the KMT, the Taiwanese elite were nothing less than traitors.

After the war Mr Kuo went to work at a sugar refinery, but in 1953 the military police came for him. He was arrested on what he says were trumped-up charges of advocating Taiwanese independence. He says he merely had a 'Taiwanese mentality', which the KMT saw as enough of a crime. He was sentenced to life imprisonment.

In prison Mr Kuo shared a cell with twenty-five other men, sleeping two per tatami mat. During the early stages of his incarceration he was beaten with wooden clubs and tortured. At one point, when his captors were trying to get him to sign a confession, they put him in a sack and submerged him in a river until he nearly drowned. On another occasion they stripped him naked, covered him with sugar water and left him out in a field tied to a chair for insects to attack. In Taiwan this is a fate worse than death. He remained in prison until 1975, when Chiang's death prompted an amnesty of political prisoners, but he has never been officially pardoned for his alleged crimes nor received any kind of apology.

What kept him going for those twenty-one years? 'I wanted to outlive Chiang Kai-shek,' he says grimly. 'I loved life. I must keep my life. I must survive in a dignified way.' His strategy was to forget time, to train himself to ignore the passing of hours, days, months. 'I wanted to be a witness to history. When I was released, I felt like I was the victor. I had won over this regime.'

Mr Kuo is beginning to tire. For my last question, I ask about the Chiang Kai-shek memorial. He would be happy to press the button to blow it up, he says. 'Put the rubble in the road and let the cars run over it.'

After I return home, I receive an email from Jason Pan. Following a fall at home, he writes, Mr Kuo slipped into a coma and, after a month in hospital on life support, died. With him goes another precious link to the past, another precious testimony.

35

Free China

Taiwan is lush and green and warm. The north is subtropical, and once you get down to the south coast it is fully tropical, but the island can also be cold. Visiting in spring, I had inadvertently hit its sweet spot, weather-wise. From May to September the typhoons and humidity are by all accounts brutal; in mid-winter the humidity renders the place ferociously cold, but right now stepping outside feels like slipping into a perfect warm bath.

Taipei combines the sophistication and modernity of Tokyo with the easy charms of a South East Asian city and, considering it is the capital of a country of 23 million, is eerily quiet. Where is everyone? Even in the rush hour there are seats on the Metro. I never see a traffic jam. There is space to breathe, a laid-back feeling, and the Taiwanese are the friendliest and most helpful people I have met on my travels. 'They are very tolerant' is how one local described the Taiwanese to me. 'Sometimes a little shy, and they can be worried about losing face.' 'My main criticism of the Taiwanese is that they only care about money,' said another. 'But the wonderful thing about the Taiwanese is they only care about money.'

These days, as well as being rich Taiwan is a beacon for democracy, freedom and progressive social policies in Asia, even more so than Japan. It was the first country in the region to legalise gay marriage and has by far the best record on gender equality: for example 38 per cent of the members of the legislature are women; in Japan the figure is around 10 per cent. The *New York Times* recently called Taiwan 'Asia's bastion of free speech' and one of the continent's 'most vibrant democracies', replacing Hong Kong in that role as Beijing tightens the noose there. It has the freest press on the continent too, according to the annual survey by Reporters Without Borders: still not that great at 42nd in the world, but South Korea is at 43rd and Japan a rather woeful 67th. China is 176th. Taiwan has decent income equality compared to China, although Japan and South Korea are among the best-performing countries in the world in this regard, and one of the most highly educated populations, placing 6th in PISA's most recent international league table of fifteen-year-olds' maths, science and reading abilities. Japan was 3rd, South Korea 9th, China 10th, the UK 23rd.

The population of Taiwan is less homogenous than that of South Korea or Japan. The island's human history starts with Austronesian tribes that migrated to Taiwan perhaps a thousand years ago from western Asia, whose ancestors are found from Sri Lanka in the west to as far south and east as New Zealand – although they are not related to Australian aborigines. Today, about 2 per cent of the population is officially indigenous.

Before Chiang Kai-shek and his 2.2 million nationalists fled to Taiwan, two main groups of mainland Chinese had already migrated there. One was the Hakka, an outcast people who moved from northern China to the south around 1,500 years ago and later started coming to Taiwan, culminating in a major migration in the 1860s after the Taiping Rebellion – which had been led by a Hakka. Around the same time the Fujianese, or Hoklo, came across from the Chinese province just across the Taiwan Strait. The Hakka have a reputation as hard workers but they were always outnumbered and so traditionally farmed land others didn't want, often hilly areas where they had to clear woodland. The Hoklo more typically farmed rice on the lowland plains. The two cultures were, and remain, very different, and have often been in conflict with one another.

Today 15 per cent of the population identifies as Hakka, and 70 per cent as Hoklo; with the 2 per cent who are Aborigines, that leaves 13 per cent as Chinese mainlanders, originating from several provinces, who came here in the late 1940s, plus other immigrants. Intermarriage and immigration is muddying the ethnic waters, and these days Taiwanese might choose to emphasise their Taiwanese-ness, their Chinese heritage, their indigenous background or something else, but in a 2016 poll more than 80 per cent considered themselves Taiwanese first and foremost, ten times the percentage who identified as Chinese. This ethnic complexity has obvious implications both in terms of domestic politics and, crucially, relations with China. Let's take domestic politics first.

The current government is headed by the Democratic Progressive Party (DPP), liberals inclined towards Taiwanese independence, who were only permitted to campaign openly in the late 1980s. The other main party is still the Kuomintang (KMT), the nationalist party founded in China by Sun Yat-sen in 1911.

'Unfortunately, the KMT still hold a lot of power in the judiciary, and a lot of their power is connected to organised crime and gangs,' Jason Pan told me. For many years the KMT was generally held to be the richest political party in the world, worth more than two billion dollars and the owner of various commercial enterprises, particularly within the media in Taiwan. 'They are still funded by China; they want to destabilise Taiwan,' he says.

The KMT has tended to enjoy solid support from those who identify as mainlanders, but also from many Hakka and aborigines. It is still seen as the party of economic prosperity thanks to its positive relations and business ties with China. But public-sector workers also tend to vote KMT, including many teachers because teaching is a high-status job in Taiwan and to qualify you need to do well academically, which means you need to attend the better schools in wealthier areas in city centres. These schools have traditionally been KMT territory and have taught the KMT version of history.

Whenever I expressed incredulity that the KMT was still popular in Taiwan, people would mention Jason Hsu. They spoke of him in the same way many Britons talked about Tony Blair in the 1990s – as the new progressive face of an increasingly moribund, ideologically worn-out party. Hsu had, for example, been a strong supporter of amending the civil code to allow same-sex marriage, for which some in the party had called for his expulsion.

I arrange to meet Hsu at his office in the centre of Taipei, close to the parliament, where I wait on a too-low sofa facing a wall covered with Blu-tacked thank-you letters in a corner of a suite of rooms cluttered with boxes and full of young volunteers. After a while Hsu sweeps out of his corner office to greet me. He has recently turned forty, is handsome in a cherubic kind of a way, and today is dressed in the uniform of the modern centrist politician – dark two-button suit and hipsterish black heavy-framed glasses.

'I was invited to become a youth adviser to the KMT when it was sliding and facing the loss of the 2016 election,' Hsu says. 'The KMT wanted someone new, fresh blood, not the traditional pedigree. I figured a party like the KMT, in transition, might be a better space for a person like me to innovate and stir things up a little bit.' Hsu grew up in the southern city of Kaohsiung. His parents, who have a Fujianese background – in other words, pre-KMT Taiwanese – worked in the night market there, and his mother also ran a beauty parlour. He describes his background as 'basically the bottom layer of society'.

Hsu is particularly concerned that the Taiwanese economy isn't modernising fast enough: China has undercut its cheap manufacturing sector and is now muscling in on Taiwan's high-tech industries. If it loses the advantage in that area, what does Taiwan have to offer the Chinese, or the rest of the world? Hsu also believes that Taiwan's relationship with China has fundamentally changed. For decades the KMT was the conduit for China–Taiwan relations, but as the KMT's popularity declined, the Communist Party of China started to bypass them and communicate with the Taiwanese people directly. In early 2018 the Chinese Taiwanese Affairs Office in Beijing announced thity-one 'preferential policies' for Taiwanese people, for instance. In essence these were bribes to lure the Taiwanese to work or invest in the mainland on the same terms as Chinese, for Taiwanese academics to apply for grants to work in China, and so on. Some saw this as a pernicious capital and human-resource grab, a kind of integration by stealth, but it is working: over three million Taiwanese now live in Shanghai. 'Taiwan is suffering from a very serious brain drain to China – in industries, academia and the education sector,' Hsu says. The Taiwanese historian I'd met in Shanghai, Chih-yun Chang, thought it was a clever strategy, 'shining the sun on Taiwan', as he put it to me.

And just as the Russians have meddled with democratic processes in the US and Europe, the Chinese government is using social media to deepen the divide between those in favour of Taiwanese independence and the pro-China/unification groups. Combined with Beijing's ongoing pressure on the international community to ignore Taiwan, it seems the Chinese are trying to squeeze the life out of this highly globalised little island of freedom and democracy. And any downturn in the economy will provide further evidence for those who say the ruling DPP is weak on economic policy and thus boost the chances of the pro-China KMT returning to power. The strategy is already working: the DPP were routed by the KMT in the November 2018 local elections, a result seen as ominous for President Tsai Ing-wen's re-election chances in 2020.

It seems paradoxical that Beijing is working so hard to support the KMT because, when Chiang Kai-shek led his followers to Taiwan in the late 1940s, he still hoped to recapture China from the communists and maintained this far-fetched fantasy as official policy for decades, his party only formally ending the state of war with China in 1991, long after his death. In schools, children were taught that it was Taiwan's role one day to civilise China, like a flea convinced of its sovereignty over the dog to whose back it clings. I don't think anyone these days believes that Taipei one day will rule China, or indeed would wish to, but China remains adamant that Taiwan is its twenty-third province. These days the CPC sees its old enemy the KMT as its best hope of unification, except of course now it would very much be on Beijing's terms.

A few weeks before my trip, in a speech to the CPC congress Xi Jinping reiterated his commitment to the 'peaceful unification of the motherland' and warned that anyone opposing this would meet 'the punishment of history'. In his new year's speech in 2019 Xi repeated his aim, calling the island's current situation 'an adverse current from history and a dead end'. But what do the Chinese people think about all this? From what I hear, not all Chinese support Xi in his determination to unify the two countries, or indeed care much either way. For one thing, the Taiwanese as a people are not greatly loved in China. 'Young people don't think of the Taiwanese as brothers and sisters any more,' one of my Chinese student correspondents told me. 'For us, Taiwanese are more like arrogant and malicious relatives. We support unification, because if it is not reunified, Taiwan is a pain in the ass.' She invited me to imagine Taiwan as a giant unsinkable American aircraft carrier, permanently moored just off the coast of China. Perhaps, as with the peoples of North and South Korea, so much time has passed that the Taiwanese and the Chinese no longer actually have that much in common.

But Beijing still continues to apply pressure in all areas, in all parts of the globe. If a country wants diplomatic ties with China, with all that means in terms of infrastructure investment, trade and brown-envelope payments, then it must cut ties with Taiwan. Burkina Faso and Panama succumbed in 2018, reducing the number of countries that formally recognise Taiwan to just nineteen – places like the Vatican, the Marshall Islands and Palau. The latter recently appealed to America and Japan for help as Beijing had banned its citizens from visiting in an attempt to change its pro-Taiwanese stance – no small matter as Chinese tourists to the Pacific island accounted for almost half of all visitors. According to the *Asia Times*, 'astronomical sums' change hands to maintain these stalwart supporters of Taiwanese independence.

Taiwanese must also tiptoe through a semantic-diplomatic mine-field regarding what they can call their own country. When his novel about twentieth-century Taiwan *The Stolen Bicycle* was nominated for the Man Booker International Prize, the author Wu Ming-yi protested when his country of birth was changed from 'Taiwan' to 'Taiwan, China' on the organiser's website, following an official complaint from the Chinese embassy in London. There was specula-tion that the decision was connected with the fact that the prize's sponsor at the time, the Man Group, had recently launched a hedge fund in China.

Beijing has also successfully pressurised forty-four foreign airlines including British Airways and Japan's two largest, ANA and JAL, along with other companies such as the Spanish clothing retailer Zara, to stop using the territorial designator 'Taiwan' in their online drop-down menus and use 'China Taiwan' instead. The Marriott hotels' website was shut down entirely in China for the crime of referring simply to 'Taiwan', as well as for listing Hong Kong and Tibet as separate countries. Presumably, somewhere in a windowless building in Beijing there is a team of people scouring the Internet, alert to the grave threat of clothing companies undermining the One China policy.

In 1945 Taiwan was one of the founding members of the United Nations, but it lost its seat to China in 1971 following Richard Nixon's rapprochement with Beijing – an attempt to bring an end to the Vietnam War – and US forces left the island shortly after. Today it is listed by the UN under 'Other Territories' along with entities like the Palestinian Authority and Northern Cyprus, which are hardly comparable to a thriving, peaceful democracy of 23.5 million people. Taiwan does not even have formal relations with its greatest regional ally, Japan; they make do with fudgy-titled organisations called things like the Japan–Taiwan Exchange Association. At the Olympics Taiwan must compete as 'Chinese Taipei'.

'China has always done this carrot-and-stick charm offensive,' says Jerome Keating, citing as evidence of the latter the test-firing of missiles in Taiwan's direction, which it tends to do just prior to elections. 'They say, if you declare independence, then we will attack, but that will never win over the minds of the Taiwanese because they have lived with democracy now and they know China. They don't need China economically either.' If anything, it is the other way round: China has benefited hugely from Taiwanese investment and know-how over the last couple of decades, and Taiwan remains its largest source of external investment. One Taiwanese-owned company, Foxconn, is the world's largest electronics manufacturer and employs more than a quarter of a million people in Shenzen, China – although that figure fluctuates, given the company's reputation for worker suicides. Neither carrot nor stick are working though, even among KMT supporters. In the last election, when a strongly pro-unification candidate came forward, she was sidelined because the KMT leadership knew full well she would be a liability at the polls.

The current president, Tsai Ing-wen, is pro-independence in theory but like most Taiwanese not in favour of a unilateral declaration any time soon and prefers to maintain the status quo. She has had her cheekier moments though, such as when she rang Donald Trump to congratulate him on his election victory, and, oblivious to the diplomatic consequences, he took her call. It was the first phone conversation between a Taiwanese leader and a US president in over forty years.

Despite the apparent stability of relations between the two countries, it was surprising to me how many people I spoke to in China and Taiwan – perhaps the majority – said that they were bracing for unification (Beijing calls it reunification; they can't even agree on the term) in the near future, the most likely scenario being a 'flash invasion' from the Fujian coast under the pretext of a military exercise. Some even claimed to know the specifics of the plan: cyber attacks would support an amphibious assault on the north coast, before paratroopers landed at Taoyuan international airport in Taipei. British journalist Steve Crook is more optimistic. 'I have been here over twenty years and throughout people have been saying China is about to invade,' he told me. 'It's like nuclear fusion. It's always just around the corner.'

Others doubt that the Chinese military would have it quite so easy. Though Taiwanese troop numbers have fallen from 270,000 in the early 2000s to 180,000 now, there are still 1.5 million reservists, and the island could be tricky to conquer. During the Pacific War the Americans considered attacking Taiwan to use as a base for the assault on Japan, but they judged it unassailable and instead attacked Okinawa.

If the Chinese were to invade, that would theoretically prompt a military response from America and Japan. According to the 1979 Taiwan Relations Act, the US has pledged to 'resist any resort to force ... that would jeopardise the security, or the social or economic system, of the people of Taiwan'. But would the Americans actually intervene? Clearly, Beijing already interferes with Taiwan's economy and constantly threatens its security, but America does little.

There has long been talk of holding an independence referendum. If that does ever happen it would make Brexit look like a show of hands at a village green bowling club. Imagine the threats and interference from mainland China. It would be fascinating to see how many of the Taiwanese vote at all (previous national referendums have been judged invalid when the turnout was low because they were boycotted by the KMT and its supporters), and how many vote in favour, with China's sword of Damocles hovering over their heads.

I meet Richard at the foot of the Taipei 101 tower, the capital's new landmark skyscraper. He is in his late sixties and is wearing a Free Taiwan Party (FTP) baseball cap and a sweatshirt proclaiming, 'My name is Xi Jinping and I am for Taiwan independence'. He and a handful of fellow protesters are standing around holding flags promoting the FTP – 'the only party who advocate Taiwan independence'.

'I am not afraid to die for independence,' Richard tells me, smiling amiably. He believes about 20 per cent of the Taiwanese population feel the same way. In a 2018 poll of 1,000 Taiwanese, 20.1 per cent wanted immediate unification with China, 24.1 per cent were satisfied with the status quo, almost 40 per cent wanted independence at some point in the future, and the rest didn't know.

Richard's parents actually came to Taiwan from the mainland with Chiang Kai-shek, but he was born here, and though he doesn't speak Taiwanese very well he considers himself Taiwanese not Chinese. The Taiwanese language is a Fujianese dialect, but since 1945 Mandarin has been the official language of Taiwan, and most people speak both. 'Taiwan should be an independent country. No question. I think it will happen within the next three years, because of international support. There is no way we will unify with Beijing.'

He admits that the possibility of Chinese military action against Taiwan is also highly likely. 'I expect it. Maybe tonight, maybe tomorrow. Soon. But just because China is big, it doesn't mean it is strong. Taiwan is small, but we are strong. We can fight back. We can defend.' Japan will help, Richard is sure of that. 'If they don't, they won't only have lost Taiwan, but their credibility internationally, and their strategic power. Once China takes Taiwan, there will be no safety for Japan.' Okinawa could be next. Some Chinese have hinted at a claim to Japan's southern archipelago in the past. Japan and China are, he feels, destined to fight. 'In the minds of the Chinese, they have a very, very deep hate towards the Japanese.' He predicts that conflict will happen sooner rather than later because the more Japan militarises, the more difficult it will be for China.

KMT politician Jason Hsu took a different view. 'I do think emotionally we think of ourselves as independent, but when people on the street say they are willing to pick up a gun to fight, that it is very much all talk.' Independence was not a priority for the younger generation, he claimed. 'There is too much at stake for China to use force against Taiwan. There are so many other ways for them to achieve what they want. They could shut down the flight routes or devalue their currency, all this could paralyse the economy.' Besides, he added, China had other priorities: the growing tension with India, Xi's Belt and Road project, North Korea, the trade war with America, corruption ...

Mr Kuo, the Japanese army veteran, was similarly optimistic about the future of Taiwan. He predicted greater openness, democracy and full independence. 'We are just waiting for the right timing, but within the next few years I believe the president will be ready to announce the end of the Republic of China. It should be now, the time for Taiwan to make a new country.'

The relationship between Taiwan and China is clearly complex, while that of Taiwan and Japan appears broadly positive. It hadn't really occurred to me to ask about the relationship between Taiwan and the third of my tigers, South Korea, but somehow it crops up while I am talking to a Taiwanese publisher, Emily Chuang, with whom I had been put in touch by a mutual Japanese friend.

'Oh, we hate the Koreans,' she tells me blithely. She and I were having dinner in a Japanese restaurant housed in a beautifully preserved old wooden Japanese house.

I stop eating, chopsticks half-raised. 'What do you mean? Why on earth ...?'

The South Koreans don't 'respect' the Taiwanese, she says, and perhaps the Taiwanese have a kind of inferiority complex towards the South Koreans.

'They cheat. They cheat a lot,' is the scathing verdict of another Taiwanese woman I am introduced to – the next day over lunch. South Korea has never done anything to Taiwan, I protest. 'But they get up people's noses. Their clannishness. You know Koreans are related to Mongolians,' she adds as if this seals her argument.

Taiwanese historian Mike Liu puts it this way: 'Taiwan became a Japanese colony in 1895. South Korea only became part of the Japanese empire in 1911, and many of the things the Japanese had done in Taiwan were copied in Korea. So, in that sense, some Taiwanese think of the Koreans as late-comers. *You learned from us.*' Another source of Taiwanese feelings of superiority is that during the colonial era the major export from Korea to Taiwan was comfort women. 'So you can see what kinds of social images we had of Koreans. There is this feeling, *We look down on you, but you don't even respect us*. How can I stand that?' he concludes.

All of this friction is compounded by the age-old geopolitical order: for centuries the Chinese looked down on Korea as a vassal state, and where did a large proportion of the Taiwanese population come from? China. 'We consider ourselves the big brother and they are the little brother,' says Liu. With this in mind, it is understandable that South Korea's economic ascendancy in the 1980s really put Taiwan's nose out of joint. Confucius still has so much to answer for in east Asia, it seems. 'We are still fighting about who should be the big brother,' agrees Liu. 'About who should be at the centre.' He is in no doubt about Taiwan's position in the hierarchy, however. 'Taiwan should learn to be a small country. We always think we should play an important role. That is what the KMT taught us – that Taiwan is a big country, that it has a role on the international platform and political arena. But, actually, no, it isn't!'

'Yes, Taiwanese people loathe South Koreans,' Jason Hsu confirms. 'It goes way back to when South Korea broke ties with Taiwan in favour of China in the early 1980s.' There has also been some ugly business with Samsung and LG poaching senior executives from Taiwanese companies, but Hsu says that the rivalry is most obvious during sporting events, particularly baseball. Taiwan is used to losing, but losing to South Korea hurts more than anything. Really, he admits, it boils down to Taiwan feeling that it doesn't get enough respect from its neighbour across the East China Sea.

After all the positive news about Taiwanese–Japanese relations, the discovery of Taiwanese animosity towards South Korea filled me with a good deal of gloom. These two nations had fought no wars against each other, had never brutalised or enslaved each other's women or exploited each others' resources; in fact they had so much in common, there were so many similarities in their recent histories: Japanese occupation followed by military dictatorship, the threat of China, American meddling, economic miracles and democracy. If the Taiwanese could find something to hate in the South Koreans, what hope was there for the entire region?

As usual, one must look to the young for hope. The young Chinese people I spoke to told me that it was to Taiwan, not Japan, Europe or the US, that they looked for popular-culture trends in fashion, design and food. 'Young Chinese are chasing authenticity,' one of them said. 'And that all comes from Taiwan. Taiwan is at the forefront in the Mandarin world in terms of the hipster scene, the artisanal baristas, craft beer, that loose, woollen, natural clothing.'

'You mean, dressing like a vegan?' I asked.

'Yes, exactly. The vegan look.'

Vegan aspiration is a straw to cling to, granted, but when one is in search of positive signs for future pan-Asian amity, one must take them where one finds them.

JAPAN

36

Tokyo

From Taiwan I have to return briefly to Japan for one final research trip. Just before I leave Taipei, I receive a slightly panicked email from my publisher in Tokyo. A 'serious problem' has arisen in Okinawa, he writes.

A Japanese newspaper is reporting that a school textbook there has chosen to publish an extract from something I wrote a decade earlier in which, with my usual sensitivity and tact, I described the Okinawan delicacy *tofuyo* as tasting like 'nuclear waste'. *Tofuyo* is the Okinawan version of the stinky tofu whose pungent aroma I had been encountering in the night markets of Taipei. When I first tasted it, I had scoffed an entire cube of the rotten soy bean snack, and deeply regretted it. The joke had been on me – one is supposed to nibble *tofuyo* using a toothpick – but the Okinawans are understandably sensitive to slights on their indigenous culture, plus in the wake of the 2011 disaster – which, in my defence, had happened after I had written the offending text – 'nuclear' has taken on an especially unfortunate resonance in Japan. They were not happy.

The next email in my inbox is from an anonymous admirer who has clearly seen the newspaper report.

Please never ever come to Japan again. all of Japanese people do not want to see you. we hate you we do not like you, because of you are racist and you are the pits as human being. please enjoy and immerse superior complex with rotten food with your sense of taste disorder. you are completely disgusting! from Japan with horrible feeling.

My publisher suggests that I might want to prepare an apology. They have arranged a few interviews with Japanese radio and print journalists to promote a new book of mine which, by coincidence, is being published in Japanese this week. Clearly, I have to be ready should any of the journalists ask me about what I am coming to think of as 'Tofuyo-gate'.

The irony of my situation – that I am concluding my journey through the fraught geopolitical relationships of east Asia by having to make my own public apology to the Japanese for a passage in one of *their* school textbooks – is so great that at first I don't even make the connection. But here I am. I am going to have to grovel. After toying with a weasely 'I am sorry if people were offended but ...' approach, or even a revisionist denial that I ever wrote the words, I go with a full mea culpa – no excuses, no mitigation – and, fortunately for me, nothing more is made of the affair.

Does this personal experience give me a fresh insight into the issues and conflicts of twenty-first-century east Asia? Not especially, but by this stage I have heard from a fairly broad range of perspectives. By definition, some of the people I spoke to for this book are deeply connected to these issues – they run museums, campaign, research, write about them, are ambassadors, anthropologists or politicians. And of course I also met veterans and the victims of war crimes, of torture and oppression. Issues of forgiveness, atonement, retribution and education understandably feature prominently in all these people's lives, but having made this journey through Japan, South Korea, eastern China and Taiwan, I offer this, not especially profound, observation: for the vast majority of the people, for the vast majority of the time, issues of the past are just that. I am fairly sure that they do not feature prominently in the day-to-day lives of the majority of the hundreds of millions who live in these countries, most of whom, like the rest of us, are just trying to get by, and many of whom are simply trying to survive.

There is a significant difference between how the Koreans and the Chinese view Japan, but then the two countries had very different experiences of the Japanese in the first half of the twentieth century. Japan only conquered parts of east and north China, perhaps a quarter of the country in total. These were densely populated territories – Beijing, Nanjing, Shanghai, Hong Kong – but large swathes of China were never ruled by Japan, and their people are unlikely to hold a grudge against the Japanese despite the best efforts of Beijing's propaganda machine.

Korea, on the other hand, was annexed in its entirety for thirty-five years. The Japanese did their best to transform the country into a kind of Outer Japan, and while Korean resistance was brave and persistent, over the decades many Koreans also collaborated with the Japanese, and many more benefited from the modernisation they brought. This leaves a complex legacy, particularly when combined with remembrance of the Imjin Wars and the familial tensions of Confucianism. The result is that Koreans have yet to forgive, let alone forget. In a 2013 Pew Poll of countries directly affected by Japan's military actions, 98 per cent of South Koreans said that Japan had not 'sufficiently apologised'; in contrast, in the Philippines only 47 per cent felt this way.

Obviously the Koreans have much stronger feelings about the Japanese than the Japanese have about the Koreans, but it seems a minor tragedy, looking from the outside in, that for all of their miraculous post-war political, cultural and economic achievements, the South Koreans still seem, at least in part, to define themselves by their oppression at the hands of the Japanese more than seventy years ago. For some proclaiming their hatred of the Japanese is a point of pride; others take this further and consider it to be intrinsic to contemporary Korean identity. According to American academic and specialist in Asian security affairs Van Jackson, 'collective suffering under Japan is an important part of understanding what makes Koreans Korean.' One Korean I spoke to confessed, 'remove our anti-Japanese feeling, then we lose half our identity'. The respected South Korea-based American political scientist Robert Kelly has written that the Korean people and their elites 'have an extraordinary, and negative, fixation with Japan. Korea's media talks about Japan incessantly, usually with little journalistic objectivity and in negative terms.' Kelly agrees that the Koreans have very good reasons to dislike the Japanese but that they 'do not stop there; they go over the top ... with no obvious point other than to provoke Japan'. And Kelly lives in South Korea, is married to a Korean and has Korean-American children.

South Korea's President Moon Jae-in was quite right when he said in a speech in March 2018 that it is not up to the perpetrator to judge their atonement sufficient or to demand that the victims 'get over it' (let alone an outsider like me), but at some point victims do usually attempt to move on, for their own sake as much as anything else. Unfortunately, magnanimity appears to be a rare commodity among his compatriots.

And if you thought the South Koreans were good at bearing a grudge, meet their cousins in the North. This is a typical recent statement on Japan from North Korea's state media: 'Japan, a matchless political dwarf, showed again its childish appearance to the world ... Enraged at the news of Japan samurais' rude action, the army and people of the DPRK are now burning their hearts with revenge on island barbarians, the sworn enemy of the Korean nation.'

In this new era of friendship between them, the North and South are already gearing up for joint efforts to take the Japanese to task for what they consider unfinished business from the occupation era. A joint body, the Korean Council for Reconciliation and Cooperation, has been discussing for some months reclaiming the remains of the thousands of Korean labourers taken to Japan during the 1930s and 40s. The Koreans say there could be tens or hundreds of thousands of sets of remains, although only 2,770 are registered at temples in Japan. This is an ominous sign for those who have hoped that improved relations, and perhaps even one day the reunification of the Korean peninsula, might present an opportunity for wiping clean the historical slate and looking ahead. Instead, the one issue which seems guaranteed to unite the North and the South is their shared hatred of the Japanese. A recent Gallup poll of 1,000 South Koreans showed that twice as many (10 per cent) had a positive view of Kim

Jong-un, a man who has for years threatened them with annihilation, as saw Shinzo Abe in the same light (5 per cent).

Towards the end of my research into all of this, it suddenly occurred to me: *I wonder whether the Korean or Chinese states have ever felt the need to offer an official apology for the actions of their armed forces?* I couldn't find anything from the Chinese, not even an apology from the CPC to its own people, but there was an interesting incident recently involving the South Korean government. South Korean forces fought alongside the Americans in the Vietnam War, during which they are alleged to have massacred civilians. In 2017 Moon Jae-in visited Vietnam. Did he apologise to the Vietnamese? In language uncannily reminiscent of that used by the Japanese, he expressed 'regret' over an 'unfortunate' aspect of their countries' two histories. As a Korean newspaper reported, 'he was not explicit' about what exactly it was he was expressing regret about. 'It looked like an apology but it was not,' the paper quoted Tran Thi Mai Xuan, a Vietnamese activist, as saying. 'I think the South Korean government should issue an official apology with sincerity.'

Perhaps Moon's vague approach was appropriate; perhaps no more explicit apology is required from the South Koreans to the Vietnamese, or indeed from the Japanese to the South Koreans. That is one of the conclusions political scientist Jennifer Lind offers in her 2011 book *Sorry States: Apologies in International Politics*, which compares Franco-German post-war relations with those of the Japanese and South Koreans. Lind acknowledges that denying atrocities seriously damages relations but points out that 'countries that offered contrition to foreign victims experienced an explosion of controversy that was *harmful* to foreign relations. Contrition, in other words, could be counterproductive.' Lind points out that America and Japan have become reconciled with virtually no atonement on Japan's part, or on America's for the atomic bombs, because both had other priorities; similarly, Italy and Austria have almost entirely escaped blame for their part in World War II. Apologies can sometimes simply make things worse: 'anger can mobilise nationalistic sentiment in the victim country, creating a spiral of acrimony that makes reconciliation even more elusive.' And it is true that Japan's apologies have usually achieved little in the long term aside from provoking its own nationalists – the men in the black vans – and have hardly mollified the Koreans and Chinese either. Eventually, the 'Few are guilty, but all are responsible' rationale might begin to ring hollow to even the most conciliatory Japanese. Apology fatigue sets in among even moderates.

Japan has said sorry so many times and in so many ways that I have often wondered if there was some linguistic nuance of which I, a foreigner, was not aware: the Koreans and Chinese seem to hear not-quite-sorries or sense fingers crossed behind backs. One Japanese academic I spoke to, Shimpei Ota, an anthropologist who has special-ised in how the Japanese and Koreans see themselves and each other, explained that part of the problem with Japan's apologies has been the overly formal language they have employed, using words which 'only normally appear in documents. It is very formal, so it doesn't really sound like an apology.'

Philip, the Gwangju pro-democracy protester I had met in Seodaemun Prison in Seoul, summed up what seems to be a common suspicion in Korea, that one can never really trust what the Japanese say: 'What they say with their face, and what they mean in their heart, these are two different things.' I have asked many Koreans to spell out their objections to the Japanese apologies for me, and they always say the same kind of thing – that the Japanese are insincere or vague, that they don't mean it, but, as I saw at the Iris Chang Museum with the TV clip of the American author challenging the Japanese ambassador, when the words are spoken in a language I understand, there seems to be no equivocation at all.

One Chinese academic, off the record, told me that part of the reason the comfort women issue continues to reverberate in South Korea is that it is 'an academic production chain'. Academics get funding to conduct research and produce theses and books, so being deaf to the apologies is profitable. That might be true of some, but it is clearly not the full explanation. To accept it as such would be to wilfully and inexcusably disregard the sincere and valid feelings of those with direct experience of the comfort stations.

The *New Yorker* magazine recently had a perhaps more enlightening take on the importance of apologies in general to Koreans. Novelist Ed Park noted the unusual frequency with which Korean public figures offer apologies – from their presidents to corporate leaders including the Korean Airlines clan. Apologies are a crucial aspect of Korea's hierarchical social structures: subordinates must apologise for their mistakes; those in charge apologise to show they are accountable. Generally, Koreans place greater importance on being apologised to by people who have wronged them than other cultures, wrote Park. From what I've seen, Japanese corporate leaders are similarly famous for their public contrition, but Park believed *han* adds an extra stubbornness to Korean grudge-bearing, calling it 'a condition born of a sense of oppression and grievance, and impossible to assuage by apologies alone'. There is a related school of thought which believes that in Korean culture whenever someone says sorry for some transgression, it gives the injured party the right to beat the guilty over the head in perpetuity. As one online commenter recently wrote, 'An apology is the beginning of eternal extortion in South Korean culture.' And as the former Japanese ambassador to China, Uichiro Niwa, put it when I met him in Tokyo, 'The Japanese will forgive even war crimes, but even for one thousand years the Chinese and Koreans will never forgive. It's a completely different culture. Even though they have never been in Japan, never read any books about Japan, still they feel unfavourable to Japanese and Japan.'

Several people I met in China and Korea mentioned that tensions would not recur quite so regularly if the Japanese would – and I paraphrase here – 'just shut up about it all'. 'The best way to solve this problem is that they agree to never speak about it any more, never visit Yasukuni again,' Dr Sun Cheng, the former adviser to the Chinese government, told me in Beijing. But Japan is a free country, a democracy, and so, as unpalatable as some aspects and members of its society are, they will always be part of the landscape.

Then again, as one Chinese student put it to me, 'Nobody is denying the Japanese right to deny their crimes or worship the criminals, but Chinese people have the right to hate them, right?'

Personally, I can't understand why any politician would go within a mile of Yasukuni, but the Japanese people are comparatively well informed about the issue; anyone can visit the shrine's museum and view its absurd revisionism. It is up to the electorate to punish or reward those public figures who do visit, although the Japanese have a fairly poor range of politicians to choose from. 'It is not that Abe is popular,' former Ambassador Niwa told me. 'It is that the opposition to Abe is so weak.'

Many I spoke to in Japan and elsewhere believed that the Chinese and the Koreans are being fed crudely propagandist narratives by their political elites. Japan-bashing is a sure-fire hit with the electorates of both countries; it guarantees a round of applause when a politician's popularity is waning or offers a useful distraction from domestic crises. Professor John Breen summed up the situation well when I met him in Kyoto: 'Neither the apology nor the demand for apology are entirely innocent. They all come out of very complex political backgrounds.' One academic I met in Taiwan tried to convince me that *all* of the animosity in South Korea (and probably also China too, for that matter) towards Japan was manufactured by politicians. 'It was very important to manufacture that hatred of Japan in South Korea because a lot of South Koreans collaborated with Japan. To hide that, everybody has to hate Japan,' he said.

Meanwhile, the opposite political strategy – rapprochement with Japan – offers few benefits to Korean and Chinese politicians and also risks providing Japanese right-wing extremists with ammunition – they can claim the 'enemy' are admitting they were wrong all along. For Japanese politicians and campaigners who urge greater contrition for their country's war crimes, the risks can be even greater – assassination attempts are not unknown – but Japanese progressives, indeed anyone who advocates a conciliatory approach towards the country's former colonies, also risk being bracketed with the ranting anti-Japanese lobby in South Korea – hardly appealing bedfellows.

But I do struggle with the notion that the people of east Asia are so passive their political leaders can easily, in Jennifer Lind's view, 'shape', 'transform' and 'craft the narrative' of their region's relationships. East Asians may not be particularly renowned for their rampant individualism, but neither are they as sheep-like as this conclusion suggests. As the recent mass protests in Seoul, which demanded – and achieved – the impeachment of a president demonstrate, the South Koreans can be notably anti-authoritarian when the fancy takes them. And if the Japanese are that passive, then how come – according to a recent poll by Kyodo News, which is consistent with most polls in the past – at least half of them oppose Shinzo Abe's long-term political goal of amending Article 9? Even in a September 2018 *Asahi Shimbun* poll of 2,000 Abe supporters, only 5 per cent considered constitutional reform important; most just wanted him to focus on the economy.

Education has a critical role to play in all of this. In an ideal world children of all nations would learn the good and bad about what their forefathers did, but this is rarely the case. Which British history textbooks mention the Bengal Famine of 1943, where perhaps as many as three million perished, many argue as a direct result of British government policy? What are American children taught about the Iraq War, I wonder? The Japanese used to be better at this than most of us, and were definitely better than their neighbours. A 2011 academic survey of Chinese, South Korean and Japanese school history textbooks by Gi-wook Shin and Daniel Sneider of Stanford University, *History Textbooks and the Wars in Asia*, showed Chinese and South Korean history books to be revisionist to an extraordinary extent, as well as aggressively nationalist and highly selective, omitting references to the role of the Americans in defeating the Japanese and all mention of the atomic bombing of Japan, for instance. Japanese books on the other hand were the least likely to stir up patriotic fervour. According to the researchers, the Japanese books offered a clear message: 'The wars in Asia were a product of Japan's imperial expansion and the decision to go to war with the United States was a disastrous mistake that inflicted a terrible cost on the nation and its civilian population.' Back in 2011 Japanese textbooks might have had a line or two about the comfort women and Nanjing, describing the latter as a 'massacre' and not merely an 'incident'.

Sadly, from what I hear, the Japanese government has now removed all references to what it considers 'masochistic' or 'unpatriotic' history teaching. Rather than simply teaching the truth about what happened using the known facts, in a direct echo of wartime indoctrination Japan's history curriculum these days aims instead to instil a 'love of country' in the country's youth. But surely in 2019 Japanese society is mature enough to teach its children the truth and encourage a critical approach to their country's history? At least then the Japanese might occupy the moral high ground in terms of education.

How have school history classes, schlocky TV war dramas and political rhetoric affected mutual perceptions between the peoples of east Asia? A 2018 Genron NPO poll of a thousand people in South Korean, Japan and China offers some slightly heartening news from the fractious siblings. The percentage of South Koreans who have a 'bad impression' of Japanese has declined since the last poll in 2017. It is still a shade over half the population, but in 2013 it had been 77 per cent. The percentage of Japanese who have a bad impression of Koreans has also declined since 2017, from 48.6 to 46.3 per cent – although five years ago it had been only 37 per cent, so the news is not completely positive. The Japanese and Chinese have more negative views of each other than the Japanese and South Koreans do. Each nation thinks the other is potentially violent, and over 80 per cent of Chinese and Japanese respondents interviewed for a 2016 Pew poll held 'unfavourable' views of the other. Only 11 per cent of Japanese looked favourably upon the Chinese, and 14 per cent of Chinese felt the same way about the Japanese. Only 10 per cent of Chinese people felt that Japan had apologised enough for the war. It looks like those TV dramas are still working, and the record numbers of Chinese tourists visiting Japan are having less of an impact that one might hope.

Encouragingly, young people (under mid-thirties) in all these countries tend to have a more favourable view of their neighbours, and herein lies hope that relations might one day improve. Without exception, the younger people I met on my journey seemed more open to friendly relations with their neighbours, were more relaxed about their admiration for each other and bore the grudges of the past with less vehemence than their parents and grandparents. As Yang Yong-hi, the *Zainichi* film maker, said of the younger genera-tion of South Koreans, 'They really want to have a good relationship with Japan. They really love Japanese culture and want to be good friends with Japanese people. Perhaps they don't feel like that about the Japanese government, but they do about the people.' Of young South Koreans, British journalist Andrew Salmon had this to say: 'They don't think about the Japanese 24/7 any more. What is happening right now with the younger generation is they are trying to find their own identity – "We're young, we're cool, we're funky. We've got big companies. We're democratic." The story of Korea is of a courageous national success. They don't see it themselves, but they're starting to.'

'They are apart from that historical colonialism, and they travel a lot to Japan,' one young Korean told me of her peers. 'They really love Japanese culture and products. Our school textbooks of course teach bad stuff about Japan, but that doesn't really affect the mentality of the younger generation. Many of my friends and I really admire Japan. There's almost no bad feeling towards Japan. They love Japan. So, there might be people who feel resentment towards what Japan did in the past, but they realise that is a different thing from the current culture.'

Such attitudes are the key to moving on from the cycle of recrimin-ations, I think, but if there is to be a meaningful long-term resolution to all of this, it will only come gradually, over a generation or two, and it will require the involvement of governments, NGOs, academics and civic groups: joint commemorations, joint memorials, joint education boards agreeing history curricula, joint panels to resolve territorial disputes.

Terrible wrongs were inflicted by Japan upon its neighbours, by the governments of all of these countries upon their own citizens, by citizens upon each other and by Western powers on Asian nations. It is a litany of inhumanity, and none of it should be forgotten. Most of the crimes will probably never be fully documented and they may at times have been exaggerated by various parties for various reasons, but there is ample evidence that they rank among the most damnable acts committed anywhere and at any time. Yet there is everything to be gained from all parties involved agreeing on what really happened, from the guilty atoning unconditionally and irrevocably for their crimes, and for the four countries to move towards a future free from denials, propaganda, populism and rhetoric. In poll after poll the people of east Asia say they want better relations with their neighbours and greatly fear the consequences of any worsening – that would be to everyone's detriment, and might even result in mutual destruction on an unprecedented scale.

If I could pass on just one message to all Chinese and South Koreans, young and old, it is this. It came from Wu Xianbing, the Chinese furniture manufacturer who had set up his own museum to the Nanjing massacre. The one thing his research had convinced him of was that the Japanese were not exceptional in any way: 'People become monsters, and it can happen to any people, to any country. Any country could do something as atrocious as the Nanjing massacre. It is not limited to a civilisation or an ethnic group.'

Index